Register Now for O
to Your B(

MW00824007

SPRINGER PUBLISHING COMPANY

C⏻NNECT™

**Includes 50
Downloadable
Worksheets**

Your print purchase of *Cognitive Behavioral Therapy in K–12 School Settings,
Second Edition* **includes online access to the contents of your book**—increasing
accessibility, portability, and searchability!

Access today at:

**http://connect.springerpub.com/content/book/978-0-8261-8313-2
or scan the QR code at the right with your smartphone
and enter the access code below.**

JWU5C5Y3

*Scan here for
quick access.*

SPC

SPRINGER ⫯ PUBLISHING COMPANY

View all our products at springerpub.com

Diana Joyce-Beaulieu, PhD, NCSP, is a faculty member in the National Association of School Psychologists–approved and American Psychological Association–accredited School Psychology Program at the University of Florida, Gainesville, Florida. She has taught numerous graduate courses, including topics in developmental psychopathology and diagnosis, as well as social–emotional assessment and counseling. She is a licensed psychologist and nationally certified school psychologist with supervision responsibilities for graduate-student practical experiences across several school districts and outpatient clinics. Her research interests include mental health services for children and adolescents, including diagnosis and counseling. Her publications include four books and numerous peer-reviewed chapters and articles. She also has served as coprincipal investigator for two professional development grants to research training models for multitiered systems of support, including applications of cognitive behavioral therapy in the school setting.

Michael L. Sulkowski, PhD, NCSP, is a faculty member in the National Association of School Psychologists–approved and American Psychological Association–accredited School Psychology Program at the University of Arizona, Tucson, Arizona. He has a conjoint appointment in the Department of Psychiatry, where he trains psychology interns and psychiatric fellows in the use of evidence-based forms of psychotherapy. He also maintains a private practice in Tucson, Arizona, in which he treats children, adolescents, and adults using variants of cognitive behavioral therapy. He is a licensed psychologist and is nationally certified as a school psychologist. His research focuses on the use of evidence-based interventions for children with mood and anxiety disorders as well as on supporting the emotional and behavioral needs of vulnerable or at-risk populations. To date, he has published three books and over 50 journal articles. His research has been highlighted by the receipt of awards from the American Psychological Association and the National Association of School Psychologists.

Cognitive Behavioral Therapy in K–12 School Settings

A PRACTITIONER'S WORKBOOK

Second Edition

Diana Joyce-Beaulieu, PhD, NCSP

Michael L. Sulkowski, PhD, NCSP

SPRINGER PUBLISHING COMPANY

Springer Publishing Company, LLC
11 West 42nd Street
New York, NY 10036
www.springerpub.com
http://connect.springerpub.com

Acquisitions Editor: Rhonda Dearborn
Compositor: Amnet Systems

ISBN: 978-0-8261-8312-5
ebook ISBN: 978-0-8261-8313-2
DOI: 10.1891/9780826183132

Supplementary Appendix: Counseling Worksheets and Handouts
Appendix ISBN: 978-0-8261-8314-9
The Appendix is available for download at www.springerpub.com/joyce-beaulieu-2e

19 20 21 22 23 / 5 4 3 2 1

The author and the publisher of this Work have made every effort to use sources believed to be reliable to provide information that is accurate and compatible with the standards generally accepted at the time of publication. The author and publisher shall not be liable for any special, consequential, or exemplary damages resulting, in whole or in part, from the readers' use of, or reliance on, the information contained in this book. The publisher has no responsibility for the persistence or accuracy of URLs for external or third-party Internet websites referred to in this publication and does not guarantee that any content on such websites is, or will remain, accurate or appropriate.

Library of Congress Cataloging-in-Publication Data
Names: Joyce-Beaulieu, Diana, author. | Sulkowski, Michael L., author.
Title: Cognitive behavioral therapy in K-12 school settings : a
    practitioner's workbook / Diana Joyce-Beaulieu, PhD, NCSP, Michael L.
    Sulkowski, PhD, NSCP.
Description: Second edition. | New York, NY : Springer Publishing Company,
    LLC, [2020] | Includes bibliographical references and index.
Identifiers: LCCN 2019035824 (print) | LCCN 2019035825 (ebook) | ISBN
    9780826183125 (paperback) | ISBN 9780826183149 | ISBN 9780826183132
    (ebook)
Subjects: LCSH: Cognitive therapy for children.
Classification: LCC RJ505.C63 J69 2020 (print) | LCC RJ505.C63 (ebook) |
    DDC 618.92/891425—dc23
LC record available at https://lccn.loc.gov/2019035824
LC ebook record available at https://lccn.loc.gov/2019035825

Contact us to receive discount rates on bulk purchases.
We can also customize our books to meet your needs.
For more information please contact: sales@springerpub.com

Diana Joyce-Beaulieu: https://orcid.org/0000-0002-6995-5038
Michael L. Sulkowski: https://orcid.org/0000-0003-3943-9136

Printed in the United States of America.

This book is dedicated to my husband, David Edmund Beaulieu.
I am immensely grateful to him, for his keen sense of humor,
encouragement, and inspiration during this endeavor.
His intelligent conversation, effervescent demeanor, and
nurturing spirit provide a sanctuary in my life each and every day.
—Diana Joyce-Beaulieu

I dedicate this book to my mother and father, Marge and Lee Sulkowski,
who have instilled the virtues of serving others in me;
it is also dedicated to the hundreds of clients I have worked with over the years
who have had the hope and courage for growth and change.
—Michael L. Sulkowski

Lastly, we dedicate this book to our colleague and friend, Dr. Thomas Oakland.
His positive and profound impact on the profession, and
on our lives personally, will never be forgotten.
—Diana Joyce-Beaulieu and Michael L. Sulkowski

Contents

Contributors

Alexa R. Dixon, MEd   Doctoral student, School of Special Education, School Psychology and Early Childhood Studies, University of Florida, Gainesville, Florida

Joseph W. Graham, BA   Doctoral student, School of Special Education, School Psychology and Early Childhood Studies, University of Florida, Gainesville, Florida

Theresa LaPuma, PhD   Postdoctoral Fellow, Commonwealth Psychology Associates, Boston, Massachusetts

Greg M. Muller, MEd BS Psychology Intern, Cornerstone Consortium, Bradenton, Florida

Janise S. Parker, PhD   Assistant Professor, School Psychology and Counselor Education, College of William & Mary, Williamsburg, Virginia

Christopher Poitevien, MEd   Postdoc, University of Florida, Gainesville, Florida

Kendra Saunders, PhD   School Psychologist, PK Yonge Developmental Laboratory School, Gainesville, Florida

Brian A. Zaboski, PhD   Postdoctoral Fellow, Yale OCD Research Clinic, Yale University, New Haven, Connecticut

Foreword

Joyce-Beaulieu and Sulkowski's first edition provided an invaluable book for school-based mental health specialists. There are millions of students who cope with complex personal issues (e.g., externalizing or internalizing). These problems are often difficult to resolve and conflicting information about how to address them abounds. In helping with these dilemmas of practice, the authors elucidated rich concepts, research findings, and valuable strategies to use in providing cognitive behavioral therapy (CBT) and other psychological treatments in school settings. To achieve this, the authors combined their professional experience as licensed psychologists and nationally certified school psychologists with the rich knowledge base contained in the extant literature. First, they analyzed a massive, complex, and often conflicting research literature. Second, they synthesized this research to provide concrete, accessible, and applicable strategies for use in school settings. Given this blending of rich practical experience and research knowledge, it is no surprise that the first edition was widely read and highly valued by the professional community. This is a valuable book, and I recommend that it should be in the library of all school psychologists and mental health specialists.

The second edition expands upon the successful first edition in many useful ways. For example, an additional chapter discusses practical and applied CBT in-session interventions. Further, two case studies illustrating how to use and document CBT in school settings have been added, as well as over 50 pages of worksheets. In addition to these dimensions that add to the practicality of the book, there is also a thorough and systematic updating of research and theory. Among this new content is a more detailed approach to conceptualizing CBT cases, planning therapy sessions, and transitioning therapy to ensure continued treatment success. More content is provided on CBT-related concepts that are now more commonly used in school settings, such as mindfulness interventions, acceptance and commitment therapy (ACT), habit reversal training (HRT), and behavioral activation. The second edition (like the first edition) is well written and based upon up-to-date research. It provides a comprehensive description of best practice and is a must-read/must-have book for mental health experts who work with students in school settings. I recommend this book with considerable enthusiasm.

Thomas L. Good, PhD
Professor Emeritus
Department of Educational Psychology, University of Arizona
American Educational Research Association Fellow
American Psychological Association Fellow
National Academy of Education Member

Preface

In *Cognitive Behavioral Therapy in K–12 School Settings: A Practitioner's Workbook*, Second Edition, we have kept all the essential components of the first edition as recommended by practitioners but also provided a number of additional features. Content is now provided on mindfulness interventions, acceptance and commitment therapy (ACT), habit reversal training (HRT), and behavioral activation. More detailed descriptions of step-by-step cognitive behavioral therapy (CBT) applications also are included (e.g., planning sessions, targeted session activity examples, therapy closure, exposure therapy), as well as two additional case studies. Essentially, the second edition goes more in-depth into translating current clinical practices for the school-based practitioner audience. Additionally, the book has enhanced coverage of culturally responsive CBT research, scholarship, and applied practice tips.

Consistent with the first edition, this book provides practitioners with an easily accessible and practical guide for implementing basic CBT counseling strategies in applied school settings. Because of the unmet mental health needs displayed by millions of students in these settings, and the advancements in the training and provision of school mental health services during the past couple of decades, school-based mental health professionals, such as counselors, school psychologists, social workers, and others, are increasingly being asked to provide evidence-based counseling and intervention services such as CBT. Therefore, to address this need, this text provides an overview of methods used to conduct effective CBT interventions in school settings. Whether the reader is a graduate student in training, beginning a career in counseling, or a seasoned practitioner, this workbook can serve as an easy how-to guide because it offers numerous counseling activities and examples as well as over 50 forms to use when planning, structuring, and conducting therapy.

The content covered in this text is nested within contemporary school-based service-delivery models, such as response-to-intervention (RtI) and multitiered systems of support (MTSS), which are commonly adopted and implemented in K–12 schools. In the first chapter, this workbook describes the need for mental health services in schools, noting the diagnoses most prevalent among school-age children, and then reviews progress-monitoring instruments for measuring counseling outcomes. The second chapter provides a theoretical foundation for CBT, including understanding the nature of internalizing compared to externalizing behaviors that may interfere with student success. Additionally, the chapter discusses cultural formation considerations and introduces the CBT triad. Chapter 3 offers a discussion of the essentials of CBT counseling from initial case conceptualization to session planning. Practical strategies for using CBT are reviewed in detail in Chapters 4 and 5. Additionally, Chapter 4 includes content on emotional and behavioral regulation strategies, including recognizing emotions and physiological triggers, relaxation training, mindfulness training, and additional behavioral regulation strategies such as behavioral activation and habit reversal training. Chapter 5 also provides a practical nuts-and-bolts approach to implementing exposure therapy and cognitive restructuring to address a range of internalizing and externalizing disorders. The content in Chapter 6 offers applied session activities that teach CBT concepts as well as a review of technology applications that may help reinforce session content. Finally, sample case studies are included in Chapter 7. The Appendix offers multiple reproducible student activity forms and resources. **The Appendix containing these forms and resources is also available for download from Springer Publishing Company's website. To download, go to www.springerpub.com/joyce-beaulieu-2e.**

This book differs from many extant CBT guides and workbooks in that it is designed for the busy practitioner who primarily works in K–12 school settings and must balance a range of different roles and responsibilities. Thus, this book is not a comprehensive review of theory; rather, it aims to serve as a workbook that can be used to help practitioners get better acclimated with CBT and then integrate this therapeutic approach into their regular practice. From decades of study, a wealth of research is available that supports the efficacy of CBT for treating various disorders and forms of psychopathology in youths; this research has been applied and referenced in the construction of this text. Because of its format and the content, it is our hope that this book will be both engaging and useful for practitioners who work with students in K–12 school settings. We have found the strategies discussed in this text have great utility in our own practice, and we trust that you will as well.

Acknowledgments

The foundational knowledge, research, and clinical expertise reviewed in this book are an invaluable gift from past and present visionaries who have dedicated their lives to meeting the mental health needs of others. Their research and legacy of scholarship have made the techniques discussed in this text possible. Thus, we are both grateful and humbled while we stand on the shoulders of great giants.

We are especially appreciative of the dedicated and scholarly contributions to this manuscript from Alexa Dixon and Joseph Graham, who coauthored Chapter 1; Dr. Brian Zaboski, who coauthored Chapter 5; Dr. Janise Parker, who coauthored Chapter 6; and Dr. Kendra Saunders, Dr. Theresa LaPuma, Chris Poitevien, and Greg Muller, who coauthored Chapter 7. It also has been a pleasure to work with Rhonda Dearborn, the senior acquisitions editor for behavioral sciences, and Mehak Massand, assistant editor, at Springer Publishing Company. Their professional support, from guiding the proposal to facilitating the final publication, has brought this project to fruition. Lastly, we wish to express our appreciation to Dr. Thomas L. Good for providing his endorsement of this book and writing the foreword. Thank you!

PART I

School-Based Cognitive Behavioral Therapy

ONE

Effective Cognitive Behavioral Therapy in Schools

INTRODUCTION

At its essence, counseling is the art of facilitating a trusted and guided conversation that fosters healthy thoughts and behaviors as well as inspires personal insight. Much like the supportive conversations that evolve around social interactions with family and friends, first understanding an individual's needs while establishing rapport is the foundation for counseling. In its most sophisticated form, counseling is the applied science of astutely recognizing thought patterns and then matching evidence-based strategies to needs in order to optimize positive change. Within the plethora of research studies on counseling techniques, cognitive behavioral therapy (CBT) is highly regarded as a first-line treatment for many mental health and personal stressor needs (Silverman et al., 2008). This text focuses on the provision of effective CBT from the initial techniques of rapport building and microskills, facilitating counseling session discussions, to the components that are most efficacious for specific mental health needs. Understanding these precision targeted components allows counselors to streamline intervention, conserving valuable time and resources, so clients are well served and institutions can effectively meet the needs of individuals.

OVERVIEW OF MENTAL HEALTH NEEDS OF CHILDREN IN THE UNITED STATES

The provision of school-based mental health support services has been a long-standing priority for best practice service delivery models in school counseling, school psychology, and school social work associations (American School Counselor Association, 2014; National Association of School Psychologists, 2010; School Social Work Association of America, 2013a). In fact, multiple educational reform efforts have called for further enhancing the integration of mental health services into schools (Atkins, Hoagwood, Kutash, & Seidman, 2010; Schelar, Lofink Love, Taylor, Schlitt, & Even, 2016).

As noted in the Individuals with Disabilities Education Improvement Act (IDEIA, 2004, Part 300 A, Section 300.34 [c][2]), highly qualified school professionals with appropriate training, such as guidance counselors, psychologists, school psychologists, and social workers, are ideally positioned to be the first-line providers of counseling services to children and youth. With training in mental health issues and counseling techniques, these related-service school personnel have valuable expertise to contribute in serving children with mental health needs (American School Counselor Association, 2015; Center for Mental Health in Schools at UCLA, 2014; Joyce-Beaulieu & Rossen, 2014; National Association of School Psychologists, 2010; School Social Work Association of America, 2013b).

In their graduate training, psychologists, school psychologists, counselors, and social workers all receive knowledge of and experience in delivering counseling services to youth and thus are well positioned to provide these services. However, studies also indicate that regardless of their initial training, practitioners also benefit from ongoing training in best practices methods, such as CBT. This continued training serves to help practitioners maintain and enhance skills as well as remain diligent in bridging the gap between practice and emerging research (Beidas & Kendall, 2010). In surveys of therapists and school psychologists, school-based practitioners cite insufficient training and knowledge as barriers to providing these mental health supports (Beidas & Kendall, 2010; Castillo, Arroyo-Plaza, Tan, Sabnis, & Mattison, 2017; Suldo, Friedrich, & Michalowski, 2010). As an example, in a nationally representative sample survey, Hanchon and Fernald (2013) discovered over 90% of school psychology practitioners indicated that they had knowledge and training in counseling techniques but nearly 40% indicated that they felt less than sufficiently prepared in providing individual counseling services in schools, whereas over 40% indicated they felt less than sufficiently prepared to provide group counseling. Other studies note general practitioner criticism of formal treatment manuals and difficulty navigating counseling services within the institutional context of schools (Beidas & Kendall, 2010). In response to these needs, this book endeavors to provide school-based practitioners, whether they are new to the field or seasoned veterans, easily accessible tools to utilize when providing effective CBT for students and offers numerous examples of practical school-based applications. This chapter provides an overview of the use of CBT within schools and the multitiered systems of support (MTSS) model, whereas Chapter 2, Cognitive Theoretical Foundations, and Chapter 3, Cognitive Behavioral Therapy Essential Components, discuss CBT theoretical foundations and essential components. The second section of the text (i.e., Chapter 4, Emotional and Behavioral Regulation Strategies, through Chapter 6, Applied Cognitive Behavioral Therapy Session Activities) offers specific counseling techniques, utilizing a number of session activities and worksheet resources (found in the Appendix). Lastly, Chapter 7, Case Studies, provides case studies that integrate CBT intervention as applied within a school setting. These case studies give a "real-world" context for many of the techniques described in the book.

The delivery of school-based counseling is important in that it removes many of the barriers to services, such as missed appointments due to transportation challenges, the hardship of lost employment time for parents, and the financial strain on families to pay for private mental health treatment. Moreover, integrating counseling as a key component of school intervention service delivery can be highly beneficial for students because youth are available multiple days per week to receive these services. Counseling plans can be coupled with classroom behavior strategies to foster generalization of skills, and a plethora of opportunities exist for teachers to reinforce concepts within their classrooms throughout the day. Additionally, school-based service delivery offers many opportunities to observe and monitor newly learned strategies in an authentic setting, which can help ensure that lasting behavioral changes are achieved. Research suggests that providing school-based mental health services also can reduce disparities in the utilization of mental health services among minority youth (Cummings, Ponce, & Mays, 2010) given that school systems provide equal access to services regardless of the financial resources of families.

A report from the U.S. surgeon general estimates that 20% of school-age children experience mental health problems in any given year. Of those students who will experience significant mental health needs, nearly 10% to 15% will suffer significant impairment in their ability to learn, be successful at school, make and keep friends, and maintain positive relationships with their caregivers (Merikangas et al., 2010; U.S. Department of Health & Human Services [USDHHS], 2000). Another indicator of student adjustment risk is school dropout. Unfortunately, within the general population, only about 82% (i.e., 4 out of every 5) of students in the United States successfully graduate from high school with a regular diploma within 4 years of entering ninth grade. This results in thousands of students dropping out of school each day in the United States (McFarland, Stark, & Cui, 2018). Regular diploma graduation rates vary significantly by state with the District of Columbia lowest at 61% and Iowa highest at 91%. Thirty-five states maintain averages at 80% or higher. Differential graduation rates also exist across gender, income, recency of immigration, race/ethnicity, and disability status. Males and students with low-income circumstances are overrepresented as dropouts across all race/ethnicities, and low-income students have a higher dropout rate than middle- or high-income students (9.4%, 5.4%, and 2.6%, respectively). Among those students with low income, students who also experience homelessness are especially vulnerable for both dropout and mental health distress (Sulkowski & Michael, 2014). Hispanic students born outside the United States have a 21% dropout rate (3.9% for non-Hispanic students) with first-generation students' dropout rates decreasing to 7.1% for Hispanic and 2.2% for non-Hispanic students (McFarland et al., 2018).

In 2013–2014, the regular diploma graduation rate within 4 years of entering ninth grade was 87% for White students, 76% for Hispanic students, and 73% for Black students (McFarland et al., 2018). For students of Hispanic heritage, the dropout rates also differed significantly by subgroups, as those of Cuban, Spaniard, Costa Rican, Panamanian, Colombian, Peruvian, and Venezuelan descent have lower than national mean dropout rates. In contrast, dropout rates for students from Guatemalan and Honduran descent are quite high: 28.7% and 19.5%, respectively (McFarland et al., 2018). Likewise, students of Asian descent generally have lower than mean dropout rates with the exception of Nepalese and Burmese descent: 19.6% and 27.5%, respectively. When data include high school completed by alternative means (e.g., general education diploma [GED]), graduation rates increase for most groups (i.e., White 94%, Black 92%, Hispanic 87%, Asian 99%, Pacific Islander 94%, American Indian/Alaska Native 79%, two or more races 97%; male 92% and female 93%). These data are lower for students with disabilities even when including alternative graduation status (with disability 84%, without disability 93%). For students receiving services for emotional disturbance (ED) under IDEIA, the dropout rate (i.e., no less than 35% from 2005 to 2015) is higher than in any other disability category, including those with intellectual disabilities (U.S. Department of Education [USDOE],Office of Special Education and Rehabilitative Services, & Office of Special Education Programs, 2018). Across the data, individuals with disabilities, especially ED, males, low income, native-born, American Indian/Alaska Native, and some subgroups within broad race/ethnicity groups appear to be most vulnerable. Therefore, they are likely to need and benefit from social–emotional and counseling supports. Given the unique life circumstances of these individuals, cultural considerations also are warranted in delivering services. Chapter 3, Cognitive Behavioral Therapy Essential Components, to Chapter 5, Exposure and Response Prevention and Cognitive Behavioral Therapy, offer additional information of cultural awareness and competencies for delivering counseling.

Lastly, mental health issues among youth are a global problem that extends well beyond the boundaries of the United States. In this regard, a study by the World Health Organization indicates that mental health problems account for nearly half of all disabilities internationally among individuals between the ages of 10 and 24 (Gore et al., 2011). Of those in need of mental health services worldwide, less than half receive services (Patton et al., 2012), illustrating the significant need. The provision of high-quality and targeted counseling interventions can assist students experiencing these difficulties to stay in school and to complete their education. Collectively, these findings highlight a critical need to provide mental health interventions to at-risk students before their problems become pervasive or chronic.

Schools and school-based mental health professionals can have a significant impact on addressing the unmet emotional, behavioral, and adjustment needs of youth. Research indicates that the majority of youth (i.e., 70%–80%) who do receive mental health services access these services through their local school districts (Bains & Diallo, 2016; Dowdy et al., 2015). Based on these data, the American Academy of Pediatrics (n.d.) has advocated for the provision of more school-based mental health services, noting the benefits of better access to assessment/evaluation or intervention compliance. As part of their initiatives, they endorsed the Mental Health in Schools Act of 2015 (H.R. 1211), which calls for increased funding and health student programs in schools to promote student well-being. Additionally, through the surgeon general's national agenda, mental health services are considered a national priority for all children, including intervention research and behavioral support delivered within the school. In particular, students from underrepresented groups, those living in poverty, and those with disabilities may demonstrate vulnerabilities that warrant considerations for early school-based intervention services (Bains & Diallo, 2016; Dowdy et al., 2015).

Counseling in schools can come in many forms, and it can be tailored to support a wide variety of developmental concerns. In elementary school, first-tier counseling services often include addressing systems-wide issues related to bullying prevention, character values, stress reduction, prosocial life skills, and consulting on educational issues. Second-tier counseling services often provide small-group and individual counseling. Examples may include friendship groups for new or shy students, self-esteem building, teaching self-regulation in regard to classroom rules or expectations, peer mediation, conflict resolution, grief counseling, organization skills, understanding body changes as puberty approaches, addressing abuse or family crisis, and advising on personal hygiene or appropriate social boundaries. Addressing all of these needs generally involves explicitly teaching skills to the child through counseling strategies or collaborating with the family to improve the student's response to temporary life stressors. In middle and high school, first-tier systems-wide counseling services may include life skills training, bullying prevention, and substance use prevention, as well as consultation as a member of leadership teams on educational issues. Second-tier, short-term, or individualized counseling interventions for older students often address increasing interpersonal communication skills, goal setting, social skills, and career planning. All of these counseling functions noted are vital in schools. However, for students with the most pervasive and severe mental health disorders, the services noted previously may not be adequate, as these students require more extensive and formalized therapeutic approaches, such as CBT, to address social and emotional dysfunction.

DSM-5 CHILD AND ADOLESCENT DIAGNOSES AND AGE OF ONSET

A brief overview of the *Diagnostic and Statistical Manual of Mental Disorders* (5th ed.; *DSM-5*; American Psychiatric Association [APA], 2013) diagnoses that are common to school-age children is provided in this section, as students with these symptoms are most likely to require more intensive or therapeutic counseling interventions. However, it is important to note that the CBT techniques expressed throughout this book also can be applied to a wide range of adjustment, behavioral, and social–emotional needs for youth even if a formal diagnosis is not indicated. A wealth of research over the past few decades indicates that very specific components of CBT are well suited and effective for treating many specific disorders and thinking distortions; however, the same CBT components are not equally effective for each type of diagnosis. For example, exposure and response prevention (E/RP, see Chapter 5, Exposure and Response Prevention and Cognitive Behavioral Therapy), a type of therapy that falls under the CBT umbrella and involves facing one's fears while abstaining from engaging in anxiety-reductive compulsions, has been found to be a first-line treatment for obsessive-compulsive disorder (OCD) in children (Jordan, Reid, Mariaskin, Augusto, & Sulkowski, 2012). In contrast, the same CBT method of E/RP could be contraindicated for a child with conduct disorder. Being aware of specific symptoms of these disorders can assist in planning CBT sessions to focus on the correct targeted skills and avoiding wasted time and counterproductive methods (Soutullo, Palma, & Joyce, 2014; Sulkowski, Joyce, & Storch, 2011).

Research suggests that over one-half of all lifetime mental health diagnoses first manifest during childhood/adolescence, and up to three-fourths of all syndromes emerge before age 24 (Kessler et al., 2005). The early emergence of a wide range of mental health issues is illustrated in Figure 1.1, which provides a review of the *DSM-5* (APA, 2013). Therefore, it is important for school-based counselors to consult the *DSM-5* when they are seeking to better understand the students they work with who have mental health diagnoses. The *DSM-5* also can offer insight for conceptualization of intervention plans, alert practitioners to common co-occurring symptoms, and offer insights on gender, race/ethnicity, socioeconomic status (SES), and cultural considerations (Joyce-Beaulieu & Sulkowski, 2016).

Elementary behavior specialists, social workers, counselors, and school psychologists are likely to receive the initial teacher referrals for disorders. Depending on the developmental course of specific syndromes, the age of onset varies and thus may be initiated at different points in a child's educational experience. Therefore,

DSM-5 Disorders—Prevalence Rate and Typical Age-of-Onset Range

Age	Percentage	Childhood											Adolescent						Postsecondary						Gender
		2	3	4	5	6	7	8	9	10	11	12	13	14	15	16	17	18	19	20	21	22	23	24	
ADHD	5.0																		▓	▓	▓				> M
Adjustment	5.0–20																		▓	▓	▓	▓	▓	▓	?
Anorexia Nervosa	0.4																					▓	▓	▓	> F
Antisocial Personality	0.2–3.3																		▓	▓	▓	▓	▓	▓	> M
Autism Spectrum	1.0																								> M
Avoidant Personality	2.4																		▓	▓	▓	▓	▓	▓	> M
Bipolar I	0.6																								> M
Bipolar II	0.3																		▓	▓	▓	▓		▓	M = F
Borderline Personality	1.6–5.9																								> F
Bulimia Nervosa	1.0–1.5																		▓	▓	▓	▓	▓	▓	> F
Conduct	2.0–10																								> M
Cyclothymic	0.4–1.0																		▓	▓	▓	▓	▓	▓	M = F
Disruptive Mood Dysregulation	2.0–5.0																								> M
Excoriation (skin picking)	1.4																								> F
Histrionic Personality	1.8																		▓	▓	▓	▓	▓	▓	> F
Generalized Anxiety	0.9																		▓	▓	▓	▓	▓	▓	> F
Hoarding	2.0–6.0																								> M
Intermittent Explosive	2.7																					▓	▓	▓	> M
Major Depressive	7.0																		▓	▓	▓	▓		▓	> F
Narcissistic Personality	≤6.2																								> M

(continued)

Disorder	DSM-5 Prevalence (%)	Sex
Obsessive-Compulsive	1.2	>M
Obsessive-Compulsive Personality	2.1–7.9	>M
Oppositional Defiant	1.0–11.0	>M
Panic	2.0–3.0	>F
Paranoid Personality	2.3–4.4	>M
Persistent Depressive	0.5	?
Posttraumatic Stress	8.7	>F
Reactive Attachment	?	?
Schizoid Personality	3.1–4.9	>M
Schizophrenia	0.3–0.7	>M
Schizotypal Personality	4.6	>M
Selective Mutism	0.03–1.0	M = F
Separation Anxiety	1.6–4.0	M = F
Social Anxiety	7.0	>F
Somatic Symptom	5.0–7.0	>F
Specific Phobia	5.0–16	>F
Tourette's	3.0–8.0	>M
Trichotillomania (hairpulling)	1.0–2.0	>F

Figure 1.1 Common *DSM-5* psychiatric disorders with prevalence rate and typical age of initial diagnosis.

Note: Data in this table are based on *DSM-5* prevalence, development, and course information related to childhood through early adulthood, unless data were available only for adults. Neurocognitive and substance use disorders are excluded. Light shading indicates pre-K to 12th grade; dark shading denotes college age.

ADHD, attention deficit hyperactivity disorder; *DSM-5, Diagnostic and Statistical Manual of Mental Disorders,* 5th edition; F, female; M, male; ?, unknown based on *DSM-5.*

practitioners who are in elementary schools may encounter significantly different child needs from those who are primarily serving students in secondary education settings (see Table 1.1). With appropriate intervention, some emotional stressors and diagnoses seem to resolve within a prescribed time frame (e.g., reactive attachment disorder, typical school adjustment), whereas others are more episodic based on stressors and temporal factors (e.g., adjustment disorders, major depressive disorder) that can recur along with negative life events throughout a student's educational years. Symptoms of other mental health disorders are chronic in nature (e.g., attention deficit hyperactivity disorder [ADHD], autism spectrum disorder, and schizophrenia). They may require more sustained school and even community services throughout the youth's educational experience. The following list denotes disorders that are most likely to occur first during specific grades and are more likely to be treated initially by counselors in those school levels.

- Preschool or elementary school: ADHD, autism spectrum disorder, reactive attachment disorder, selective mutism, separation anxiety, specific phobia, and Tourette's disorder
- Middle and high school: excoriation (skin-picking) disorder, social anxiety disorder, and trichotillomania (compulsive hair-pulling disorder)
- Postsecondary/college: antisocial personality disorder, avoidant personality disorder, bipolar type I disorder, borderline personality disorder, histrionic personality disorder, narcissistic personality disorder, obsessive-compulsive personality disorder, and paranoid personality disorder

Other disorders are more variable in their onset range, as noted in Table 1.1, with onset ages that span from childhood to adolescence or preadulthood. These disorders include the following: adjustment disorder, anorexia nervosa, bulimia nervosa, conduct disorder, disruptive mood dysregulation disorder, generalized anxiety disorder, hoarding disorder, major depressive disorder, OCD, oppositional defiant disorder (ODD), panic disorder, persistent depressive mood disorder, posttraumatic stress disorder (PTSD), schizoid personality disorder, schizophrenia, schizotypal personality disorder, and somatic symptom disorder. As the onset of these disorders spans across different academic years, practitioners serving children of all ages will likely need counseling skills to help students who are affected by these disorders.

Specific mental health supports and transition services are often needed to help students with disorders that present during adolescence and young adulthood. School-based mental health service providers may be involved with formal efforts to prepare students with mental health needs for successful entrance into postsecondary education settings and related opportunities through their participation in federally mandated transition planning efforts (Joyce & Grapin, 2012; Joyce-Beaulieu & Grapin, 2014; Sulkowski & Joyce, 2012).

Beginning at age 16, written transition supports are legally mandated and written into the individualized education plans of students with disabilities (USDOE, 2011). Depending on the student, these supports may include counseling interventions that build self-efficacy, mental health wellness, and/or self-advocacy for continuing mental health supports in college or in workplace transitions. Services for students with disabilities also extend to direct service provision in postsecondary education mental health centers and college disability centers for traditional college enrollment. Now more than ever, the lines are blurred between high school

TABLE 1.1   Behavior Modification Strategies

Technique	Description and Goals	Key Points for Implementation
Shaping	Shaping is utilized to encourage an individual to exhibit a target behavior by reinforcing successive approximations of that behavior over time. It is best applied when there is a large gap between a student's current behaviors and the desired behaviors.	■ Identify target or desired behavior goal. ■ Identify a behavior in the individual's present repertoire as a starting point for reinforcement. ■ Select an appropriate reinforcer. ■ Create a sequence of successive approximations of the behavior. ■ Reward successive approximations of the behavior until the child arrives at the target behavior. ■ For example, if targeting completing math worksheets, start by rewarding completion of one item, then two items, and so on, to completion.
Fading	Fading is used to encourage an individual to demonstrate a target behavior across multiple settings. This is accomplished by gradually changing one setting, in which the behavior already occurs, to a second setting. *Note: This technique calls for changes in settings rather than changes in behaviors.*	■ Identify the setting in which the behavior is already occurring. ■ Identify a setting in which the behavior should occur (i.e., target environment). ■ Create a sequence of successive approximations of the target environment. ■ Use a token economy to reward the display of appropriate behaviors in the target setting as the child progresses through this sequence. ■ For example, if a child learns to control anxiety in counseling sessions but cries when in class, gradually increase the number of persons in counseling activities, until she or he is more comfortable with others, and then move to a classroom full of students.
Chaining	Chaining is used to encourage the student to exhibit a series of related behaviors (i.e., to strengthen a sequence of new responses that ultimately elicit the target behavior). Chaining can also be used to weaken maladaptive behavior patterns.	■ Identify response patterns in the old behavior chain, starting back far enough to include responses that prompt the undesired behavior. ■ Write a new behavior chain that prompts the target behavior. ■ Model the new behavior chain, and have the child follow the new sequence. ■ Reinforce the child for successfully implementing the new chain. ■ For example, if a student is chronically late from lunch, teach a new response (e.g., clean lunch tray up earlier, quicker route back to class), model and remind her or him; if she or he forgets, walk back to cafeteria and rehearse.
Contingency contracting	Contingency contracting is used to increase the occurrence of a low-frequency behavior. In this technique, permission to engage in high-frequency behaviors is made contingent on the performance of a low-frequency behavior.	■ Establish a contract to determine the terms of contingency between the low- and high-frequency behaviors. ■ Reward the child frequently with smaller amounts of the preferred or high-frequency activity and only after he or she has executed the low-frequency behavior (i.e., do not provide noncontingent reinforcement). ■ For example, give 10 minutes of preferred computer time for 1 hour of work completion.

(continued)

TABLE 1.1   Behavior Modification Strategies (*continued*)

Technique	Description and Goals	Key Points for Implementation
Token reinforcement	The purpose of token reinforcement is to increase the occurrence of desirable behaviors and/or to decrease the occurrence of problematic behaviors by systematically reinforcing the goal behavior.	■ Identify and define problematic behaviors as well as appropriate replacement behaviors. ■ Identify tokens, feasible reinforcers, and a schedule of reinforcement. ■ Provide reinforcers when desired behavior occurs. Implement a response cost when inappropriate behaviors are exhibited. ■ For example, a child earns tokens toward a reinforcer for work completed; not turning in assignments could result in token reduction.
Replacement behavior training	Replacement behavior training is used to teach new behaviors and skills that can be used in place of problematic behaviors.	■ Identify and define the problematic behavior. ■ Identify and teach the individual replacement behaviors. This may require modeling and opportunities for student practice. ■ Implement schedule of reinforcement for replacement behaviors. ■ For example, each time a student prone to impulsive anger says "excuse me" or uses an "I" statement, offer points toward earning a reinforcer.
Interdependent group-oriented contingency management	This technique is a group management system that reinforces the behaviors of a group as a whole. The goal of this strategy is to increase appropriate behaviors while simultaneously decreasing classroom disruptions; groups also may persuade individuals to cooperate.	■ Divide the class into groups or teams. ■ Model appropriate behaviors and instruct students to role-play behavior. ■ Identify a group reinforcer (e.g., points, reward). ■ Post a visual representation of points earned or lost. ■ Reinforce the winning team at predetermined intervals. ■ For example, groups caught displaying good social skills earn points (e.g., helping others, quiet group projects, saying "thank you").
Precorrection and prompting	This technique is designed to encourage the display of appropriate or desirable behaviors, especially when it is likely that the individual will need reminders to do so.	■ Identify the context in which problem behaviors typically occur and clarify behavioral expectations for that setting. ■ Define/model expected behaviors, have student role-play behavior. ■ Provide reinforcement for appropriate behaviors. ■ Provide cuing and prompting as needed for appropriate behaviors. ■ For example, prompting a withdrawn student to join a group or cuing the student on introductory comments (e.g., "Say hello to Juan").
Differential reinforcement of alternative or incompatible behavior	The purpose of this technique is to weaken maladaptive behaviors by simultaneously strengthening an incompatible or competing response.	■ Identify and define the problematic behavior. ■ Identify a competing behavior (i.e., one that will be incompatible with the problem behavior). ■ Reinforce occurrences of the competing behavior while ignoring or redirecting the student when the problematic behavior occurs. ■ For example, when targeting classroom running, reward in-seat behavior or walking behaviors.

(continued)

TABLE 1.1   Behavior Modification Strategies (*continued*)

Technique	Description and Goals	Key Points for Implementation
Self-monitoring	Self-monitoring is used to increase the individual's awareness of his or her behaviors and to encourage him or her to self-regulate while working toward a goal.	■ Identify target behavior to be monitored. ■ Set intervention goals as well as time frame for goal. ■ Provide child with a cuing graphic, list, or behavior chart. ■ Define and describe steps for self-monitoring the behavior and model them for the student. ■ For example, a shy student might mark his or her own behavior chart each time he or she initiates a conversation with someone; try to increase total interactions each day or weekly.
Self-reinforcement	This technique is used to encourage students to reinforce their own appropriate behaviors with either tangible or intangible rewards.	■ Identify an appropriate reinforcer. ■ Determine contingencies for earning the reinforcer. ■ Describe and model steps for earning and accessing the reinforcer. ■ For example, student can self-initiate a 2-minute Internet surfing break after 30 minutes of work completion in the library.

Source: Alberto, P. A., & Troutman, A. C. (2012). *Applied behavior analysis for teachers* (9th ed.). New York, NY: Pearson; Kaplan, J. S., & Carter, J. (1995). *Beyond behavior modification: A cognitive-behavioral approach to behavior management in the school* (3rd ed.). Austin, TX: Pro-Ed.

and college, as 82% of high schools offer dual enrollment, according to the National Center of Education Statistics (NCES) report (Marken, Gray, & Lewis, 2013). The number of students in adolescence receiving instruction in college settings for at least part of the day is on the rise (National Research Center for Career and Technical Education, 2010; USDOE, 2011). Students utilizing dual enrolment are typically in ninth grade or higher (although some states, such as Arizona, have no age limit). Therefore, counseling for high-school students may occur within the postsecondary institution in which they are dual enrolled.

COUNSELING WITHIN MTSS IN SCHOOLS

Although a wide range of mental health high-quality services are available through community agencies and private practitioners, a review of the status of national mental healthcare for youth indicates that those services are most often accessed in a fragmented and noncomprehensive manner. This has often resulted in low service effectiveness, especially for more chronic or severe mental health problems (USDHHS, 2000). Response to intervention (RtI) and MTSS are models of school-based service delivery that have evolved over the past few decades to provide schools with the infrastructure to offer a continuum of multifaceted counseling and behavioral supports to students who display a range of academic, behavioral, and mental health needs (Cook et al., 2015; Sulkowski & Michael, 2014; Sulkowski, Wingfield, Jones, & Coulter, 2011). When mental health services are well integrated into a systematic model, academic outcomes improve, behavioral referrals decrease (Hussey & Guo, 2003), and there are reduced disparities for students who receive services (Cummings et al., 2010).

The overarching RtI/MTSS frameworks incorporate a multitiered approach to service delivery to help students at varied levels of need (Elliott & Morrison, 2008; Kurns & Tilly, 2008). At the first tier of service delivery (tier I), general emotional and behavioral health as well as preventive universal or school-wide services are delivered. Examples may include prosocial social–emotional learning curricula embedded within the classroom instruction and positive behavioral intervention and supports (PBIS) framework for structuring school environments for all students. Tier I services meet the needs of approximately 80% to 85% of students. At the second tier (tier II), interventions are provided for students who display needs that cannot be adequately addressed by tier I services alone and are at risk for academic failure or other negative outcomes. Tier II services are predicted to serve 5% to 15% of the population, and these services are designed as short-term, low-intensity interventions that may be structured around a protocol or prescribed curricula. They often are provided once or twice a week for 6- to 12-week periods and can be delivered in group settings. Tier II interventions tend to address more common student needs and may include elements of CBT as needed (e.g., relaxation training, identifying negative emotional states, understanding cognitive triad), although other methods may be employed as well. Examples of tier II counseling interventions might include friendship groups, social skills training groups, self-esteem building exercises, problem-solving skills, test anxiety, or conflict resolution strategies. Within a typical school setting, there is generally a continued and revolving need for tier II counseling groups, especially around key student transitions (e.g., adapting to a new school, bereavement or loss, coping with teen relationship stressors). When students respond well to the intervention, a problem-solving team may decide to discontinue. If it is determined that a more intensive intervention is needed, students are provided more individualized, longer-term, and often more frequent intervention. This third tier (tier III) often supports 1% to 5% of the student population. Examples might include a semester or more of CBT therapy sessions, meeting two or more times per week, to address depression or a sequence of anger management/self-regulation interventions.

Students requiring tier III services often have a multifaceted support plan that also may include other behavioral interventions in addition to counseling (e.g., mentoring, daily behavior report cards, positive reinforcement plans to increase generalization of new behaviors taught in counseling sessions). For students with needs that require sustained intervention, special education eligibility may be considered with a classification of ED. Once identified, individuals receiving ED services may continue to require a structured counseling regimen for multiple years as well as supplemental mental health supports (e.g., behavior modification, outside counseling or family therapy coupled with school counseling, and sometimes psychopharmacology). A quick review of behavioral modification strategies that school personnel can utilize to supplement counseling or enhance multifaceted interventions is noted in Table 1.1.

Progress Monitoring

A key factor in well-implemented RtI/MTSS intervention models is the mandate for data-based decision-making and the utilization of progress-monitoring measures to track student outcomes. Progress monitoring offers a number of benefits, including feedback to the counselors on how well interventions are working, information to decide when goals are met and therefore when counseling can be ended, as well as guidance on when students may require more intense services or multifaceted intervention plans. This section reviews several easy methods for collecting progress-monitoring data on the effectiveness of counseling interventions: naturally occurring school performance data, observational data, knowledge/skills testing, daily behavioral report cards, behavior rating scales, subjective units of distress (SUDs) data, and the *DSM-5* cross-cutting symptomology measures.

Best practices associated with psychoeducational assessment involve employing a multifaceted approach that includes gathering information across multiple settings, at multiple times, and from multiple sources, using multiple data collection methods (American Educational Research Association, American Psychological Association, & National Council on Measurement in Education, 2014; Saklofske, Joyce, Sulkowski, & Climie, 2013). Although originally written for comprehensive test design, these principles also are valuable for conducting brief intervention outcome-related measurements, such as pre- and postintervention assessments. By acquiring data across multiple settings, personnel can ensure that the student is applying the new skills throughout the day and generalizing to other contexts outside the counseling sessions. These data provide strong evidence that a student has adopted the new strategies and the counseling has had positive impact. A benefit of gathering information multiple times is to establish that new knowledge or improved emotional mood is stable. For example, measuring a child's feelings of sadness across several sessions and establishing a period of time that their mood improves and stabilizes can indicate effectiveness and perhaps a good rationale for closing the intervention, whereas a couple of session of not feeling sad does not provide enough information to determine whether intervention should be withdrawn. Additionally, if the first measures are made prior to the counseling, the data will provide information on the student's baseline level of functioning in a particular domain (e.g., anxiety, social skills) that can be compared to later levels of functioning that are assessed during or after counseling to provide stronger evidence of improvement. By collecting information on a student's level of functioning across multiple sources (e.g., teacher, parent, self-report), possible rater biases can be controlled. For example, a parent's overly optimistic perceptions of his or her child may not be supported by data provided by another caregiver or by adults at school.

Of course, to rule out or control for rater biases, high-quality rating measures are needed. These include validity scales that alert practitioners to inconsistent or overly negative/positive rating patterns. Through measuring multiple variables, practitioners also can ensure that complex sets of skills are thoroughly assessed before recommendations to change or discontinue services are made. An example of this might include measuring an adolescent's knowledge of new relaxation techniques and problem-solving strategies as well as obtaining his or her self-rated feelings of anger.

Additionally, interviewing the student directly can provide qualitative information on state-of-mood, attitudes, and perceptions, which will be important to informing therapy sessions. For students who are reticent to share their thoughts verbally, therapists may find sentence completion exercises or if/then questionnaires helpful (see Appendix Exhibits 1.1–1.3 for examples). These data coupled with observations of her or his use of the relaxation techniques in a natural setting (e.g., in class when frustrated, during competitive physical education activities) and decreasing discipline referrals for angry outbursts would offer a well-rounded set of data for intervention decision-making that would be consistent with an RtI model of assessment and service delivery.

Traditionally, intervention effectiveness decisions have relied on anecdotal evidence (e.g., teacher report of improvement), which subsequently left unanswered questions about whether reported changes were stable, enduring, adequately learned, and generalizable to other settings, thus transportable to other contexts or applicable in similar situations that the student may encounter. Fortunately, there are many quick and easy progress-monitoring methods available that offer greater validity and reliability than anecdotal reports. The following sections offer a brief review of counseling progress-monitoring methods with the understanding that the practitioner's choice of specific methods (or combinations of measures) will depend on the complexity of the presenting problems displayed by the student and the targeted goals of CBT.

Naturally Occurring School Data

A number of readily available sources of behavioral data can be easily accessed by school-based mental health practitioners. These sources do not require extra data collection effort or time for counselors and thus are highly efficient. Often, these data are directly related to the counseling referral concerns and the preferred outcomes that are desired after intervention. As an example, for students with externalizing or acting-out behavioral problems, important and relevant school data to track include office discipline referrals (ODRs), in-school suspensions (ISSs), and incidents of out-of-school suspensions (OSSs). For youth with the aforementioned problems and a significant discipline history, counseling strategies often aim to foster self-regulation, anger management, or conflict resolution skills, which, if successfully learned and applied, likely will result in reductions in ODR, ISS, and OSS incidents. Similarly, for students who are disengaged academically, do not participate in class, have low work completion, and have difficulty meeting deadlines for projects, monitoring work completion and grades related to assignments can provide a direct measure of whether counseling to address academic motivation is being effective.

For students with social anxiety who may avoid performance assignments (e.g., oral presentation, group projects) and also may exhibit high rates of absenteeism, attendance data, number of days tardy, and completion of key assignments requiring public evaluation are easily accessible data sources that can help with measuring the efficacy of intervention. As another example, for anxious students with high numbers of unjustified nurse visits and unnecessary requests to go home for somatic complaints (e.g., headaches, stomach pains), their nurse visit data can be tracked across the counseling intervention sessions to show improvements. Nurse visits are logged daily and thus are easy-to-access and naturally occurring data within school systems.

Figure 1.2 provides an example of using naturally occurring school data for progress monitoring during the course of counseling intervention. To assess therapeutic progress, ODR, ISS, and school absences were reviewed, as these data were tracked by schools as part of their general operating procedures and readily available for review. Weeks 1 to 3 are baseline data, and weeks 4 to 12 represent data during counseling. The counseling sessions aimed to address impulse control difficulties in

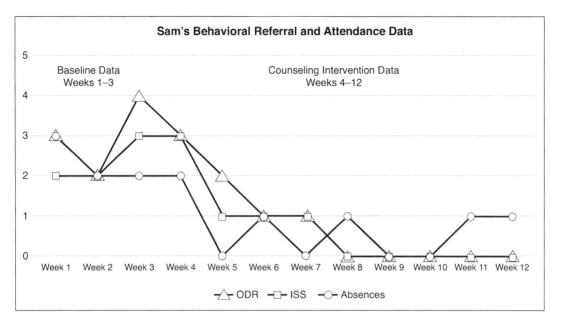

Figure 1.2   Naturally occurring school data progress-monitoring sample.
ISS, in-school suspension; ODR, office discipline referral.

a student that resulted in numerous altercations with classmate, disciplinary referrals, and subsequent school avoidant problems.

To help this student, cognitive restructuring was provided to challenge two cognitive distortions: jumping to negative conclusions and mind reading. In addition, anger management skills were taught that aimed to increase the student's emotional regulation skills, and the use of "I" statements was taught to help the student communicate his needs better in a nonconfrontational manner. Lastly, the student was taught conflict resolution skills (i.e., generating nonaggressive yet effective solutions for addressing interpersonal conflicts). Counseling for this student was individualized and delivered two times a week (30 minutes per session) for 9 weeks, totaling 18 sessions. Additionally, avoidance issues related to school attendance were addressed. Data indicate the student's ODR and ISS incidents steadily diminished to zero incidents and stabilized there for several weeks, so counseling appears to have had a positive effect, at least on part of the goals for better self-regulation. However, absences were only modestly improved during the intervention time frame; thus, additional interventions to address attendance were warranted.

Observational Data

School-based mental health professionals are highly familiar with observational data, as these data are often requested by teachers who are trying to better understand puzzling or maladaptive student behaviors, physicians who are diagnosing ADHD or monitoring medication effects, as well as parents who have concerns regarding the interpersonal actions of their children. Observational data also can be utilized to measure counseling outcomes. Examples might include pre- and postintervention data for on-task behaviors when the goals of counseling are addressing self-regulation, attention, frustration tolerance, withdrawal, or work completion.

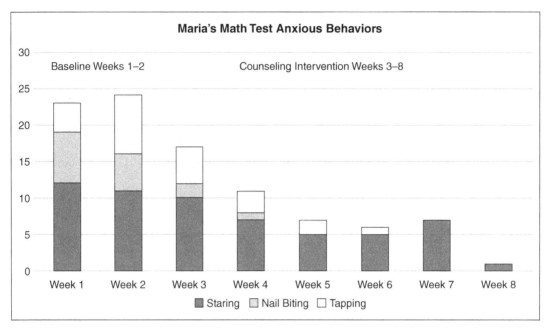

Figure 1.3 Observational data progress-monitoring sample; frequency of maladaptive behaviors during math quizzes.

Several factors can increase the utility of observational data: assuring that baseline functioning is documented for comparison to intervention measures, collecting samples across classes and times of day, and establishing peer comparisons.

An example of observational data is noted in Figure 1.3 for an anxious student with a history of maladaptive test behaviors that included significant nail biting, loud finger tapping, and episodes of staring off. These behaviors were interfering with her test performance specifically in math, a class she struggled in academically as she was preoccupied with worry and not finishing quizzes in the allotted time. Therefore, a goal of counseling was to challenge her cognitive distortions associated with catastrophizing: "I'll never pass math," "I can't get answers right on math tests," and "I'll never graduate or go to college without math." Further, a second goal was to teach her more appropriate replacement strategies that she could employ when she was anxious (e.g., four-square breathing relaxation technique, positive self-affirmations). Observations were taken each Friday using time sampling method for 20 minutes with 30-second intervals during the weekly math quiz. The first 2 weeks' baseline data were collected. Weeks 3 to 8 counseling intervention was implemented twice weekly with 20-minute sessions (total of 12 counseling sessions). Results of this case study indicate that the student improved because she displayed fewer maladaptive behaviors related to her test anxiety. Additionally, teacher data on number of test items completed also indicated improvement. By the 9th week, she was completing all quiz items. Although, not all items were always correct, the interference from math test anxiety behaviors was important to her success. The discrete math skill components continued to be addressed in tier II math intervention. A technique for measuring how well she is applying replacement strategies taught in counseling (e.g., breathing technique) could also be acquired through observing her use of the new strategies during quizzes.

Knowledge/Skills Testing

Often through the CBT process, a number of new skills are taught. These skills might include being able to identify and describe one's feelings, employing self-calming and relaxation techniques (e.g., diaphragmatic breathing, progressive muscle relaxation), challenging negative self-talk or cognitive distortions, interacting more effectively with peers, or becoming more assertive in getting one's needs met in a prosocial manner. The student's awareness of these skills can provide a good comparison of pre- and posttest knowledge. For example, this might occur by having the counselor inquire during the first session as to how many (and what) self-calming techniques a student knows or how many (and what) feeling words he or she can recall and pair with facial expressions (e.g., sad, mad, angry). When measuring this knowledge, it is important to have the child recall without providing her or him with cues that can give away answers or simply stating his or her opinion of how many new strategies he or she has acquired. Having the child demonstrate the skill also is a strong measure of knowledge acquisition.

Figure 1.4 illustrates pre- and posttest progress-monitoring data for a small-group application of CBT addressing social skills. In general, the goal of the CBT sessions was to provide support for four third-grade students from different classrooms who had similar needs. Teacher referrals indicated that the students were socially withdrawn and awkward in interacting with others, and they had been observed to voice maladaptive and self-deprecating statements when they were encouraged to contribute to group projects. These negative statements sometimes also caused others to avoid playing or working with them. Examples of statements were as follows: "Nobody ever likes me" (overgeneralizing), "They won't like my drawing on the group poster" (fortune-telling), and "I'm just stupid" (labeling). Counseling sessions addressed several of the cognitive distortions displayed by the

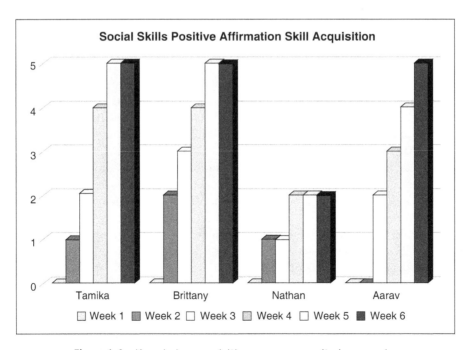

Figure 1.4   Knowledge acquisition progress-monitoring sample.

students by teaching the students to identify and employ more adaptive positive self-affirmations as replacement thoughts and also building prosocial skills in interacting with others (e.g., joining a group, reciprocity in sharing ideas).

One 20-minute group counseling session was provided per week for 6 weeks. Over the 6 weeks, each student had to create five positive replacement thoughts he or she could use in difficult situations and memorize the affirmations. These were acquired one per week, and they were given practice scenarios in sessions to build fluency. The affirmations they came up with and began to apply to replace their cognitive distortions included "Some people like me," "The group poster might be hard but I can try my best," "I am good at ____, so maybe I'll be good at this too," and "Sometimes I may feel stupid but everyone does. I actually do good at school sometimes." As one can see, all of the replacement self-affirmations are more adaptive, objective, and rational than the cognitive distortions were. Additionally, these statements are not overly Pollyannaish or unreasonably or illogically optimistic. One of the goals in CBT is to be realistic and adaptive but not to be dismissive of real stressors students may encounter. Instead, the positive replacement statements provide relief by reducing students' use of negative thoughts as opposed to artificially inflating their use of positive ones.

In the example provided in Figure 1.4, Tamika, Brittany, and Aarav memorized and demonstrated fluency in applying five different positive replacement affirmations when presented a variety of social scenarios, by the 6th week. Although their progress was different, they each reached the goal. Verification by the teachers that the children also were heard using healthier responses in the classroom and were improving both the number and quality of interactions with others also supported invention effectiveness. Adding classroom observations would also strengthen confirmation that the skills were being applied. As noted in the graph, Nathan made little progress and stagnated at week 4. Thus, a rationale could be made for continuing and individualizing intervention for him.

Daily Behavioral Report Cards

Daily behavioral report cards are often utilized as a behavioral modification strategy, and they involve identifying observable and objectively defined target behaviors that are positively phrased that the child strives to achieve each day. Examples might include "Sally will raise her hand before asking questions" or "Juan turns in his homework at the beginning of each class." The child may be asked to have each teacher throughout the day note whether the behavioral goal is achieved. Usually, this strategy requires a parent review and/or signature at the end of the day, and it is tied to a specific reward if a certain number of points are earned. Often, rewards can be delivered at both home and school to ensure the generalizability of the plan across settings as well as the presentation of desired behaviors. Rewards may be tangible objects or preferred activities. Rewards should be coupled with praise and recognition for demonstrating positive or desired behaviors. The goals are set to be obtainable 75% or more of the time, and the criterion for reward is moved up as the child reaches his or her behavioral goals. When used as counseling outcome data, the results from daily behavioral report cards may be confounded with the behavioral management/incentive effects, as goal lines are often moved up over time. In other words, changes to behavior plans and related contingencies may make it challenging to generalize from these plans across different time points. However, it is

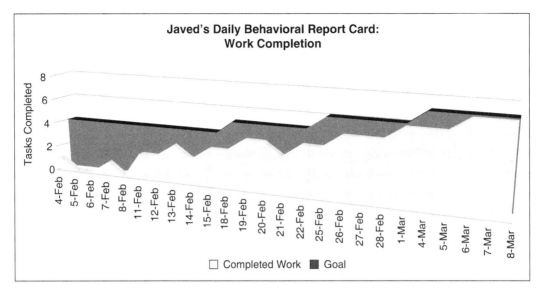

Figure 1.5   *Daily behavioral report card progress-monitoring sample.*

not uncommon for students with high needs to require multifaceted interventions, and coupling more than one method of support with the counseling effort is often a necessary strategy.

An example of a daily behavioral report card is given in Figure 1.5. The child's referral concern was task avoidance due to the student's perfectionistic tendencies, resulting in immediately giving up or throwing away a paper if he felt he made a mistake. Counseling targeted challenging an all-or-nothing (e.g., "I can't turn it in if it is not just right") thinking cognitive distortion, and it involved conducting behavioral exposures (i.e., managing distress associated with submitting less than perfect papers). Counseling also was coupled with a behavior plan that rewarded completion of class assignments. As reflected in the daily behavior report card data, the goal was graduated over time. It was first set at completing four tasks per day (e.g., worksheets, assignments, art activity) and then moved up one point each week after the 2nd week of the plan. The teacher also initially provided prompting, cueing, and positive praise for attempts at work, even if the answer was incorrect during the 1st week of intervention. Counseling was provided twice weekly for 4 weeks, and results showed notable improvement by the 3rd week.

Subjective Units of Distress

SUDs measurement is simply based on self-reported feelings (e.g., anxiousness, fear, and anger) that individuals experience in the moment when asked. The method can be utilized for a number of counseling purposes but is often applied during behavioral exposures to assess the degree of anxiety that an individual is experiencing when facing a feared situation or stimulus. A more detailed explanation for the procedure of using SUDs is provided in the section on the exposure/response prevention therapy technique in Chapter 5, Exposure and Response Prevention and Cognitive Behavioral Therapy; however, a basic review of this process is worth mentioning in this chapter. The student and the therapist can work together to help create the SUDs scale, and it can have a wide or small range of points (e.g., 1–100, 1–10). For

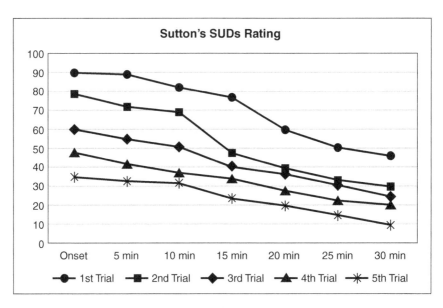

Figure 1.6 Subjective units of distress (SUDs) data progress-monitoring sample; exposures to crowded situations at school.

younger children, it may be helpful to use a smaller number of points and to provide descriptors on the scale adjacent to the numbers that the student chooses to make it personally more meaningful (e.g., "10 = freaking out," "4 = a little scared," 1 = "easy"). However, for assessing and interpreting progress-monitoring data, it will be important to report the scale number rather than the qualitative descriptors. Additionally, using pictorial representations may assist younger students in conceptualizing the scale (e.g., thermometers, rulers, rising stars). Pictorial themes may be especially appealing if they reflect the child's personal interests (e.g., sports, animals, rockets blasting off). Two samples of pictorial feelings scales for younger students are provided in the Appendix (see Exhibits 1.4 and 1.5).

SUDs data can be collected at each session, across the duration of intervention at select points (e.g., every 3 weeks), or multiple times within a session (particularly when E/RP is occurring). Figure 1.6 provides an example of SUDs progress-monitoring data on an anxiety scale with a range of 1 to 100 (100 = extremely high anxiety, 0 = absolute calm). This example reflects self-reported SUDs scale measurement every 5 minutes across five exposure counseling sessions. In this example, an adolescent student was afraid of crowds or being in dense groups of people (e.g., in crowded hallways). This fear resulted in her avoiding the cafeteria, missing required auditorium meetings, and avoiding participating in large-group activities (e.g., band practice).

Prior to engaging in the counseling intervention, the student and the school psychologist worked together to come up with a hierarchy of feared situations, and the student agreed to confront these situations. Therapy was first structured to have the student confront her anxious thoughts associated with being in crowded places through engaging in imaginal exposures. Then, a series of graduated in vivo (i.e., in real life) exposures (e.g., sitting in back of cafeteria during lunch, joining a band practice, attending the all-school meeting in the auditorium) were attempted, with the counselor accompanying and monitoring the student's self-reported stress level. According to the student's subjective report, her initial level of anxiety was a 90/100 SUDs during the first exposure trial. However, this decreased throughout the 30-minute exposure. In subsequent trials, her anxiety started to drop lower than the previous trial start point. Additionally, the pattern of data within each session indicated that the student's SUDs quickly dropped within about 5 to 10 minutes after exposure, which is relatively common for many youth experiencing anxiety problems. During trials 4 and 5, the student reported below-50 initial distress via her SUDs ratings. Overall, these data indicate the student was responding favorably to E/RP and benefiting from treatment as evidenced by reductions in overall distress at the outset of each exposure session as well as reductions in distress following each exposure.

Behavioral Rating Scales

Rating scales come in a wide variety of formats and degrees of complexity, and they may or may not have norm-referenced scores. Four basic types of behavior rating scales have obvious utility for progress monitoring associated with implementing CBT in the schools:

- Omnibus measures sample psychopathology across a number of internalizing and externalizing domains and allows comparison to a nationally representative sample of children. The Behavior Assessment System for Children, Third Edition (BASC-3) is one example of an omnibus measure that has multiple mental health scales (e.g., anxiety, depression, withdrawal, somatization, social skills, aggression, attention; Reynolds & Kamphaus, 2015). Although not necessarily intended to be used as a repeated measure of progress over a short period of time (e.g., instructions often ask for ratings of behavior over the past several weeks), this type of measure offers clinical norms and can be useful for measuring progress over time for students who fall in the clinical range. A limitation of omnibus measures is often their length, as many have over 100 items.
- A second generation of rating scales also has emerged to provide quick options for tier I screening in RtI/MTSS models. These measures typically contain 10 to 30 items and offer a single *T*-score that can be compared to national norms for identifying emotionally at-risk students. The BASC-3 Behavioral and Emotional Screening System (BASC-3 BESS) and the Conners 3 Global Index (Conners 3 GI) are examples of rating screener measures (Kamphaus & Reynolds, 2015; Conners, 2008). These instruments can be used repeatedly to track progress; however, one limitation of these measures is that they only give one global score rather than tracking progress on specific symptoms.
- Third-generation rating scales have added progress-monitoring forms that are short/quick measures addressing targeted areas of intervention need. They are norm referenced and designed for repeated measures over short periods of time. Many also offer scoring and tracking software programs that create intervention progress-monitoring graphs. Examples include the BASC-3 Flex Monitor forms. The instrument also offers the option of selecting items from a pool of 600 questions to customize the ratings (Reynolds & Kamphaus, 2016). Additional examples include the Conners 3 ADHD Index (Conners 3 AI), the Children's Depression Inventory–Second Edition, Short Form

TEST-TAKING SURVEY	Never	Sometimes	Always
1. Tests make me nervous.	1	2	3
2. I have to read questions over and over.	1	2	3
3. I have trouble concentrating during a test.	1	2	3
4. My mind goes blank during the test.	1	2	3
5. My head or stomach hurts before a test.	1	2	3
6. I worry about what grade I will get on a test.	1	2	3
7. My hands get shaky during a test.	1	2	3
8. During a test I forget things I knew before.	1	2	3
9. I don't sleep well the night before a big test.	1	2	3
10. I usually feel sick on the day of a test.	1	2	3

Figure 1.7   Test anxiety Likert scale progress-monitoring sample.

(CDI-2), and the Social Skills Improvement System (SSIS), as well as short versions of the Anger Regulation and Expression Scales (ARES-S; Conners, 2008; DiGiuseppe & Tafrate, 2011; Gresham & Elliot, 2008; Kovacs, 2004).

■ Self-made Likert scales can be created by the counselor to specifically target questions for the student, and they can be highly individualized. Decisions made based on these scales must be made with caution, as they lack norm-referenced comparison information. Figure 1.7 provides an example of a therapist-created Likert survey with specific questions based on targeted counseling goals and teacher-reported referral needs.

DSM-5 *Cross-Cutting Symptomology Measures*

For the first time, the *DSM-5* manual offered a series of freely accessible measures of psychiatric symptoms that also can be used as progress-monitoring measures. The measures can be downloaded and reproduced without charge by clinicians for use with their patients from the APA's *DSM-5* website (www.psychiatry.org/practice/dsm/dsm5/online-assessment-measures). Forms include ages 6 through adult and offer self-ratings, parent ratings, and some clinician ratings. The following categories are available:

■ Level 1 cross-cutting symptom measure includes adult symptom self-report (i.e., ages 18 and older), parent/guardian measures for ages 6 to 17, and child self-report measures (i.e., ages 11–17) with 25 items across 12 domains: depression, anger, irritability, mania, anxiety, somatic symptoms, inattention, suicidal ideation/attempt, psychosis, sleep disturbance, repetitive thoughts and behaviors, and substance use.

- Level 2 cross-cutting symptom measures include several brief adult (i.e., age 18 and older), parent report (i.e., ages 6–17), and child self-report (i.e., ages 11–17) symptom domain-specific measures (e.g., depression, anger, mania, anxiety).
- Disorder-specific severity measures offer symptom severity ratings for several syndromes (e.g., depression, separation anxiety disorder, social anxiety) that may be particularly important to diagnosis criteria where severity specifiers are indicated. Adult, child, and clinician-rated forms are available.
- Disability measures are based on the World Health Organization Disability Assessment Schedule 2.0 (Üstün, Kostanjsek, Chatterji, & Rehm, 2010). They include 36 items and assess disability impact across six domains: understanding/communicating, getting around, self-care, getting along with others, daily life activities, and integration/participation in society.
- Personality inventories are provided for adult (i.e., age 18 and older), child (i.e., ages 11–17), and parent report (i.e., ages 6–17). Five personality domains are included (i.e., negative affect, detachment, antagonism, disinhibition, and psychoticism).
- Additionally, the *DSM-5* site offers early development and home background interview forms as well as cultural formulation interviews that may be helpful during the case conceptualization stage of planning for CBT sessions. An example of *DSM-5* rating data (i.e., level 2 cross-cutting measure for somatic symptoms and severity measure for separation anxiety disorder) is included in the sample report in Chapter 7, Case Studies.

CBT EFFICACY IN SCHOOL-BASED APPLICATIONS

There are many different theoretical orientations for counseling; however, CBT is one of the most effective approaches as noted by the American Psychological Association's Task Force on Promotion and Dissemination of Psychological Procedures (Silverman et al., 2008). CBT has a long history of empirical support among clinical service providers for helping students with a wide range of needs, including ADHD, austism spectrum disorder, anxiety, bullying, OCD, depression, PTSD, panic attacks, and phobias (Abdulkader, 2017; Albano & Kendall, 2002; Bella-Awusah, Ani, Ajuwon, & Omigbodun, 2016; Kendall, 2006; Luxford, Hadwin, & Kovshoff, 2017; Rones & Hoagwood, 2000; Salloum, Sulkowski, Sirrine, & Storch, 2009). In fact, some researchers have found that CBT has more enduring results than medication for moderate and mild needs, and coupling CBT with medication can extend positive effects over medication alone for anxiety and depression (Carpenter et al., 2018; Cuijpers et al., 2014).

CBT also has been successfully adapted to provision of services within school settings for a wide range of disorders, including depression, anxiety, ODD, PTSD, and OCD (Creed, Reisweber, & Beck, 2012; Masia-Warner, Fisher, Shrout, Rathor, & Klein, 2007; Ruocco, Gordon, & McLean, 2016). Research indicates that the efficacy of CBT extends across a range of school settings serving diverse student populations (Mychailyszyn, Méndez, & Kendall, 2010; Neil & Christensen, 2009). Studies support both individual and small-group counseling delivery; however, results may vary by specific counseling needs (Eiraldi et al., 2016; Zaboski et al., 2019). For example, Ginsburg, Becker, Kingery, and Nichols (2008) found CBT services delivered in school-based mental health clinics were highly efficacious for high-risk populations of inner-city schools.

In addition to direct positive mental health outcomes, CBT intervention also has been shown to improve school academic performance. In a nonmanualized CBT intervention study that delivered 14 weeks of counseling to high school students, attendance was improved, discipline referral rates were lowered, and one half of the participants had higher grade point averages following services (Michael et al., 2013). A national review of school-based counseling literature found that positive impact was also documented for improving general social competency, reading and math scores, and personal engagement and commitment to school success (Foster et al., 2005).

CONTRAINDICATIONS FOR COUNSELING THERAPY

The application of CBT is dependent on a student's ability to understand causal connections among thoughts–feelings–behaviors, insightful self-awareness, and a motivation to participate in a meaningful way. Therefore, cognitive ability and maturity are essential considerations in selecting CBT as a counseling method. For students with significant intellectual disabilities, CBT may not be the most effective intervention methods. A second consideration is the child's developmental stage. Early Piagetian developmental theory noted that preoperational children (i.e., ages 2–7 years old) tend to function primarily from an egocentric view. Thus, it is unlikely that they will have great insight into their own thinking patterns or insight into others' perspectives during social interactions. Concrete operational age children (i.e., ages 7–11) can reason better than younger children, especially if concepts are demonstrated or put into concrete examples. Thus, CBT counseling that incorporates concrete activities and examples is likely to be somewhat effective. In comparison, children in the formal operational stage (i.e., ages 12 and older) can reason deeply, even about abstract concepts; therefore, the CBT framework is a good match for their metacognitive skills. In fact, research by Durlak, Fuhrman, and Lampman (1991) found CBT outcomes consistent with early Piagetian developmental theory in that children in the formal operations stage (ages 11 and older) have twice the positive effects utilizing CBT as children ages 2 to 10.

Additional contraindications for the use of CBT include suicidality, abuse, and psychosis. Suicidal thoughts and ideation require mood stabilization, a safety plan, and sometimes psychopharmacological intervention first before the underlying core belief system of the individual can be addressed. In circumstances of abuse, protective measures for safety and reporting the incident are the first considerations. Often, abused children are quickly separated from caregivers or other significant persons in their lives, which can also introduce complex guilt and abandonment feelings. For these children and adolescents, a more specialized counseling approach, trauma-focused cognitive behavioral therapy (TFBT), may be more appropriate. TFBT combines components of traditional CBT with family therapy elements and behavioral modification (Child Welfare Information Gateway, 2018; Silverman et al., 2008). Youth who are receiving treatment for psychosis typically require a combined treatment plan that includes antipsychotic medications and social support systems and may include CBT. However, if the child or adolescent is having a psychotic episode or quickly cycling between episodes, he or she will not have the reasoning and insight required for effective CBT.

REFERENCES

Abdulkader, W. F. A. K. (2017). The effectiveness of a cognitive behavioral therapy program in reducing school bullying among a sample of adolescents with learning disabilities. *International Journal of Educational Sciences, 18*(1–3), 16–28. doi:10.1080/09751122.2017.1346752

Albano, A. M., & Kendall, P. C. (2002). Cognitive behavioural therapy for children and adolescents with anxiety disorders: Clinical research advances. *International Review of Psychiatry, 14*, 129–134. doi:10.1080/09540260220132644

Alberto, P. A., & Troutman, A. C. (2012). *Applied behavior analysis for teachers* (9th ed.). New York, NY: Pearson.

American Academy of Pediatrics. (n.d.). *Promoting children's mental health.* Retrieved from https://www.aap.org/en-us/advocacy-and-policy/federal-advocacy/Pages/mentalhealth.aspx

American Educational Research Association, American Psychological Association, & National Council on Measurement in Education. (2014). *The standards for educational and psychological testing.* Washington, DC: American Educational Research Association.

American Psychiatric Association. (2013). *Diagnostic and statistical manual of mental disorders* (5th ed.). Arlington, VA: American Psychiatric Publishing.

American School Counselor Association. (2014). *ASCA National Model: A framework for school counseling programs: Executive summary.* Retrieved from https://schoolcounselor.org/ascanationalmodel/media/anm-templates/anmexecsumm.pdf

American School Counselor Association. (2015). *The school counselor and student mental health.* Retrieved from http://www.schoolcounselor.org/asca/media/asca/PositionStatements/PS_Student MentalHealth.pdf

Atkins, M. S., Hoagwood, K. E., Kutash, K., & Seidman, E. (2010). Toward the integration of education and mental health in schools. *Administration and Policy in Mental Health and Mental Health Services Research, 37*(1–2), 40–47. doi:10.1007/s10488-010-0299-7

Bains, R. M., & Diallo, A. F. (2016). Mental health services in school-based health centers: Systematic review. *The Journal of School Nursing, 32*(1), 8–19. doi:10.1177/1059840515590607

Beidas, R. S., & Kendall, P. C. (2010). Training therapists in evidence-based practice: A critical review of studies from a systems-contextual perspective. *Clinical Psychology (New York), 17*(1), 1–30. doi:10.1111/j.1468-2850.2009.01187.x

Bella-Awusah, T., Ani, C., Ajuwon, A., & Omigbodun, O. (2016). Effectiveness of brief school-based, group cognitive behavioural therapy for depressed adolescents in south west Nigeria. *Child and Adolescent Mental Health, 21*(1), 44–50. doi:10.1111/camh.12104

Carpenter, J. K., Andrews, L. A., Witcraft, S. M., Powers, M. B., Smits, J. A. J., & Hofmann, S. G. (2018). Cognitive behavioral therapy for anxiety and related disorders: A meta-analysis of randomized placebo-controlled trials. *Depression and Anxiety, 35*(6), 502–515. doi:10.1002/da.22728

Castillo, J. M., Arroyo-Plaza, J., Tan, S. Y., Sabnis, S., & Mattison, A. (2017). Facilitators of and barriers to model school psychological services. *Psychology in the Schools, 54*(2), 152–168. doi:10.1002/pits.21991

Center for Mental Health in Schools at University of California, Los Angeles. (2014). *Mental health in schools: New roles for school nurses.* Retrieved from http://smhp.psych.ucla.edu/pdfdocs/nurses/unit1.pdf

Child Welfare Information Gateway. (2018). *Trauma-focused cognitive behavioral therapy for children affected by sexual abuse or trauma.* Retrieved from https://www.childwelfare.gov/pubPDFs/trauma.pdf

Conners, C. K. (2008). *Conners 3rd edition™ (Conners 3®).* North Tonawanda, NY: Multi-Health Systems.

Cook, C. R., Frye, M., Slemrod, T., Lyon, A. R., Renshaw, T. L., & Zhang, Y. (2015). An integrated approach to universal prevention: Independent and combined effects of PBIS and SEL on youths' mental health. *School Psychology Quarterly, 30*, 166–183. doi:10.1037/spq0000102

Creed, T. A., Reisweber, J., & Beck, A. T. (2012). *Cognitive therapy for adolescents in school settings.* New York, NY: Guilford Press.

Cuijpers, P., Sijbrandij, M., Koole, S. L., Anderson, G., Beekman, A. T., & Reynolds, C. F. (2014). Adding psychotherapy to antidepressant medication in depression and anxiety disorders: A meta-analysis. *World Psychiatry, 13*(1), 56–67. doi:10.1002/wps.20089

Cummings, J., Ponce, N., & Mays, V. (2010). Comparing racial/ethnic differences in mental health service use among high-need adolescent populations across clinical and school-based settings. *Journal of Adolescent Health, 46,* 603–606. doi:10.1016/j.jadohealth.2009.11.221

DiGiuseppe, R., & Tafrate, R. C. (2011). *Anger Regulation and Expression Scale (ARES): Technical manual.* North Tonawanda, NY: Multi-Health Systems.

Dowdy, E., Furlong, M., Raines, T. C., Bovery, B., Kauffman, B., Kamphaus, R. W., . . . Murdock, J. (2015). Enhancing school-based mental health services with a preventive and promotive approach to universal screening for complete mental health. *Journal of Educational and Psychological Consultation, 25*(2–3), 178–197. doi:10.1080/10474412.2014.929951

Durlak, J., Fuhrman, T., & Lampman, C. (1991). Effectiveness of cognitive-behaviour therapy for maladaptive children: A meta-analysis. *Psychological Bulletin, 110,* 204–214. doi:10.1037/0033-2909.110.2.204

Eiraldi, R., Power, T. J., Schwartz, B. S., Keiffer, J. N., McCurdy, B. L., Mathen, M., & Jawad, A. F. (2016). Examining effectiveness of group cognitive-behavioral therapy for externalizing and internalizing disorders in urban schools. *Behavior Modification, 40*(4), 611–639. doi:10.1177/0145445516631093

Elliott, J., & Morrison, D. (2008). *Response-to-intervention: Blueprint for implementation—District level.* Alexandria, VA: National Association of State Directors of Special Education. Retrieved from https://buildingrti.utexas.org/sites/default/files/resource_files/39_eca4d94d-4cc3-4cda-9f1b-62640978ddd8%20%281%29.pdf

Foster, S., Rollefson, M., Doksum, T., Noonan, D., Robinson, G., & Teich, J. (2005). *School mental health services in the United States, 2002–2003.* Rockville, MD: Substance Abuse and Mental Health Services Administration.

Ginsburg, G. S., Becker, K. D., Kingery, J. N., & Nichols, T. (2008). Transporting CBT for childhood anxiety disorders into inner-city school-based mental health clinics. *Cognitive and Behavioral Practice, 15,* 148–158. doi:10.1016/j.cbpra.2007.07.001

Gore, F. M., Bloem, P. J., Patton, G. C., Ferguson, J., Joseph, V., Coffey, C., . . . Mathers, C. D. (2011). Global burden of disease in young people aged 10–24 years: A systematic analysis. *Lancet, 377,* 2093–2102. doi:10.1016/S0140-6736(11)60512-6

Gresham, F., & Elliott, S. N. (2008). *Social Skills Improvement System (SSIS) rating scales.* Bloomington, MN: Pearson Assessments.

Hanchon, T. A., & Fernald, L. N. (2013). The provision of counseling services among school psychologists: An exploration of training, current practices, and perceptions. *Psychology in the Schools, 50*(7), 651–671. doi:10.1002/pits.21700

Hussey, D. L., & Guo, S. (2003). Measuring behavior change in young children receiving intensive school-based mental health services. *Journal of Community Psychology, 31,* 629–639. doi:10.1002/jcop.10074

Individuals with Disabilities Education Improvement Act, 20 U.S.C. § 1400 *et seq.* (2004).

Jordan, C., Reid, A. M., Mariaskin, A., Augusto, B., & Sulkowski, M. L. (2012). First-line treatment for pediatric obsessive-compulsive disorder. *Journal of Contemporary Psychotherapy, 42,* 243–248. doi:10.1007/s10879-012-9210-z

Joyce, D., & Grapin, S. (2012). School psychologists' role in facilitating successful postsecondary transitions for students with disabilities. *Communiqué, 41*(3), 1–22. Retrieved from https://www.nasponline.org/publications/periodicals/communique/issues/volume-41-issue-3

Joyce-Beaulieu, D., & Grapin, S. (2014). Support beyond high school for those with mental illness. *Phi Delta Kappan, 96*(4), 29–33. doi:10.1177/0031721714561443

Joyce-Beaulieu, D., & Rossen, E. (2014). Preparation of school psychologists in the United States. *International Journal of School and Educational Psychology, 2,* 166–171. doi:10.1080/21683603.2014.934643

Joyce-Beaulieu, D., & Sulkowski, M. (2016). The *Diagnostic and Statistical Manual of Mental Disorders: Fifth Edition (DSM-5)* model of impairment. In S. Goldstein & J. A. Naglieri (Eds.), *Assessing impairment: From theory to practice* (2nd ed., pp. 167–189). New York, NY: Springer.

Kamphaus, R. W., & Reynolds, C. R. (2015). *BASC-3 behavioral and emotional screening system (BASC-3 BESS).* Minneapolis, MN: Pearson Assessments.

Kaplan, J. S., & Carter, J. (1995). *Beyond behavior modification: A cognitive-behavioral approach to behavior management in the school* (3rd ed.). Austin, TX: Pro-Ed.

Kendall, P. C. (2006). *Child and adolescent therapy: Cognitive-behavioral procedures* (3rd ed.). New York, NY: Guilford Press.

Kessler, R. C., Berglund, P., Demler, O., Jin, R., Merikangas, K. R., & Walters, E. E. (2005). Lifetime prevalence and age-of-onset distributions of DSM-IV disorders in the National Comorbidity Survey Replication. *Archives of General Psychiatry, 62,* 593–602. doi:10.1001/archpsyc.62.6.593

Kovacs, M. (2004). *Children's depression inventory, second edition (CDI-2)*. Toronto, ON, Canada: Multi-Health Systems.

Kurns, S., & Tilly, W. D. (2008). *Response-to-intervention: Blueprint for implementation—School building level*. Alexandria, VA: National Association of State Directors of Special Education. Retrieved from https://buildingrti.utexas.org/sites/default/files/resource_files/schoolbuildinglevel_blueprint.pdf

Luxford, S., Hadwin, J. A., & Kovshoff, H. (2017). Evaluating the effectiveness of a school-based cognitive behavioural therapy intervention for anxiety in adolescents diagnosed with autism spectrum disorder. *Journal of Autism and Developmental Disorders, 47*(12), 3896–3908. doi:10.1007/s10803-016-2857-7

Marken, S., Gray, L., & Lewis, L. (2013). *Dual enrollment programs and courses for high school students at postsecondary institutions: 2010–11. First look* [NCES 2013-002]. Washington, DC: National Center for Education Statistics.

Masia-Warner, C., Fisher, P. H., Shrout, P. E., Rathor, S., & Klein, R. G. (2007). Treating adolescents with social anxiety disorder in school: An attention control trial. *Journal of Child Psychology and Psychiatry, 48,* 676–686. doi:10.1111/j.1469-7610.2007.01737.x

McFarland, J., Stark, P., & Cui, J. (2018). *Trends in high school dropout and completion rates in the United States: 2014. Compendium report* [NCES 2018-117]. Washington, DC: National Center for Education Statistics.

Merikangas, K. R., He, J. P., Burstein, M., Swanson, S. A., Avenevoli, S., Cui, L., . . . Swendsen, J. (2010). Lifetime prevalence of mental disorders in U.S. adolescents: Results from the National Comorbidity Survey Replication–Adolescent Supplement (NCS-A). *Journal of the American Academy of Child & Adolescent Psychiatry, 49,* 980–989. doi:10.1016/j.jaac.2010.05.017

Michael, K. D., Albright, A., Jameson, J. P., Sale, R., Massey, C., Kirk, A., & Egan, T. (2013). Does cognitive behavioral therapy in the context of a rural school mental health program have an impact on academic outcomes? *Advances in School Mental Health Promotion, 6,* 247–262. doi:10.1080/1754730X.2013.832006

Mychailyszyn, M. P., Méndez, J. L., & Kendall, P. C. (2010). School functioning in youth with and without anxiety disorders: Comparisons by diagnosis and comorbidity. *School Psychology Review, 39,* 106–121. doi:10.1002/ pits.20548

National Association of School Psychologists. (2010). *Model for comprehensive and integrated school psychological services*. Bethesda, MD: Author.

National Research Center for Career and Technical Education. (2010). *Programs of study: Year 2 joint technical report*. Louisville, KY: Author.

Neil, A. L., & Christensen, H. (2009). Efficacy and effectiveness of school-based prevention and early intervention programs for anxiety. *Clinical Psychology Review, 29,* 208–215. doi:10.1016/j.cpr.2009.01.002

Patton, G. C., Coffey, C., Cappa, C., Currie, D., Riley, L., Gore, F., . . . Ferguson, J. (2012). Health of the world's adolescents: A synthesis of internationally comparable data. *Lancet, 379*(9826), 1665–1675. doi:10.1016/S0140-6736(12)60203-7

Reynolds, C. R., & Kamphaus, R. W. (2015). *Behavior assessment system for children* (3rd ed.). Bloomington, MN: Pearson Assessments.

Reynolds, C. R., & Kamphaus, R. W. (2016). *BASC–3 flex monitor*. Bloomington, MN: NCS Pearson.

Rones, M., & Hoagwood, K. (2000). School-based mental health services: A research review. *Clinical Child and Family Psychology Review, 3,* 223–241. doi:10.1023/A:1026425104386

Ruocco, S., Gordon, J., & McLean, L. A. (2016). Effectiveness of a school-based early intervention CBT group programme for children with anxiety aged 5–7 years. *Advances in School Mental Health Promotion, 9*(1), 29–49. doi:10.1080/1754730X.2015.1110495

Saklofske, D. H., Joyce, D. J., Sulkowski, M. L., & Climie, E. (2013). Models of personality assessment for children and adolescents. In C. R. Reynolds (Ed.), *The Oxford handbook of child psychological assessment* (pp. 348–365). New York, NY: Oxford University Press.

Salloum, A., Sulkowski, M. L., Sirrine, E., & Storch, E. A. (2009). Overcoming barriers to using empirically supported therapies to treat childhood anxiety disorders in social work practice. *Child and Adolescent Social Work Journal, 26,* 259–273. doi:10.1007/s10560-009-0173-1

Schelar, E., Lofink Love, H., Taylor, K., Schlitt, J., & Even, M. (2016). *Trends and opportunities for investment in student health and success: Findings from the 2013-2014 Census of School-Based Health Centers (SBHCs)*. Washington, DC: School-Based Health Alliance.

School Social Work Association of America. (2013a). *National school social work practice model.* Retrieved from https://www.sswaa.org/copy-of-school-social-worker-evalua-1

School Social Work Association of America. (2013b). *School social workers' role in addressing students' mental health needs and increasing academic achievement.* Retrieved from https://www.sswaa.org/copy-of-about-school-social-work

Silverman, W. K., Ortiz, C. D., Viswesvaran, C., Burns, B. J., Kolko, D. J., Putnam, F. M., & Amaya-Jackson, L. (2008). Evidence-based psychosocial treatments for children and adolescents exposed to traumatic events. *Journal of Clinical Child and Adolescent Psychology, 37*, 156–183. doi:10.1080/15374410701818293

Soutullo, O., Palma, L., & Joyce, D. (2014). DSM-5 depression symptoms and interventions: What school psychologists need to know. *Florida Association of School Psychologists Newsletter, 40*, 34–47. Retrieved from http://www.fasp.org/PDF_Files/Newsletter/FASP_Winter_2014.pdf

Suldo, S. M., Friedrich, A., & Michalowski, J. (2010). Personal and systems-level factors that limit and facilitate school psychologists' involvement in school-based mental health services. *Psychology in the Schools, 47*(4), 354–373. doi:10.1002/pits.20475

Sulkowski, M. L., & Joyce, D. (2012). School psychology goes to college: The emerging role of school psychology in college communities. *Psychology in the Schools, 49*, 809–815. doi:10.1002/pits.21634

Sulkowski, M. L., Joyce, D. K., & Storch, E. A. (2011). Treating childhood anxiety in schools: Service delivery in a response-to-intervention paradigm. *Journal of Child and Family Studies, 21*, 938–947. doi:10.1007/s10826-011-9553-1

Sulkowski, M. L., & Michael, K. (2014). Meeting the mental health needs of homeless students in schools: A multi-tiered system of support framework. *Children and Youth Services Review, 44*, 145–151. doi:10.1016/j.childyouth.2014.06.014

Sulkowski, M. L., Wingfield, R. J., Jones, D., & Coulter, W. A. (2011). Response to intervention and interdisciplinary collaboration: Joining hands to support children and families. *Journal of Applied School Psychology, 27*, 1–16. doi:10.1080/15377903.2011.565264

U.S. Department of Education. (2011). *Questions and answers on secondary transition.* Retrieved from https://sites.ed.gov/idea/files/Transition.QA_.September_2011_FINAL.pdf

U.S. Department of Education, Office of Special Education and Rehabilitative Services, & Office of Special Education Programs. (2018). *39th annual report to Congress on the implementation of the Individuals with Disabilities Education Act, 2017.* Retrieved from https://www2.ed.gov/about/reports/annual/osep/2017/parts-b-c/39th-arc-for-idea.pdf

U.S. Department of Health & Human Services. (2000). *Report of the Surgeon General's conference on children's mental health: A national action agenda.* Washington, DC: Author. Retrieved from https://www.ncbi.nlm.nih.gov/books/NBK44233

Üstün, T. B., Kostanjsek, N., Chatterji, S., & Rehm, J. (2010). *Measuring health and disability: Manual for WHO disability assessment schedule–WHODAS 2.0.* Geneva, Switzerland: World Health Organization.

Zaboski, B. A., Joyce-Beaulieu, D., Kranzler, J. H., McNamara, J. P., Gayle, C., & MacInnes, J. (2019). Group exposure and response prevention for college students with social anxiety: A randomized clinical trial. *Journal of Clinical Psychology, 75*(9), 1489–1507. doi:10.1002/jclp.22792

TWO

Cognitive Theoretical Foundations

INTRODUCTION

This chapter covers theoretical formations that undergird cognitive behavioral therapy (CBT) and applied practice. An overview of the CBT theoretical model is provided and contextualized with the work of leading scholars. The medical model of psychopathology is then discussed because much of the CBT literature focuses on ameliorating internalizing and externalizing psychopathology. Key features of various disorders are discussed to inform practitioners of unique considerations for treatment planning. In this regard, specific treatment goals are listed, and CBT interventions are proposed for various disorders. The chapter includes a discussion on tailoring CBT to be culturally responsive to meet the needs of an increasingly diverse student population.

AN OVERVIEW OF THE CBT THEORETICAL MODEL

The CBT model of counseling simply proposes that (a) individuals' thoughts influence their behaviors; (b) their behaviors influence their emotions; and (c) their emotions influence their thoughts (Kendall, 2011). See Figure 2.1 for a visual description of the CBT model (also Appendix Exhibits 2.1 and 2.2). Additionally, consistent with the CBT model, an individual's behavioral responses to life circumstances and events affect both short- and long-term consequences for the individual (Kendall, 2011). Slightly different variations of the CBT model exist for different forms of psychopathology, and they are discussed under sections related to internalizing and externalizing psychopathology.

The theory that undergirds CBT has its origins in the work of A. T. Beck (1991; A. S. Beck, 1995, 2011) and Albert Ellis (1991). Beck's contributions are numerous and varied; however, central to his work is a framework for understanding how automatic thoughts (and sometimes images) occur spontaneously in people's thinking. Within this framework, maladaptive automatic thoughts (automatic negative thoughts [ANTs]) cause distress when present and, depending on the theme and content, can contribute to the development of mental health problems. For

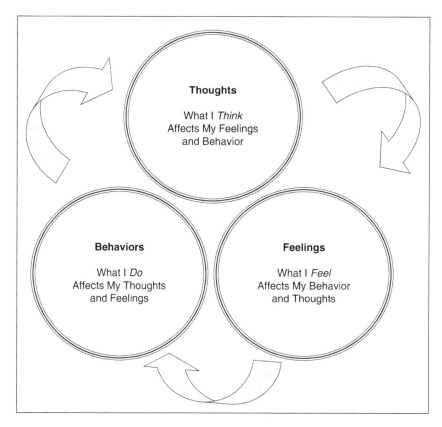

Figure 2.1 Cognitive behavioral therapy model.

example, a person with ANTs such as "I'm not good enough" or "I'm worthless" likely will feel shut down and may start to feel depressed if these thoughts are prevalent and perceived to be validated by negative experiences (e.g., failing a test, not making a sports team, being rejected for a date).

Common patterns emerge in the ANTs experienced by individuals with various forms of psychopathology and mental health problems. For example, individuals affected by depression often experience ANTs related to feeling inadequate, unlovable, unworthy, worthless, and powerless. Individuals who are highly anxious tend to have ANTs related to feeling threatened, unsafe, vulnerable, socially awkward, or potentially rejected. Lastly, individuals who are prone to anger often experience ANTs related to perceived injustice, entitlement, or feeling threatened.

Ellis's contributions to CBT theory compliment the work of Beck and are best expressed through his development of rational-emotive behavioral therapy (REBT). According to Ellis, beliefs (or the way that a person interprets circumstances) can be categorized as either rational or irrational (see Appendix Exhibits 2.3–2.10 for varied model diagrams and worksheets that explain this concept by applying differing complexity and sophistication for use with a wide range of children/adolescents during sessions). Consistent with this perspective, rational beliefs would lead to a healthier, well-balanced perspective. Conversely, irrational beliefs would contribute to greater degrees of distress and dysfunction. Irrational beliefs are at variance with reality, and maintaining them inherently eventually results in frustration because of the discrepancy between the expectancy associated with the belief and actual reality.

It is important to note that both Beck's and Ellis's perspectives are confident in the ability to change thought patterns through a logical process of helping individuals find evidence to determine if their ANTs or irrational beliefs are valid and grounded in reality. Thus, their early work sets the foundational "C" in the CBT theoretical model. Moreover, through evaluating thoughts with a therapist and coming up with more rational, accurate, or adaptive thoughts, a person is effectively engaging in cognitive therapy.

Cognitive therapy is effective because replacing irrational or maladaptive thoughts with more adaptive, positive, or rational thoughts can result in better behavioral choices that then result in better outcomes. By nature, positive outcomes are reinforcing and are more likely to be repeated. Thus, the skill of making good choices becomes better developed over time through successful application and reinforcement. For example, if a student is notified of a test, one possible related thought could be "I need to make a plan to study." If the student follows through on this thought, studies, and does well on the test, then over time, it is more likely that this behavior (i.e., studying) will occur in the future, and, if reinforced, will influence future thoughts and behaviors. These principles also apply to negative thought patterns in that maladaptive or irrational thoughts that regularly occur and influence behavior ("Why bother studying? I'm just going to fail anyway") are more likely to automatically occur and influence future thoughts and behaviors. Essentially, as maladaptive behaviors are repeated, they become habits and contribute to a cycle of recurring negative consequences, which can then reduce motivation to change or adapt to life circumstances.

Because the CBT model is multifaceted and there is a reciprocal relationship between thoughts, feelings, and behaviors, different points of intervention are possible. As discussed, modifying or changing maladaptive and irrational thoughts is one intervention point because thoughts influence feelings and behaviors. A second intervention point involves modifying maladaptive behaviors, which then influence feelings and behaviors. Take, for example, teaching a student a new adaptive skill. Once learned, the student may feel more efficacious, empowered, and happier. Moreover, previous maladaptive thoughts also could be replaced with more adaptive ones whether the student is consciously aware or not. Thus, behavioral interventions or the "B" in CBT also is a key intervention point, and for some disorders, the "C" and the "B" in the CBT theoretical model should be reversed to highlight the importance of behavioral interventions (Hayes, Levin, Plumb-Vilardaga, Villatte, & Pistorello, 2013). For example, when working with individuals who have obsessive thoughts as part of their psychopathology (e.g., obsessive-compulsive disorder [OCD], autism spectrum disorder), it is important to ensure that cognitive interventions do not interact with already problematic or maladaptive thought patterns—there is little utility with obsessing over one's obsessive thoughts. However, if one is capable of making positive behavioral changes, such changes can spill over to influence feeling and thinking: "I usually obsess over getting perfect grades; however, this time, I just did my best, and I can live with the outcome."

The concept of "experience before explanation" (Taibbi, 2015) related to positive therapeutic change grounds the CBT theoretical model when the primary intervention point involves changing behavior. In other words, when "BCT" is involved, a therapist works with a student to change his or her behaviors through trying to engender positive experiences (e.g., facing a feared situation or event, being able to apply self-calming strategies, disengaging from a conflict situation with a peer) that can then be generalized and explained by a therapist: "Wow, I'm proud of you! You read your report in front of the whole class even though you were anxious, and it wasn't as scary as you initially thought." Therefore, with BCT, "explanation" can be a potential avenue to then engage in cognitive interventions following therapeutic behavioral experiences. In this regard, the therapist could juxtapose how maladaptive and irrational thoughts influenced problematic patterns of behavior ("You used to think that you couldn't read in front of the class because your peers would think you're dumb") and how making behavioral changes can result in more adaptive thinking patterns ("However, this time you did it. You read in front of the class and you did well").

Although discussed less in the literature on the theoretical foundations of CBT, emotion is the third and last intervention point (Suveg, Sood, Comer, & Kendall, 2009). However, an important caveat exists related to intervening with emotion. In this vein, telling someone to change his or her feelings can be highly invalidating and nontherapeutic: "Just stop feeling depressed. Every teenager goes through a breakup at some point—you'll get over it."

Therefore, when intervening at the "E" or emotional intervention point within the cognitive behavioral framework, emotional intervention is mostly related to teaching emotion regulation strategies. Further, similar to intervening at the cognitive or behavioral level, intervening on the emotional level influences thinking and behaving. Perhaps, then, should CBT be rebranded as "BCET"? However, perhaps the acronym is a needless mouthful, especially because emotion regulation strategies are now generally included in CBT treatment manuals and protocols. Therefore, suffice it to say that interviewing on the emotional level also influences thinking and feeling. Common emotion regulation strategies within the CBT theoretical framework include diaphragmatic breathing, progressive muscle regulation, meditation, and yoga. Although such strategies have been inconsistently included within CBT frameworks and models, it is now hard to argue against the positive therapeutic cognitive, behavioral, and emotional effects associated with the aforementioned emotion regulation strategies.

Considering the former, the CBT theoretical model has evolved conceptually—and it continues to evolve. From being strongly tied to the seminal work of specific prominent psychotherapists, CBT is now a much more established and open enterprise for practitioners to use to help students. The model is still grounded on a simple theoretical framework: Thoughts influence feelings that influence behaviors. And then behaviors influence thoughts, and the cycle continues. However, this theoretical model can be modified for different forms of psychopathology or common and overarching psychological problems. Thus, consistent with the medical model of describing psychopathology primarily encompassed in the American Psychiatric Association (APA)'s *Diagnostic and Statistical Manual of Mental Disorders* (5th ed.; *DSM-5*; 2013) and the World Health Organization's *International Classification of Disease and Related Health Problems* (*ICD-10*) manual (2016), CBT has been used extensively to treat two prominent forms of psychopathology that are discussed in the following sections.

THE MEDICAL MODEL OF PSYCHOPATHOLOGY

Most forms of psychopathology that are amenable to CBT fall along a spectrum of internalizing and externalizing psychopathology. In general, internalizing psychopathology involves excessively trying to overcontrol one's behavior and is related to the presentation of anxiety, depression, and social withdrawal. On the other hand, externalizing psychopathology is characterized by inadequate efforts to regulate one's behavior and is characterized by excessive anger, aggression, conduct problems, and oppositional and defiant behavior. It is important to note, however, that many students present with mixed forms of internalizing and externalizing psychopathology. For example, irritability is common in students experiencing depression, and some highly anxious youth become reactive when they must confront anxiety-provoking stimuli and situations. Similarly, many students with externalizing psychopathology will also feel depressed, anxious, or socially withdrawal in response to experiencing adjustment problems at school, at home, or in other settings.

Therefore, the preponderance of presenting symptoms or psychopathology should govern clinical impressions as well as how the CBT theoretical model can be applied to address the needs of students. In this vein, students presenting with mixed internalizing and externalizing forms of psychopathology may benefit from receiving various CBT components related to their presenting issues. For example, a student with a specific phobia might also benefit from learning relaxation and self-calming strategies that he or she can use when he or she is feeling hypervigilant at school while he or she also participates in behavioral exposures and cognitive restructuring. The relationships between presenting forms of psychopathology, the CBT theoretical model, and the implementation of specific CBT components should be convergent and mutually informative.

Internalizing Psychopathology

Although perhaps not as much or to the same degree as students with externalizing problems that disrupt the school environment, many students with internalizing challenges also are referred to school practitioners to receive CBT and other intervention services (Kutash, Duchnowski, & Lynn, 2006). Such students tend to display symptoms that can be clustered under the following subheadings: anxiety and related disorders, depressive disorders, and obsessive-compulsive and related disorders. Each of these subsections is discussed here with a focus on the presentation of specific disorders and their clinical features and evidence-based components of CBT used in their treatment.

Anxiety and Related Disorders

Generalized anxiety disorder (GAD). The diagnostic criteria for GAD require persistent, excessive anxiety and worry that is difficult to regulate (APA, 2013, pp. 222–226). The worry must not be in the presence of another mental disorder and should not be attributed to substance use. Additionally, significant impairment in social, occupational, or other aspects of functioning must be present. Out of the six possible symptoms, three or more must be present, which can include but is not limited to the following: irritability, muscle tension, and being easily fatigued (APA, 2013, p. 222). Only one of the six possible symptoms needs to be present in

TABLE 2.1 Treatment Goals and Interventions for General Anxiety Disorder

Treatment Goals	CBT Interventions
■ Reducing automatic negative thoughts	■ Cognitive restructuring, mindfulness
■ Reducing physical symptoms of anxiety	■ Relaxation training, emotional regulation strategies
■ Reducing avoidant behavior	■ Exposure therapy
■ Reducing beliefs about the world being dangerous	■ Cognitive restructuring, exposure therapy/ behavioral experiments

CBT, cognitive behavioral therapy.

children to warrant diagnosis. Prevalence rates are lower among adolescents (0.9%) than adults (2.9%) in the United States. In other countries, prevalence rates range from 0.4% to 3.6%. In regard to gender, GAD occurs twice as often in females than males. Comorbidities include other anxiety and unipolar depressive disorders (i.e., OCD, social anxiety disorder, substance/medication-induced disorder, posttraumatic stress disorder [PTSD]). Risk factors include a temperament that is neurotic, behaviorally inhibited, and harm avoidant. Like major depressive disorder (MDD), genetics accounts for one third of the risk of developing GAD (APA, 2013, pp. 223–226). Table 2.1 lists common treatment goals and CBT interventions for GAD.

Social anxiety disorder (social phobia). The criteria for social anxiety disorder require a fear or anxiety of being scrutinized by individuals in a social setting (APA, 2013, pp. 202–208). Similar to specific phobia, the actual social situation typically produces fear that is out of proportion with the actual situation and is generally avoided or endured with great effort. Behavior examples in children include crying, tantrums, clinging, or inability to speak in social situations. Specifiers include performance only if the fear is restricted to public speaking or performances (typically seen in musicians, dancers, athletes), but the individual does not avoid the social situation. Additionally, performance fears may impair school, work, or social settings where public speaking is often required (APA, 2013, p. 203).

Prevalence rates are much higher in the United States (7%) than in other countries (0.5%–2.0%). Females have a rate of social anxiety disorder that ranges from 1.5 to 2 times higher than that of males. American Indians and non-Hispanic Whites have the highest social phobia rates in the United States. Comorbidities include MDD, substance use disorders, delusional disorders, and body dysmorphic disorder. Social anxiety disorder (performance-only type) also is often comorbid with avoidant personality disorder. More specifically, children with high-functioning autism and selective mutism often present with comorbidities to social anxiety disorder. Risk factors include fear of negative evaluations and child abuse. Behavioral inhibition is strongly regarded as a genetic component of social anxiety disorder and is exhibited through socially anxious parents. As with specific phobia, people are two to six times more likely to develop social anxiety disorder if the first-degree relatives have social anxiety (APA, 2013, pp. 204–208). Table 2.2 lists common treatment goals and CBT interventions for social anxiety disorder.

Selective mutism disorder. The diagnostic criteria for selective mutism disorder require a consistent failure to speak when the expectation is to speak and is not attributed to a communication disorder or inability to use spoken language

---

TABLE 2.2   Treatment Goals and Interventions for Social Anxiety Disorder

Treatment Goals	CBT Interventions
■ Reducing fear of negative evaluation	■ Exposure therapy, cognitive restructuring
■ Eliminating safety behaviors	■ Self-monitoring, exposure therapy
■ Reducing avoidant behavior	■ Exposure therapy
■ Reducing need for approval, acceptance, and self-scrutiny	■ Cognitive restructuring

CBT, cognitive behavioral therapy.

TABLE 2.3   Treatment Goals and Interventions for Selective Mutism Disorder

Treatment Goals	CBT Interventions
■ Increasing verbal approximations	■ Shaping, chaining, successive approximations, differential reinforcement
■ Reducing physical symptoms of anxiety	■ Relaxation training, emotional regulation strategies
■ Reducing avoidant behavior	■ Exposure therapy
■ Generalizing verbal behavior	■ Practicing in the presence of family members/ familiar people

CBT, cognitive behavioral therapy.

(APA, 2013, pp. 195–197). It is important to note that selective mutism disorder should only be diagnosed alongside schizophrenia, autism spectrum disorder, or other psychotic disorder if the child is able to produce speech in some social situations (APA, 2013, p. 197). The prevalence rate for selective mutism disorder is extremely rare, ranging between 0.03% and 1% with no variation regarding race or gender. Comorbidities include separation anxiety disorder, social anxiety disorder, and specific phobia. Risk factors include receptive language difficulties, shyness, social isolation/anxiety, and overprotective parents. There is evidence to suggest a genetic component in selective mutism disorder that is similar to social anxiety disorder (APA, 2013, pp. 196–197).

Table 2.3 lists common treatment goals and CBT interventions for selective mutism disorder.

Separation anxiety disorder. The *DSM-5* criteria for separation anxiety disorder require a persistent and distressing fear of separation from an attached individual that results in significant impairment across multiple domains (e.g., social, academic, occupational). There are eight possible symptoms (e.g., repeated nightmares, repeated complaints of physical symptoms, recurrent or excessive distress when facing separation from home or attachment figures), of which three must be present (APA, 2013, pp. 190–197). For children, the disturbance or fear must persist for at least 4 weeks and in adults, 6 months.

Prevalence rates in the United States are highest in children (4%), followed by adolescents (1.6%), and then adults (0.9%–1.9%). It should be noted that separation anxiety is the most common disorder among children and is equally common

TABLE 2.4 Treatment Goals and Interventions for Separation Anxiety Disorder

Treatment Goals	CBT Interventions
■ Increasing time and distance from attachment figures	■ Graduated exposure therapy
■ Reducing physical symptoms of anxiety	■ Relaxation training, emotional regulation strategies
■ Reducing "clingy" behavior or tantrums when separated	■ Differential reinforcement, successive approximations
■ Reducing worry about separation and harm befalling attachment figures	■ Cognitive restructuring, graduated exposure therapy

CBT, cognitive behavioral therapy.

in males and females (APA, 2013, p. 192). Comorbidities include generalized anxiety disorder, specific phobia, PTSD, panic disorder, social anxiety disorder, agoraphobia, OCD, and personality disorders. Risk factors include parent overprotection/intrusion and life stressors, such as loss or illness of a loved one or parental divorce. Other notable risk factors, typically seen in young adults, are leaving the parental home, entering a committed relationship, and becoming a parent. Females are more frequently seen with separation anxiety disorder than males, and 73% of community samples indicate genetic correlates. Suicidality may be associated with separation anxiety disorder in the presence of comorbid mood disorders, anxiety disorders, or substance use (APA, 2013, pp. 192–195). Table 2.4 lists common treatment goals and CBT interventions for separation anxiety disorder.

Specific phobia. Specific phobias are marked by an intense, persistent fear of a specific object or situation that causes clinical distress and is out of proportion to the actual danger posed by the stimulus (APA, 2013, pp. 197–202). The phobia-inducing or phobic object or event provokes immediate fear or anxiety when it is actively avoided or endured. Specifiers should be distinguished for each specific phobia as evidenced by the majority of individuals (75%) experiencing more than one specific phobia (e.g., animal, situational, natural environment).

Prevalence rates are approximately 7%–9% with similar percentages across the United States and European countries, whereas lower percentages are noted in Asian, African, and Latin American countries (2%–4%). Prevalence rates are highest among adolescents aged 13 to 17 years of age (16%), followed by children (5%) and the elderly (3%–5%). Females are twice as likely as males to possess a specific phobia. All of the specifiers, except for blood injection injury, are experienced more in females. Comorbidities include depression symptoms, personality disorders, bipolar disorders, eating disorders, OCD, schizophrenia, panic disorder, social anxiety disorder, and separation anxiety disorder. Risk factors include parental loss, separation, or overprotectiveness; abuse (physical or sexual); or a traumatic event with the feared object or situation. Genetic correlates include an increase in the likelihood of having a specific phobia if a close relative has a specific phobia (APA, 2013, pp. 200–202). Table 2.5 lists common treatment goals and CBT interventions for specific phobia.

Panic disorder. The criteria for panic disorder are consistent with an unexpected panic attack. There are 13 possible symptoms (e.g., sweating, chills, feeling dizzy), of which four must be present in conjunction with either persistent worry

TABLE 2.5   Treatment Goals and Interventions for Specific Phobia

Treatment Goals	CBT Interventions
■ Habituating to phobic stimuli or situations	■ Exposure therapy
■ Reducing physical symptoms of anxiety	■ Relaxation training, emotional regulation strategies
■ Eliminating avoidance of phobic stimuli or situations	■ Exposure therapy
■ Modifying beliefs that a stimulus or situation is dangerous	■ Cognitive restructuring, exposure therapy

CBT, cognitive behavioral therapy.

TABLE 2.6   Treatment Goals and Interventions for Panic Disorder

Treatment Goals	CBT Interventions
■ Habituating to feelings of panic	■ Exposure therapy (interoceptive exposure therapy)
■ Reducing physical symptoms of anxiety	■ Relaxation training, emotional regulation strategies, muscle relaxation
■ Reducing automatic negative thoughts	■ Cognitive restructuring
■ Engaging in previously avoided places or activities	■ Exposure therapy

CBT, cognitive behavioral therapy.

about future panic attacks or a significant shift in behavior as a result of the panic attacks (APA, 2013, pp. 208–214). It should be noted that panic disorder is not to be confused with panic attacks because the disorder occurs when the panic attacks are unexpected and not explained by a mental disorder, and panic attacks should be used as a specifier with other mental disorders when explained by such (APA, 2013, p. 214).

Prevalence rates for panic disorder are consistent across the United States and European countries (2%–3%) but lower in Asian, African, and Latin American countries (0.1%–0.8%). Panic disorder is more evident in non-Latino Whites and American Indians, and in females. Panic disorder increases at the onset of puberty and peaks in adulthood. Comorbidities include anxiety disorders (more specifically, agoraphobia), MDD, bipolar disorders, and substance use disorder, particularly with alcohol. Risk factors include neuroticism and increased anxiety sensitivity, as well as childhood sexual and physical abuse and substance use (e.g., smoking). There is a genetic component of panic disorder, and it is evident through activity in the brain's amygdala, children of parents with mental disorders, and respiratory disturbances (e.g., asthma). Comorbidities of panic disorder and child abuse may attribute to higher rates of suicidality (APA, 2013, pp. 210–213). Table 2.6 lists common treatment goals and CBT interventions for panic disorder.

Somatic symptom disorder. Somatic symptom disorder requires excessive thoughts, feelings, or behaviors that are distressing and impair daily functioning, as they are related to health concerns (APA, 2013, pp. 311–315). Behavioral examples include the following: pervasive thoughts about the seriousness of symptoms,

TABLE 2.7 Treatment Goals and Interventions for Somatic Symptom Disorder	
Treatment Goals	**CBT Interventions**
■ Habituating to health worries, concerns, and somatic sensations	■ Exposure therapy
■ Reducing physical symptoms of anxiety	■ Relaxation training, emotional regulation strategies, muscle relaxation
■ Reducing catastrophic and automatic negative thoughts	■ Cognitive restructuring
■ Reducing checking behaviors associated with health concerns	■ Self-monitoring

CBT, cognitive behavioral disorder.

persistent levels of high anxiety in regard to personal health, and excessive time and energy devoted to health concerns (APA, 2013, p. 311). Severity is categorized using mild, moderate, and severe terminology and can be specified across two categories (e.g., predominant pain and persistent). Prevalence rates are unknown, but it is estimated to be around 5% to 7% and presents more in females than males. Comorbidities include medical, anxiety, and depressive disorders. Degree of impairment is heightened when comorbid with a medical illness. Risk factors include a temperament that aligns with neuroticism, environment that is consistent with low socioeconomic status and limited education, and stressful life events, such as sexual abuse and concurrent physical illness or psychiatric disorder (APA, 2013, pp. 312–315).

To rule out legitimate physical ailments, it may be important to consider a physician's well-check visit before beginning intervention for persistent somatic complaints. Given the nature of somatic complaints, students with this disorder will often visit the school nurse and request to leave school. Therefore, collaboration with the school nurse to monitor clinic visits can be an important source of progress monitoring data. If these students are permitted to leave school frequently because of somatic complaints and the home activities they return to are enjoyable (e.g., watching TV, playing), it is possible that this school policy can be reinforcing the behaviors. Therefore, an agreement on when and if the child is permitted to leave school, between the parents and school administration, could be an important consideration. Table 2.7 lists common treatment goals and CBT interventions for somatic symptom disorder.

Depressive Disorders

Major depressive disorder. MDD (often just called depression) is characterized by a very low mood, decreased pleasure or interest in activities, or irritability in children/adolescents that persists in most circumstances for at least 2 weeks (APA, 2013, pp. 160–163). Additional criteria include noticeable differences in weight, appetite, sleep, or movement; chronic fatigue; inability to concentrate; feeling insignificant or experiencing undue guilt; and suicidal ideation or attempts (APA, 2013, pp. 161–163). MDD is always categorized as either a single or recurrent episode, and particular descriptors are used to delineate severity (mild, moderate, severe), psychotic features, partial or full remission, and unspecified manifestations of MDD. The course of MDD is specified through additional labels where applicable (e.g., with anxious distress, with atypical features, with seasonal pattern; APA, 2013, p. 162). Individuals with unremitting symptomology generally have poorer outcomes than those whose symptoms recently appeared or are less severe (APA, 2013, p. 165).

MDD affects 7% of the population annually and is notably more common in females (approximately 1.5 to 3 times more likely compared to males) and in adolescents or young adults (approximately three times more likely compared to older adults; APA, 2013, p. 165). Several other internalizing disorders may be comorbid with MDD, including eating disorders, OCD, and panic disorder. Co-occurrence with substance abuse or borderline personality symptoms is also common (APA, 2013, p. 168). Risk factors include negative affect or temperament, traumatic life events, and immediate family members who have or previously had MDD.

Persistent depressive disorder (PDD). Previously known as dysthymia, PDD is characterized by a chronically low or irritable mood that persists for an extended period of time (at least 2 years, or 1 year for children or adolescents). This may be accompanied by changes in appetite or sleep, loss of energy, inability to concentrate, low self-worth, or feelings of despair and helplessness (APA, 2013, p. 168). PDD uses similar specifiers to those accompanying MDD. PDD often develops early in life and persists over time but affects approximately 0.5% of the population in a given year (APA, 2013, pp. 169–170). In addition to comorbidities noted for MDD, individuals with PDD are more likely to have anxiety and substance abuse disorders as well as personality disorder symptoms when PDD occurs early in life. Loss of a parent and having relatives with PDD are both risk factors, and individuals who have PDD with lowered overall functioning generally have poorer outcomes (APA, 2013, p. 170). Table 2.8 lists common treatment goals and CBT interventions for MDD and PDD.

Disruptive mood dysregulation disorder (DMDD). DMDD is a new addition to the *DSM-5* that was created to curtail the overdiagnosis of bipolar disorder in children (APA, 2013, p. 157). The diagnosis must be made between ages 6 and 18, with the first symptoms occurring before age 10. The hallmark symptom of DMDD is a pattern of chronic and intensely irritable mood that has appeared in multiple settings for at least 1 year. This irritability manifests as either "temper outbursts" at least three times per week or a persistently short-tempered, angry mood easily observed by others. Irritability must be severe and beyond developmental expectations (APA, 2013, p. 156).

TABLE 2.8   Treatment Goals and Interventions for Major Depressive Disorder and Persistent Depressive Disorder

Treatment Goals	CBT Interventions
■ Eliminating suicidal ideation	■ Consider an emergency involuntary commitment recommendation, ensure the safety of the environment, remove the means, cognitive restructuring
■ Improving social activity and energy	■ Behavioral activation strategies
■ Reducing automatic negative thoughts	■ Cognitive restructuring
■ Increasing social contact	■ Reinforce social activities and planning of such activities

CBT, cognitive behavioral therapy.

TABLE 2.9 Treatment Goals and Interventions for Disruptive Mood Dysregulation Disorder

Treatment Goals	CBT Interventions
■ Reducing irritability	■ Self-monitoring and management strategies
■ Reducing behavior outbursts and tantrums	■ Parent behavior management training
■ Improving motivation for desirable behavior	■ Token economies, differential reinforcement
■ Improving compliance	■ Giving effective praise and behavioral prompts

CBT, cognitive behavioral therapy.

DMDD occurs in approximately 2% to 5% of children and adolescents with elevated prevalence noted in males and elementary-age children (APA, 2013, p. 157). Additional psychiatric symptoms frequently occur with DMDD, and comorbidity with oppositional defiant disorder (ODD) is the most common; however, individuals with DMDD also have elevated health concerns and may be diagnosed with other behavior-related disorders (APA, 2013, p. 160). Table 2.9 lists common treatment goals and CBT interventions for DMDD.

Obsessive-Compulsive and Related Disorders

Obsessive-compulsive disorder. OCD encompasses a pattern of obsessions (recurring, intrusive, and disturbing thoughts that are actively avoided or suppressed) and/or compulsions (excessive or illogical behaviors or thoughts that the individual believes will alleviate distress) that lead to significant life stress or time spent engaging in such behaviors (APA, 2013, p. 237). OCD can occur with good, poor, or absent insight regarding the inaccuracy of OCD-related beliefs and compulsions. Symptoms are often accompanied by anxiety or repulsion and may occur in multiple domains (e.g., contamination, harm, symmetry or organization, inappropriate or taboo thoughts; APA, 2013, pp. 238–239).

OCD occurs in about 1.2% of Americans with slightly higher prevalence reported in males during youth. About one-quarter of males report symptoms before age 10 (APA, 2013, p. 239). Risk factors for OCD involve traumatic life events (including abuse), a family history of OCD, the presence of other internalizing disorders, negative affect, and a history of restrictive behaviors. Differential brain functioning in areas related to decision-making, emotionality, and inhibition has also been observed (APA, 2013, pp. 239–240). Over half of adults with OCD also experience internalizing disorders, including anxiety, depressive, or bipolar disorders. Tic disorders and other OCD-related disorders also regularly co-occur (APA, 2013, p. 242). Table 2.10 lists common treatment goals and CBT interventions for OCD.

Excoriation (skin-picking) disorder and trichotillomania (hair-pulling disorder). Excoriation disorder entails the habitual picking of one's skin (to the point of sores and sometimes bleeding), and trichotillomania entails the habitual pulling out of one's hair (to the point of hair loss). Both are characterized by unsuccessful attempts to modify the behavior and impaired life functioning (APA, 2013, pp. 251, 254). Excoriation behaviors commonly occur on the face and arms and can involve picking healthy or damaged skin (APA, 2013, p. 255). Trichotillomania often involves pulling out hair from the head or eyebrows/eyelids and is regularly accompanied by hair-pulling rituals (APA, 2013, p. 252). Symptoms of both disorders may occur in reaction to stress or without active awareness and can result in feelings of

TABLE 2.10   Treatment Goals and Interventions for Obsessive-Compulsive Disorder

Treatment Goals	CBT Interventions
■ Reducing compulsions	■ Exposure/response prevention
■ Reducing obsessive thoughts	■ Exposure/response prevention, acceptance/commitment therapy
■ Reducing avoidant behavior	■ Exposure/response prevention
■ Reducing family involvement with rituals	■ Family accommodation reduction therapy

CBT, cognitive behavioral therapy.

TABLE 2.11   Treatment Goals and Interventions for Excoriation Disorder and Trichotillomania

Treatment Goals	CBT Interventions
■ Reducing hair pulling and skin picking	■ Habit reversal training
■ Reducing hair-pulling and skin-picking urges	■ Habit reversal training, exposure/response prevention
■ Reducing stress and distress	■ Relaxation strategies
■ Reducing shame, guilt, and embarrassment	■ Cognitive restructuring

CBT, cognitive behavioral therapy.

satisfaction (APA, 2013, pp. 252, 255). Excoriation disorder and trichotillomania are more common in females than males in adult populations, but trichotillomania is more common in male children than female children (APA, 2013, pp. 252, 255). Prevalence rates for both disorders are less than 2% in adults. Both typically originate in adolescence and feature a family history of OCD-related disorders as a risk factor (APA, 2013, pp. 253, 255). Excoriation disorder and trichotillomania are often comorbid with each other as well as MDD and other OCD-related disorders (APA, 2013, pp. 254, 257). Table 2.11 lists common treatment goals and CBT interventions for excoriation disorder and trichotillomania.

Externalizing Psychopathology

The *DSM-5* criteria for externalizing disorders in this chapter are divided into two categories consistent with the *DSM-5* manual: disruptive and neurodevelopmental (APA, 2013). Disruptive disorders are often first diagnosed in elementary or middle school as they tend to have onset in early childhood or adolescence, whereas neurodevelopmental disorders have onset during the preschool developmental period. It should be noted that although *DSM-5* criteria are reviewed, this text does not provide a comprehensive listing of all qualifiers, and the *DSM-5* should be consulted for greater diagnostic detail prior to identifying or confirming any diagnosis. Although aggression and bullying may not be diagnoses, they do represent a constellation of inappropriate actions that are all too frequent in schools and can be harmful and disruptive in educational settings. Each syndrome also provides information on a national website with family and clinician resources that are empirically supported. The sites may provide helpful parent education materials and self-help materials, and some also sponsor blogs and chat rooms as a source of support.

Disruptive, Impulse Control, and Conduct Disorders

Unlike internalizing disorders that can be overlooked because they do not often interfere with the learning of classmates, disruptive disorders have long been a source of concern in school systems, as they often disturb the entire classroom. The three *DSM-5* disruptive disorders covered in this section—conduct disorder (CD), intermittent explosive disorder (IED), and oppositional defiant disorder (ODD)— are more often diagnosed in males. Similarly, attention deficit hyperactivity disorder (ADHD) also is far more commonly diagnosed in males.

Conduct disorder. The criteria for CD require a persistent and recurring pattern of actions that violates the rights of others and/or societal norms. There are 15 possible symptoms across four categories (e.g., aggression to animals or people, destruction of property, theft or deceit, and violating serious rules), of which three must be present (APA, 2013, pp. 469–475). Behavior examples include bullying, fighting, cruelty to animals or people, mugging, setting fires, burglary, conning others, and stealing. Specifiers include childhood-onset type (poorest prognosis), adolescent-onset type, and unspecified onset type with severity ratings of mild, moderate, or severe. Additionally, significant impairment in school, work, or interpersonal functioning must be present (APA, 2013, p. 470).

Prevalence rates range from 2% to 10% and appear to be consistent across race, ethnicity, and countries. Comorbidities include ODD, ADHD, specific learning disorders, anxiety, and depressive/bipolar disorders. Risk factors include a temperament that is undercontrolled, lower intelligence (especially verbal skills), harsh parenting, family substance abuse, deviant peers, and parental mental health diagnoses (e.g., CD, depression, ADHD). Physiological correlates include less automatic fear response than typical and abnormalities in the prefrontal lobe and amygdala interfering with how affect is processed. It also is noted that CD is associated with a "slower resting heart rate … and this marker is not characteristic of any other mental disorder" (APA, 2013, p. 474). Table 2.12 lists common treatment goals and CBT interventions for CD.

Oppositional defiant disorder. The *DSM-5* requires a pattern of angry, argumentative, vindictive, defiant behaviors over a 6-month time frame for a diagnosis of ODD (APA, 2013, pp. 462–466). There are eight possible symptoms, including being angry or resentful, arguing with authority, and blaming or annoying others. The severity of symptoms can range from mild to moderate. Additionally, the behaviors should have a negative impact on the student's school, work or interpersonal functioning and cause distress to those closest to the child (APA, 2013, p. 470). Prevalence rates range from 1% to 11% and are consistent across race, ethnicity, and countries. Risk factors include emotional reactivity, low frustration tolerance, and a

---

TABLE 2.12   Treatment Goals and Interventions for Conduct Disorder

Treatment Goals	CBT Interventions
■ Reducing aggressive and threatening behavior	■ Multisystematic family therapy
■ Reducing irritability	■ Self-calming strategies, relaxation strategies
■ Reducing tantrums and conflict	■ Use a neutral tone of voice, provide alternatives
■ Protecting other students	■ Wraparound care

CBT, cognitive behavioral therapy.

history of poor parenting. ODD has several physiological correlates, including brain anomalies in the amygdala and prefrontal cortex as well as lower basal cortisol reactivity and lower heart rate (APA, 2013, p. 464). Table 2.13 lists common treatment goals and CBT interventions for ODD.

Intermittent explosive disorder. The diagnostic criteria for IED require a repeated pattern of impulsive (not premeditated) aggressive outbursts (APA, 2013, pp. 466–469). Outbursts can manifest verbally (e.g., tantrums) or physically (property damage, harm to animals or people). The prevalence rate for IED is estimated at 2.7%; it occurs more often among persons under age 40, and the occurrence is lower in some other countries (e.g., Asia). Comorbidities include depression, anxiety, and substance abuse, CD, ODD, and ADHD. Risk factors include early childhood trauma experiences and first-degree relatives with IED. Brain abnormalities related to the limbic system and amygdala (especially related to anger) are known physiological correlates (APA, 2013, p. 468). Table 2.14 lists common treatment goals and CBT interventions for IED.

Attention deficit hyperactivity disorder. The diagnosis of ADHD is based on a recurring "pattern of inattention and/or hyperactivity-impulsivity" (APA, 2013, p. 59). Inattentive symptoms may include not attending to details, resulting in making mistakes; difficulty listening or following directions; and struggles with organization skills and forgetfulness. Hyperactive/impulsive symptoms present as fidgeting, restlessness, and excessive nonproductive motor movement (e.g., running), as well as a propensity to blurt answers and interrupt conversations (APA, 2013,

TABLE 2.13   Treatment Goals and Interventions for Oppositional Defiant Disorder

Treatment Goals	CBT Interventions
■ Reducing oppositionality and defiance	■ Provide effective commands, pick and choose conflicts
■ Reducing irritability	■ Self-calming strategies, relaxation strategies
■ Reducing tantrums and conflict	■ Use a neutral tone of voice, provide alternatives
■ Reducing conflicts with authority figures	■ Develop meaningful relationships with authority figures

CBT, cognitive behavioral therapy.

TABLE 2.14   Treatment Goals and Interventions for Intermittent Explosive Disorder

Treatment Goals	CBT Interventions
■ Reducing impulsivity	■ Self-management and calming strategies
■ Reducing aggression	■ Self-calming strategies, relaxation strategies, distraction strategies
■ Reducing anger	■ Cognitive restructuring, self-calming strategies, relaxation strategies
■ Preventing future explosive episodes	■ Restitution, undoing, making valid apologies

CBT, cognitive behavioral therapy.

TABLE 2.15 Treatment Goals and Interventions for Attention Deficit Hyperactivity Disorder

Treatment Goals	CBT Interventions
■ Reducing inattention, hyperactivity, and impulsivity	■ Stimulant medication
■ Reducing inattention	■ Organizational strategies, self-monitoring
■ Reducing hyperactivity	■ Scheduled breaks, self-monitoring
■ Reducing disorganization	■ Organizational strategies, self-monitoring

CBT, cognitive behavioral therapy.

pp. 59–65). Additionally, significant impairment in school, work, or interpersonal functioning must be present (APA, 2013, p. 60).

Prevalence rates are estimated at 5%, and the diagnosis is more often applied to Caucasian children in the United States. High comorbidity rates are reported for ODD, CD, and disruptive mood dysregulation. Specific learning disabilities and anxiety can be comorbid as well, although the rate is lower. Risk factors include lower behavior inhibition, higher risk taking, low birth weight, and maternal use of alcohol during pregnancy. A strong heritability factor is indicated, especially in first-degree relatives with ADHD (APA, 2013, pp. 59–65). Table 2.15 lists common treatment goals and CBT interventions for ADHD.

CULTURALLY RESPONSIVE CBT

The literature on CBT and its clinical application has been criticized for its omission of cultural, ethnic, and linguistic information (Hays & Iwamasa, 2006). This probably is because the majority (about 84%) of therapists identify as being White or having European American heritage (Lin, Stamm, & Christidis, 2018). Thus, whether directly or inadvertently, with CBT and other forms of psychotherapy more generally, predominant cultural values, norms, and patterns of communication can be reinforced through the therapeutic process. This could then be alienating to culturally and linguistically diverse individuals, especially for individuals who find CBT's emphasis on personal independence, self-disclosure, and assertiveness in opposition to culturally held values of interdependence, protecting the family reputation, and being subtle (Hays & Iwamasa, 2006).

However, the previous concerns do not invalidate the utility of using CBT with culturally and linguistically diverse clients. Instead, emerging research and literature discuss ways in which CBT can be culturally mindful and responsive. This literature base does not debase elements of CBT; in fact, it enhances or infuses CBT with elements from multicultural counseling models that pertain to working with specific groups of clients (Norcross, Hedges, & Prochaska, 2002).

Although a review of culturally responsive CBT requires a book in itself (see Hays & Iwamasa, 2006), it is important to highlight some salient ways in which the treatment can be adapted for culturally and linguistically diverse clients. First, culturally responsive CBT requires therapists to engage in self-reflection to identify biases they may harbor because of personal reasons, ignorance, inexperience, or gaps in knowledge associated with potential clients. Additionally, the therapists should consider how prevailing cultural norms and messages influence their own communication patterns and styles. Ultimately, through developing greater self-awareness regarding the former, the CBT practitioner can be more sensitive and better calibrate treatment. However, it is important to note that self-reflection is an ongoing and interactive process that never is fully complete.

The second step of culturally responsive CBT involves obtaining information about specific cultures and ethnicities from credible sources. This might include information that is published by outlets in these communities themselves, attending cultural events, talking to community leaders or experts, seeking supervision or consultation from an individual from the specific culture, accessing materials and individuals who are members of cultural diversity professional organizations and groups, and developing relationships with individuals from the same or similar culture as clients (Hays & Iwamasa, 2006). As a concluding note, it is important to recognize that culture influences every therapist and client in unique and dynamic ways. Therefore, cultural considerations are an essential part of the CBT process.

REFERENCES

American Psychiatric Association. (2013). *Diagnostic and statistical manual of mental disorders* (5th ed.). Arlington, VA: American Psychiatric Publishing.

Beck, A. T. (1991). *Cognitive therapy and the emotional disorders.* New York, NY: Penguin.

Beck, J. S. (1995). *Cognitive therapy: Basics and beyond.* New York, NY: Guilford Press.

Beck, J. S. (2011). *Cognitive behavior therapy: Basics and beyond* (2nd ed.). New York, NY: Guilford Press.

Ellis, A. (1991). The revised ABC's of rational-emotive therapy. *Journal of Rational-Emotive and Cognitive-Behavior Therapy, 9,* 139–172. doi:10.1007/BF01061227

Hayes, S. C., Levin, M. E., Plumb-Vilardaga, J., Villatte, J. L., & Pistorello, J. (2013). Acceptance and commitment therapy and contextual behavioral science: Examining the progress of a distinctive model of behavioral and cognitive therapy. *Behavior Therapy, 44,* 180–198. doi:10.1016/j.beth.2009.08.002

Hays, P. A., & Iwamasa, G. Y. (Eds.). (2006). *Culturally responsive cognitive-behavioral therapy.* Washington, DC: American Psychological Association.

Kendall, P. C. (Ed.). (2011). *Child and adolescent therapy: Cognitive-behavioral procedures.* New York, NY: Guilford Press.

Kutash, K., Duchnowski, A. J., & Lynn, N. (2006). *School-based mental health: An empirical guide for decision-makers.* Tampa, FL: University of South Florida, The Louis de la Parte Florida Mental Health Institute, Department of Child & Family Studies, Research and Training Center for Children's Mental Health.

Lin, L., Stamm, K., & Christidis, P. (2018). *Demographics of the U.S. psychology workforce: Findings from the 2007–16 American Community Survey.* Washington, DC: American Psychological Association. Retrieved from https://www.apa.org/workforce/publications/16-demographics/report.pdf

Norcross, J. C., Hedges, M., & Prochaska, J. O. (2002). The face of 2010: A Delphi poll on the future of psychotherapy. *Professional Psychology: Research and Practice, 33,* 316–322. doi:10.1037/0735-7028.33.3.316

Suveg, C., Sood, E., Comer, J. S., & Kendall, P. C. (2009). Changes in emotion regulation following cognitive-behavioral therapy for anxious youth. *Journal of Clinical Child & Adolescent Psychology, 38,* 390–401. doi:10.1080/15374410902851721

Taibbi, R. (2015). *Doing family therapy: Craft and creativity in clinical practice.* New York, NY: Guilford Press.

World Health Organization. (2016). *International classification of disease and related health problems (ICD-10).* Retrieved from https://icd.who.int/browse10/2016/en

THREE

Cognitive Behavioral Therapy Essential Components

INTRODUCTION

Much of the work involved in effective counseling occurs outside the therapy sessions through preplanning and astute matching of client needs with specific intervention components most likely to be effective. Although scripted cognitive behavioral therapy (CBT) manuals are available, the lessons take a broad and sequential approach, often covering more concepts than may be necessary for a particular child or group. Within the umbrella of CBT are a plethora of techniques and strategies, thus giving room to individualize therapy. By being familiar with these basic principles and techniques, the counselor can customize sessions to optimize precious time within the school settings for intervention. Use of progress-monitoring measures can serve as a guide for practitioners when deciding what components are proving to be effective or not effective for a specific student and when advancing the goals of counseling. Thus, this chapter offers an overview of essential components to counseling therapy planning, starting with case conceptualization through first session considerations. Chapter 4, Emotional and Behavioral Regulation Strategies, and Chapter 5, Exposure and Response Prevention and Cognitive Behavioral Therapy, offer detailed application instructions for CBT principles, whereas Chapter 6, Applied Cognitive Behavioral Therapy Session Activities, adds activities and Chapter 7, Case Studies, provides case examples.

CASE CONCEPTUALIZATION

Case conceptualization (also called case formation) involves a process of understanding the student's needs from all the data gathered about the individual (e.g., referral concern, interviews, classroom observations, student records, medical files, assessment data) and then formulating hypotheses regarding the mechanisms maintaining her or his emotional and behavioral challenges. Some authors have described the process of case conceptualization as creating a road map or blueprint for services that best suit the individual. Examples of individualized life experiences may include culture, identity, past trauma, socioeconomic circumstance, education level, and family and community resources, as well as diagnoses and coping skills. This process of understanding the client also can reveal strengths from which to build on in therapy (e.g., supportive extended family, faith-based supports, hobbies, and talents). Mechanisms may include a range of triggers, life circumstances, thinking errors, or even neurological anomalies involving memory or learning abilities. The hypotheses are based on sound theoretical frameworks as a guide to understanding the child's functioning (e.g., helpless/hopelessness common to depression). Once hypotheses are created, intervention methods used to address those factors can be applied to test the hypotheses. It is not unusual for new hypotheses to emerge throughout the counseling sequence, as there is more time for observing the student and the child also begins to reveal more about him- or herself. Many experts in the field consider case conceptualization to be a core competency for the practice of counseling (Betan & Binder, 2010; Sperry, 2010).

Case Conceptualization Models

There are a number of prescriptive case conceptualization processes in the literature that counselors may wish to utilize. Beck (2011, pp. 29–30) offers a case formulation model that suggests the counselor ask her- or himself a series of questions (e.g., What are the student's problems? What distortions are associated with those problems?) to help provide clarity on the counseling goals and methods. Her method includes investigating the child's core beliefs, assumptions, rules, compensatory strategies, and situation, as well as the automatic thoughts and subsequent affect and behavior. The temporal/contextual model reviews connections between behavior, cognition, and affect within the child and also as connected to the external world. Consideration is given to the client's perceptions of information, beliefs, interaction style, emotional awareness, self-regulation, and environmental experiences (Zubernis & Snyder, 2015). Bronfenbrenner (1981) postulated a model that juxtaposes a child's interaction with his or her surrounding micro- and mesosystems (e.g., family, school, neighborhood), an exosystem (e.g., family friends, parent work setting, social/community services), and society at large (e.g., macrosystem of social, cultural, and historical influences). Although a review of the numerous case conceptualization models is beyond the scope of this book and counselors may adopt a variety of models, the common factor is that each model considers the child holistically within the context of his or her life experience, unique attributes, and surrounding environments. During case conceptualization, considerations should be given also to parent–caregiver collaboration and child diversity factors. The American Counseling Association recommends that counselors maintain an awareness of their own attitudes, beliefs, and potential biases as well as the worldview and beliefs of the child and family when making intervention decisions and assessing student needs (Arredondo et al., 1996). Additional information on cultural formation considerations can be found in Chapter 2, Cognitive Theoretical Foundations, and in this chapter.

Home–School Collaboration

Most case conceptualization models include parents and caregivers as a crucial consideration in planning effective intervention for children and youth. It is important to acknowledge that students spend more time at home and with family than school as well as the fact that learning in early formative years occurs at home and caregivers are most often highly invested in the well-being of their children. Although school can be a busy institution, taking the time to include parents offers many benefits, as they best understand a child's history, culture, and current supports. Researchers have found that school-based mental health and behavioral interventions are more effective when caregivers are involved (Shucksmith, Jones, & Summerbell, 2010), and this collaboration is especially important for children from diverse backgrounds (Lines, Miller, & Arthur-Stanley, 2010). Children benefit in other ways as well, including improved grades, higher test scores, better attendance, and fewer special education placements (Christenson & Reschly, 2010). Additionally, by including families, clinicians can help develop rapport, ensure better compliance with homework, and generalize treatment across different settings.

Adapting for Developmental Factors

Following case conceptualization and establishing a strong home–school collaboration, consideration for the developmental level of individuals participating in counseling needs to be considered. Although the core concepts of CBT remain the same across ages of clients, the way those precepts are taught, the activities that reinforce the concepts, and the applications will vary based on the student's developmental level. In general, younger children understand ideas in a more concrete manner, and the use of manipulatives, visual aids, fun practice exercises, and simple vocabulary are helpful. As an example, teaching a concept, such as the relationship between thoughts, feelings, and behaviors, can use a simple schematic or a more sophisticated model; both approaches teach the same core principle (see Appendix Exhibits 2.1–2.9). Illustrating thinking errors might include simple fun activities, such as modeling/role-playing exercises or animated video clips, for younger children and more sophisticated exercises, such as thought journaling or perspective taking, for adolescents (see Appendix Exhibits 5.12–5.17). Chapter 6, Applied Cognitive Behavioral Therapy Session Activities, offers a number of session activities that reflect differentiation by age.

Emergency Indicators

As noted in Chapter 2, Cognitive Theoretical Foundations, there are a number of contraindications for CBT, including limited intellect, low receptive/expressive language, and very young children. Additionally, there are some emergency indicators that, although rare, can occur during counseling, and there should always be a plan to address those. If students are experiencing psychosis, panic attack, significant grief, intoxication, ill effects of drug use/misuse, or physical distress, an immediate transport to the school nurse and emergency services is warranted. Should this occur during a small group counseling session, the therapist also needs to simultaneously have a plan for the safety of the rest of the children. Each school generally has a way to quickly alert personnel for support (e.g., radios, call buttons, office phone), and being aware of these procedures is important. Knowing where the surrounding adults in close proximity are and who is easily accessible for backup can also be important. By having awareness of these contingencies ahead of time, the counselor remains supportive of all the children's needs. In the case of expressions of suicidal ideation or intent, therapy should immediately switch to implementation of the school's suicidal assessment procedure. Lastly, documenting any emergency responses will be important to informing later intervention plans.

THERAPY SESSION PLANNING

Psychoeducation

Psychoeducation is one strategy used to address *cognitive deficiency* or a lack of accurate information that can have a negative impact. Within the broader social context of mental health, there is often a stigma and negative connotation associated with a psychiatric diagnosis, atypical behavior, and in some cases even participation in counseling services. Additionally, families do not always have access to rigorous scientific reviews of syndromes and effective interventions. Thus, it is easy for parents and their children with behavior challenges and/or mental health diagnoses to misunderstand their own symptoms, risk factors, and prognosis. It also is common for children to feel their spontaneous behaviors or diagnosis is insurmountable or overwhelming. Part of the psychoeducational component within a CBT context includes providing accurate information to the child and parents regarding the nature of disorders and challenging behaviors. Parents may misunderstand symptoms as "bad" behavior without fully appreciating the complex physiological influences. Some children may feel powerless, and one of the goals of psychoeducation is to empower them. This concept may be expressed as "taking charge of my ADHD [attention deficit hyperactivity disorder]," "kicking my anxiety away," or "I'm more than OCD [obsessive-compulsive disorder]; it doesn't rule me." Psychoeducation also involves teaching students and their families about the interventions, both the purposes and implementation, especially if parents will be asked to extend the strategies to the home. In addition to sharing *Diagnostic and Statistical Manual of Mental Disorders,* Fifth Edition (*DSM-5*; American Psychiatric Association [APA], 2013) information with parents, clinicians can also share a wide range of nationally funded resources for specific behavioral needs and interventions with empirical rigor with families as part of the psychoeducation process. Table 3.1 lists national child/adolescent mental health centers that provide empirically supported intervention resources.

Getting Started

Counseling children and youth requires the ability to adapt theoretical terms and concepts to their personal developmental level, as well as the ability to build rapport and trust. In essence, these are basically good communication skills, or more specifically for counseling, they are often called microskills. Microskills can be easily developed and applied to most interpersonal relationships even beyond the counseling paradigm and generally include the following abilities:

- Rapport: This involves establishing an empathic and caring alliance with a client. Strategies may include good eye contact, caring voice tone and inflection, sharing common interests, chair/desk positioning that is not

TABLE 3.1   National Child/Adolescent Mental Health Centers With Empirically Supported Intervention Resources

National Resource Center	Website
American Psychological Association	www.apa.org
Association for Behavioral and Cognitive Therapies	www.abct.org/home
Autism Speaks	www.autismspeaks.org
Center for Autism and Related Disorders	www.centerforautism.com
Centers for Disease Control and Prevention	www.cdc.gov/ncbddd
Collaborative for Academic, Social, and Emotional Learning	www.casel.org
International OCD Foundation	www.ocfoundation.org
American Academy of Child and Adolescent Psychiatry	www.aacap.org
National Child Traumatic Stress Network	www.nctsnet.org
National Dissemination Center for Children with Disabilities	www.parentcenterhub.org
National Institute of Mental Health	www.nimh.nih.gov
Tourette Association of America	www.tsa-usa.org
Positive Youth Development in the United States: Research Findings on Evaluations of Positive Youth Development Programs	
What Works Clearinghouse	http://ies.ed.gov/ncee/wwc

OCD, obsessive-compulsive disorder.

intimidating (e.g., removing desk barriers), and body language that communicates the therapist is attentive.

- Listening skills: This involves the ability to identify core emotions and key facts and sustain alert attention.
- Questioning skills: The ability to select closed-ended questions to elicit facts when needed or open-ended question formats to facilitate a richer context of information, as well as avoidance of *why* questions and leading questions are important to skilled questioning.
- Reflecting skills: This includes the ability to use paraphrasing and summarizing to communicate that the counselor hears and understands the client's conversation. Within the summarizing technique, two more nuanced communication skills can also be important: The signal summary lets the client know you understand the essence of his or her comments, and it is time to move to another topic; the planning summary provides a brief recap and telescopes that it is time for closure of the conversation or to end the session.

Although this section focuses on getting started in counseling for the first session, having at least a tentative written outline of targeted skills and activities for the counseling sequence will be helpful. This outline can improve treatment implementation and fidelity, as it serves to remind the therapist of the purposes and goals for the sessions. Goals for the initial session should include ample opportunities for the student(s) to introduce him- or herself, ask questions, and get to know the counselor and others if the format is small group counseling. Rapport can be established by maintaining good eye contact, having a warm demeanor, exploring interests important to the student(s), and using vocabulary that is consistent with their developmental level. A counselor's knowledge of pop culture consistent with the student's age also can foster common ground and rapport. Additionally, there are a plethora of icebreaker exercises available online to help small groups get to know each other. Several are listed here:

- Get-to-Know-You Bingo (Bingo cards, chips, and a way to select random numbers are needed. As numbers are called, the individual places a chip on his or her bingo card and answers the question for that row and column. Including a valued prize for the winner can increase enthusiasm for participating.)
- Roll and Respond (Students are asked to roll dice and then respond to questions on cards labeled 1–6—the card corresponding to the number on the dice is answered.)
- Sentence Completion Jenga (Jenga blocks can be purchased at most toy stores and labeled with sentence stems in permanent marker. As a block is pulled, that individual answers the question. Question stems might include the following: "My favorite activity at school is…," "On weekends I like to…," "The best vacation would be….")
- Word Card Stories (A variety of word cards, primarily verbs and nouns, are placed face down on the table. Students randomly choose 10 cards and create a short story, including every word on their cards. Students can vote on the "wildest," "silliest," and "best" story.)
- Rumor Control (This game starts with the counselor or a student sharing a partial sentence whispered to a neighbor; each child in turn adds to the words and whispers the information to the next student until everyone has participated. The last student shares the rumor, which has usually evolved in surprising ways.)
- Pat-on-the-Back (Students are provided with a stiff sheet of paper hung on their back with a string and pencils. Each student anonymously writes two to three compliments on all the other students' backs. At the end, students may comment on notes if they wish to.)

The first session will also need to include a discussion of boundaries and expectations. For group counseling, it may be helpful to have the students generate the session rules (e.g., "We will all take turns talking," "We only talk when we are holding the sponge ball, and we must pass it to someone else when the timer goes off"). It also is important to share the goals of the counseling intervention and to elicit student input on activities they may enjoy (e.g., video clips, board games, prizes for participation, phone apps). Additionally, the limits of confidentiality need to be discussed in terms of not sharing what others say in the group outside the therapy session; also, it may be noted that if someone is in danger of being hurt, hurting others, or hurting him- or herself, the counselor will seek appropriate help for the student.

Given the important role that progress-monitoring measures (see Chapter 1, Effective Cognitive Behavioral Therapy in Schools) and therapy homework assignments have in reinforcing counseling concepts, it will be helpful to establish expectations for these at the first session. The counselor may say "I am going to ask you to rate your feelings from time to time on a scale of 1 to 10" or "We are going to use a feeling thermometer to show how you feel." (See Appendix Exhibit 1.4.) Additionally, it may be noted that students will be asked to practice things they learn in session at home or other locations to improve their skills. Counselors may inform students that parents have a copy of the strategies used in counseling (e.g., progressive muscle relaxation) and they also will help remind them to use the techniques at home. If teachers are coupling a classroom positive behavioral incentive program with the counseling goals, it may also be important to review the contingencies (e.g., "Your teacher also will be noticing how often you use your deep breathing relaxation technique and will provide points you can use toward a treasure box reward at the end of the day").

TERMINATING THERAPY

When the counselor and/or school intervention team decide that counseling goals are met, it is helpful to give the student advance notice of the termination of therapy. This is especially important for counseling interventions because there is a supportive relationship with the student and she or he may feel nervous about the withdrawal of services or, in some cases, may even feel abandoned. Informing the student of the impending last session, offering a way to contact counseling services if needed later, and celebrating new skills acquired are strategies to ease the transition. Lastly, there is support in the literature for the use of follow-up booster sessions several weeks or months following intervention (Foxx, 2013; Utz, 2016). When these are proactively set at the last session, the student is assured that she or he has the opportunity to meet again. Booster sessions offer a review of strategies as well as a method to document the stability of counseling effects.

REFERENCES

American Psychiatric Association. (2013). *Diagnostic and statistical manual of mental disorders* (5th ed.). Arlington, VA: American Psychiatric Publishing.

Arredondo, P., Toporek, M. S., Brown, S., Jones, J., Locke, D. C., Sanchez, J., & Stadler, H. (1996). *Operationalization of the multicultural counseling competencies*. Alexandria, VA: American Counseling Association.

Beck, J. S. (2011). *Cognitive behavior therapy: Basics and beyond* (2nd ed.). New York, NY: Guilford Press.

Betan, E. J., & Binder, J. L. (2010). Clinical expertise in psychotherapy: How expert therapists use theory in generating case conceptualizations and interventions. *Journal of Contemporary Psychotherapy, 40*, 141–152. doi:10.1007/s10879-010-9138-0

Bronfenbrenner, U. (1981). *The ecology of human development: Experiments by nature and design*. Cambridge, MA: Harvard University Press.

Christenson, S. L., & Reschly, A. L. (Eds.). (2010). *Handbook of school-family partnerships*. New York, NY: Routledge/Taylor & Francis.

Foxx, R. M. (2013). The maintenance of behavioral change: The case for long-term follow-ups. *American Psychologist, 68*(8), 728–736. doi:10.1037/a0033713

Lines, C., Miller, G., & Arthur-Stanley, A. (2010). *The power of family-school partnering (FSP): A practical guide for school mental health professionals and educators*. New York, NY: Routledge.

Shucksmith, J., Jones, S., & Summerbell, C. (2010). The role of parental involvement in school-based mental health interventions at primary (elementary) school level. *Advances in School Mental Health Promotion, 3*(1), 18–29. doi:10.1080/1754730X.2010.9715671

Sperry, L. (2010). *Core competencies in counseling and psychotherapy: Becoming a highly competent and effective counselor.* New York, NY: Routledge.

Utz, M. (2016). *When a therapist leaves a client: Closing the therapeutic relationship effectively.* Retrieved from https://sophia.stkate.edu/msw_papers/686

Zubernis, L., & Snyder, M. (2015). *Case conceptualization and effective interventions: Assessing and treating mental, emotional, and behavioral disorders.* Thousand Oaks, CA: SAGE.

PART II

Counseling Techniques

FOUR

Emotional and Behavioral Regulation Strategies

INTRODUCTION

Although the cognitive behavioral therapy (CBT) model directly emphasizes the use of cognitive and behavioral interventions as part of the therapeutic process, emotional and behavioral regulation strategies are included in CBT protocols. Such strategies are varied in nature, application, and efficacy depending on the clinical presentation of students as well as their own particular needs. In other words, different emotional and behavioral regulation strategies will be effective for different students, and it might not be clear which will work the best. Therefore, therapists should feel free to try several different strategies. In doing so, the therapist might identify one strategy that works particularly effectively. Alternatively, however, several effective strategies might be identified, which can then help fill up the student's CBT toolkit.

As implied, emotional and behavioral regulations strategies are applied to help students manage difficult emotions and behaviors—emotions and behaviors that either cause personal distress or result in negative consequences for the student and others. These emotions are anxiety, stress, agitation, irritability, and depression, and these behaviors typically are inattentiveness, hyperactivity, impulsivity, tics, and problematic habits, such as hair pulling and skin picking. It is important to note that overlap typically exists between students with emotional and behavioral problems. For example, a child with attention deficit hyperactivity disorder (ADHD) likely will have problems with impulsivity and emotional regulation as well as hyperactivity and behavior management problems. Similarly, a child experiencing clinically significant depression may appear agitated and impulsive in addition to sad and moody and may benefit from combined treatment strategies. Therefore, therapists should consider both emotion and behavior regulation problems when working with students using these strategies.

RECOGNIZING EMOTIONS AND PHYSIOLOGICAL TRIGGERS

Recognizing Feelings

The first step toward applying emotional or behavioral strategies is to be able to identify one's feelings and triggers. However, this is not easy for most students to do, regardless of their age or developmental level. In fact, many adults struggle to identify their feelings, especially nuanced ones. Therefore, students need to develop a feeling vocabulary that will allow them to label their feelings and emotional state. Elementary school students and middle school students typically have a smaller emotional vocabulary. When asked how they are feeling, they might say "happy," "mad," "sad," or "bad"—but probably not "ecstatic," "blissful," disgruntled," or "indignant." It is not important for students to develop a complete list of feelings (and such a list would be just about impossible to learn because certain emotion-related words are specific to certain languages, cultures, and subcultures). However, it is important for students to learn a developmentally appropriate list of feeling words, be able to describe them, and be able to identify them in themselves. The ways to teach students to recognize feelings are numerous, and CBT therapists are always developing new creative strategies using new technologies. However, some basic techniques are commonly used; four are described here:

> **Emotion labeling**. A plethora of different worksheets are freely available online, and some are more complex than others. These worksheets typically include cartoons that exaggerate facial expressions to illustrate how they look in contrast to each other. Some worksheets are blank, and the therapist has the student label the faces with the emotions that he or she thinks are most fitting. This can then stimulate a dialogue of why the student labeled the pictures with specific emotions and what it feels like to experiencing the emotion. Alternatively, if the emotions are present under the cartoon, the therapist can focus on what physical features are present in the pictures and why they indicate the respective emotion. For example, the student might say "He looks really happy because he is smiling from ear to ear."
>
> **Feeling cards**. Another approach to foster feeling identification skills involves using feeling cards. As an example of this approach, the therapist and the student could both write down as many feeling words they can think of (within reason). Put the cards into a deck, shuffle them, and then take turns pulling cards from the deck and describing the emotion to the best of their ability, when they recently felt this emotion, and what was happening when they did. Using feeling cards to identify emotions is particularly useful because the therapist can model for the student to help scaffold his or her ability to identify feelings. For example, if the therapist pulled a card that said "excited," he or she might say something like "I feel like I have a lot energy, and I can't wait for something to happen—like right before going trick-or-treating on Halloween." "I felt very excited when I took my children to Disneyland because I knew they would love it."

Guessing feelings. A third feeling identification approach involves watching age-appropriate TV shows or cartoons with the volume on mute and asking the student to say what feeling the character(s) is feeling and why. This can help stimulate a dialogue between the therapist about a range of feelings, which can then be leveraged to talk about personal emotions, what these feelings are like, and which feelings are similar or different from each other. As a caveat, it is important not to choose TV shows or cartoons that are overly familiar to the student, as the student might already have a sense of the character dialogue.

Order that feeling. A fourth strategy to help students identify feelings involves providing them with a list of words that can be used to express a positive or negative feeling and then have them move the words along a ruler from "least" to "most" to indicate their intensity. For example, given the words *calm, unsettled, upset, agitated, frustrated, mad, angry*, and *furious*, the student would be expected to order them from the least (i.e., calm) to the most significant expression (i.e., furious).

When to Use/Not Use Recognizing Feeling Strategies

Special sensitivity is warranted for teaching feeling vocabulary in group settings when children have speech difficulties and may find the exercises embarrassing. For those children, individual practice may be more appropriate. It also is important to consider the reading and developmental level of children when setting up expectations for expanding feeling vocabulary. Even for children of younger ages, there is a wide range of simple feeling words to express emotions. Additionally, for students prone to using profanity, setting boundaries and expectations for nonconfrontational word choices will be important.

Identifying Physiological Precursors/Triggers

In particular, many students with externalizing behavior problems and disorders (e.g., conduct disorder [CD], oppositional defiant disorder [ODD], intermittent explosive disorder [IED]) are highly reactive to perceived provocation and display an impulsive temper. The goal of improving students' awareness of physiological precursors to problematic behavior (e.g., aggressive, oppositional, explosive) is to provide them with an advanced warning system they can use to manage their feelings and behaviors. Improving awareness in this regard also offers students time to stop and think of alternative actions in lieu of acting in ways that result in negative consequences. Common physiological precursors or triggers of increasing distress or some other negative emotional state include a racing heartbeat, sweaty palms, shaky hands, clenched hands, pacing, tense muscles, or a flushed face or neck. However, children with externalizing disorders may have limited insight into such precursors, indicators, or triggers when they occur. They typically will describe their anger as instantaneous ("I go straight to red-hot mad") and beyond their control ("I was born with a temper; I can't stop it"). Therefore, they may need more explicit instruction on a process that seems to happen automatically. In other words, they might need this process to be broken down into specific steps. These are delineated here:

Step 1. The first step in the process, often called normalizing, involves understanding that feelings and emotions are real and everyone has them. The therapist also acknowledges that emotions can be very powerful but still can be moderated. Additionally, the initial sessions should emphasize that even negative emotions can be put to good use. Generally, examples of common innocuous incidents that may spark anger are discussed (e.g., losing money from a hole in one's pocket, being splashed with mud when another student jumps in a puddle). Then, examples of multiple response options are provided, and the therapist encourages the child to generate ideas as well (e.g., search for the money, wash off the mud, and laugh about it). The therapist also discusses how even a negative feeling could result in a good consequence if the individual chooses to learn from it (e.g., sew up the hole in the pocket, walk further away from the street).

Step 2. The next step in this process involves identifying the student's particular physiological stress responses. This can be accomplished by having the student recall a time when he or she was upset and then talk about what body changes he or she noticed. For students with limited insight, the therapist may need to suggest common ways that people feel stress and ask them to identify which ones are personally applicable. For younger students, it may be necessary to provide a *body map* drawing to explain the location of specific physiological reactions (e.g., stomachaches). An example of a physiological stress reaction list and a body map are provided in the Appendix Exhibits 4.1 and 4.2.

Step 3. In addition to physiological precursors, if students can identify the *triggers* that immediately precede stressful reactions, they have an opportunity to interrupt the stress-building process and perhaps change any habitual negative reaction patterns. Therapists will need to assure understanding of the cognitive model first (see Appendix Exhibit 2.1) and assist students in keeping thought records to identity circumstances or actions that tend to elicit maladaptive thoughts and behavior responses. Information from teacher referrals and observational data also may help the clinician identify triggers for the child (e.g., teacher's report indicates that child becomes angry when called on to answer questions).

Step 4. Once students can identify *triggers and physiological precursors* that suggest impending stress, they have the opportunity to implement a relaxation technique to manage their distress. Several commonly used CBT-based relaxation strategies are discussed later (for more information, see Appendix Exhibits 4.3–4.8).

Step 5. The next step in this process includes teaching the student problem-solving skills with the goal of establishing the ability to self-generate alternative and positive behavior choices. Sometimes, students with externalizing behavior problems employ maladaptive strategies to solve their problems that may include acting-out with verbal or physical aggression, noncompliance, and manipulative and covert actions (e.g., revenge, pitting parents against each other, sabotage). It would be hard to argue that those methods are not effective, as they do often accomplish a temporary goal for the student despite the long-term consequences being negative. Instead of debating the effectiveness of maladaptive behaviors, the therapist should strive to reinforce "win-win" long-term positive outcomes. It may take some time and several sessions to accomplish this aim. The ABCD form in the Appendix Exhibit 2.7 may be useful to help encourage students to differentiate between immediate and long-term consequences.

Finding the Pros and Cons

Another strategy to help to brainstorm alternative strategies to problematic behavior involves examining the pros and cons of options. However, it is important to note that some students with externalizing problems have a propensity to debate or negatively judge ideas too quickly. Therefore, the instructions for brainstorming should include an emphasis on quickly jotting down possible positive solutions without immediately evaluating them. After the list is generated, the second step is to evaluate the pros and cons of each idea. Lastly, the student is guided to select a *best* solution from the brainstorming list based on which item has the most pros and no major downside. As these may be new choices or behaviors for the student, it also may be important to practice the new behavior in session through role-play scenarios before encouraging the student to try the strategies in a real-life situation. Therapists may wish to make the brainstorming exercise a homework assignment to be completed when the student encounters stressful situations outside the therapy session and then review his or her choices and outcomes in the following session. In particular, a review of the student's thoughts following efforts to try a new solution can help guide future counseling sessions that may need to address obvious skill deficits or thinking errors.

When to Use/Not Use Identification of Physiological Precursors/Triggers Strategies

As with other counseling interventions, identification of physiological precursors and triggers will require the cognitive skills and maturity to understand and accurately assess one's own thoughts, feelings, and behaviors. Therefore, the student's cognitive ability level should be considered and perhaps this approach should not be used with students with any significant limitations in this regard. Additionally, the authenticity of reported feelings and efforts at brainstorming require self-disclosure, motivation, and honesty. For students with significant malingering, manipulative, or covert behavior tendencies, this method may be less effective. Regarding homework assignments for students with externalizing problems, often coupling assignments can be combined with a positive reinforcement plan (e.g., small incentives/rewards for returning completed worksheets) to ensure compliance. It also may be helpful to elicit parent participation in prompting, encouraging, and assisting with therapy-related homework exercises.

RELAXATION TRAINING

Relaxation training is a therapeutic technique that is used to help individuals reduce high levels of anxiety and stress (see Appendix Exhibits 4.3–4.8). Relaxation training is based on the idea that while most people encounter stressful, frustrating, and anxiety-producing events, some people respond to related distress in different ways (Otto, Simon, Olatunji, Sung, & Pollack, 2011). Overwhelming events can compromise an individual's ability to cope with adversity and warrant strategies to self-regulate. Therefore, relaxation training is generally implemented to help students cope more effectively with stress, anxiety, hyperarousal, or agitation in a healthy manner by learning how to remain calm, feel more in control of their bodies, delay impulse, and reduce their physiological responses (e.g., manage racing a heartbeat, slow rapid breathing).

The first step in teaching relaxation training involves explaining to students the purpose of relaxation training and what they can expect from it. This explanation can include a description of different reactions that people often have when faced with stressful, anxiety-provoking, frustrating, or provocative events (e.g., unhealthy versus healthy responses). With internalizers, the therapist may also want to discuss how relaxation training can be a viable and beneficial coping strategy for anxiety reduction. However, for externalizers, the therapist might want to describe how relaxation strategies can help when staying calm and when angry or frustrated. Several commonly used relaxation strategies are described here.

Diaphragmatic Breathing

Diaphragmatic breathing (also called belly breathing) implies taking deep breaths—much deeper than usual breaths. Essentially, the student should robustly engage the diaphragm, a thin skeletal muscle that sits at the base of the chest and separates the abdomen from the chest to allow for deep breaths. To accomplish this, students are first taught to sit or lie down with good spinal alignment and then to breathe slowly (1–3 seconds) and deeply through the nose. This assures that they breathe deeply as noted by stomach area expansion (in and out). Then, the student should hold the breath for 2 to 3 seconds. Following this, the student should exhale slowly through the mouth (1–3 seconds). It also may help to put a heavy book on the chest of the student and encourage the student to try to push the book up with inhalations, which suggest that the student is taking deep breaths. The purpose of belly breathing is to counteract the shallow, fast breathing that persons prone to explosive anger or anxiousness exhibit. Additionally, by increasing the amount of oxygen in the blood, it can help produce a sense of calmness, relaxation, dizziness, and even mild elation. It may take about 5 to 15 minutes for students to feel the effects of diaphragmatic breathing, and once they do, they might feel lightheaded or dizzy, so it is best to prepare them for these possible reactions in advance. Overall, the utility of diaphragmatic breathing lies in its ability to help some students "take the edge off a little." Therefore, it should not be applied to address serious anxious, avoidant, or anger problems.

Progressive Muscle Relaxation

Progressive muscle relaxation (PMR) technique involves teaching students to tense and then relax muscle groups to release tension and stress. Therapeutically, PMR is based on the premise that relaxing our muscles can help reduce our overall tension, stress, frustration, and anxiety. Through successive application, students will be able to identify the areas in which they hold tension (e.g., pulling shoulders up too high) and use those indicators for self-awareness of their own emerging distress. Common areas where muscle tension tends to accumulate include the shoulders, neck, chest, arms, and back. Therefore, using PMR, the therapist typically reads a script or uses a recording that includes instructions for tensing and releasing sequential muscle groups (e.g., close eyes and tense forehead, release; shoulder, torso, abdomen, legs, and feet are also tensed and relaxed, in turn). Appendix Exhibit 4.8 includes a sample PMR script.

Guided Imagery

Guided imagery is most applicable to school intervention and is a form of meditation or "safe place" visualization. It involves temporarily alleviating emotional distress by replacing intrusive thoughts with a mental picture of a place or event that is calming to the child. Typically, students are asked to identify favorite places (e.g., the beach, the forest), and a script is utilized initially by the therapist and later self-administered by the student as needed. Students are asked to sit in a comfortable place, close their eyes, and then listen to a recording of the script or imagine the location. Recorded guided imagery will typically have background sounds consistent with the described location. Some newer applications include visual images as well (see Table 6.1, Low-Intensity Cognitive Behavioral Therapy (CBT) Applications). The script usually describes a location emphasizing multiple senses (e.g., "You are standing on a pristine beach, hearing the waves gently caress the shore, smelling the fresh salt air, and feeling the warm sand beneath you"). It is important not to confuse guided imagery with two other CBT imagery techniques: imagery exposure and imagery rescripting. Imagery exposure involves recalling a particularly emotional event in detail and examining the feelings/thought of those moments with the help of the therapist to identify their feelings and better understand behaviors they exhibited (e.g., the fight or flight response). Imagery rescripting can be utilized with more significant mental health needs, including intrusive images, contamination, bulimia, and suicidality (Holmes, Arntz, & Smucker, 2007). These two particular imagery methods require additional training and are beyond the scope of this text.

When to Use/Not Use Relaxation Training

Relaxation training is generally used to reduce anxiety, stress, and frustration. In particular, relaxation training often is implemented to help students who express somatic complaints, including those who may frequently visit the school nurse for nonjustified headaches and stomachaches. This form of treatment can also be used with individuals who exhibit problems with emotional regulation, such as being overly dramatic or demonstrating disproportional anxious responses to daily demands. However, relaxation training should not be used for individuals who display significant compulsive symptomology, as they may use this method to ruminate over their problems more. Further, relaxation training should not be used for children/adolescents who display extreme avoidant behaviors, as they may utilize the relaxation to enhance their avoidant tendencies. Lastly, although part of a more comprehensive treatment approach, relaxation training should not be used with students who display serious anger or aggression problems.

MINDFULNESS TRAINING

Mindfulness originated from ancient Buddhist and Eastern perspectives, and it relates to awareness and alertness on the present moment, whatever it might be (e.g., one's breath, sounds, one's consciousness, physiological sensations, the passing of thoughts). As translated for school-based practice, Renshaw and Cook (2017, p. 6) describe mindfulness training as involving two components: (a) "Checking in with what's happening with you right now" and (b) "Being friendly to your thoughts and feelings," "ungluing from unhelpful insides," and "seeing yourself as the storyteller, not the story." Therefore, although not initially conceived as such and vice versa, CBT and mindfulness overlap in that they involve a focus on the relationship between thoughts, feelings, and behaviors. However, in contrast to CBT, mindfulness involves observing thoughts and emotions—not changing or restructuring them. Additionally, in contrast to behavior modification, mindfulness involves watching the desire to engage in a behavior instead of actively trying to modify antecedents and consequences related to its occurrence.

Considering the former, deciding whether to take an active CBT or reflective approach to addressing thoughts, feelings, and behaviors, the main determination should be that it is more important either to change or to accept mental and emotional experiences as they occur in various contexts. Inherently, both CBT and mindfulness-based therapeutic approaches are behavioral in nature as they involve making specific choices that influence thoughts and feelings in turn. For example, a student with social anxiety disorder could be encouraged to engage in an exposure that involves reading aloud in front of peers (a behavioral approach) and taught specific replacement thoughts (a cognitive restructuring approach): "I don't have to be perfect—nobody is"; "Everyone gets nervous sometimes. It's normal." Conversely, the same student could be encouraged to do the same (a behavioral approach) and taught to observe thoughts, feelings, and experiences (a mindfulness approach): "Okay, my mind is racing—that's where it is at; it won't always be racing"; "My palms are sweaty. Sometimes that happens when I am nervous or hot." Thus, although not commonly described in the literature, habituation to thoughts and feelings likely undergirds the therapeutic benefit of CBT and mindfulness approaches (Hayes & Shenk, 2004).

Many different approaches exist for teaching students' mindfulness skills, and research on applying mindfulness in school settings has ballooned over the past couple of decades (Felver, Celis-de Hoyos, Tezanos, & Singh, 2016). In general, and like more traditional variants of CBT, research on the application of mindfulness suggests that it is an effective approach for working with a range of students who display both internalizing and externalizing problems (Felver et al., 2016). Therefore, although mindfulness is an ancient approach to experiencing life—yet a relatively new approach within the school-based treatment literature in Western settings—it displays considerable promise as it is an evidence-based approach to address thoughts, feelings, and behaviors. Three components of using mindfulness in the schools follow:

> **Self-regulation of attention.** Self-regulation involves maintaining focused attention and interpreting one's mental states. Attention control varies based on a range of factors (e.g., amount of sleep,

hunger, emotional state) and is highly variable across different individuals. However, consistent with the mindfulness perspective, all individuals can make improvements with regulating their attention. In application, self-regulating one's attention might involve training students to focus on their breathing, orient toward a specific sound (e.g., the ring of a bell), or orient to whatever is happening the present moment. The key is for students to try to orient their attention toward a singular thing or stimulus and then return their attention back to where it is interned to be focused when it drifts without self-judgment.

Mindful meditation exercises. Mindfulness meditation exercises are numerous and vary in degrees of difficulty and duration of implementation. However, regarding school-based practice, simplicity is key. As an emotional and behavioral regulation strategy, the implementation of mindful meditation should aim to reduce distress and increase well-being. Therefore, similar to strategies to regulate attention, school-based meditation tends to aim to focus one's mind on sensations, feelings, stimuli, thoughts, or intentions. These exercises aim to follow the same process as attention regulation mindfulness strategies; however, the focus of the meditation may be varied. For example, among countless others, some topics could be on gratitude, love, the well-being of others, body sensations, or passively observing thoughts as they arise. It also may be beneficial to use developmentally appropriately guided meditation scripts that are readily available for free online. Many of these scripts include CBT components, such as encouraging self-acceptance, empowerment, reflection, and compassion. Moreover, many also are similar to the guided imagery strategies that were discussed earlier. In many ways, the distinction between relaxation training and mindfulness has broken down to be mostly arbitrary.

Meditative drawing. Meditative drawing involves sketching and/or coloring various designs and patterns (e.g., mandalas) to induce a sense of relaxation or even flow (i.e., experiencing a pleasurable sense of hyperconcentration and connection to the process of what one is doing). It also is thought to stimulate creativity and shift attention away from stressful or mildly anxiety-provoking thoughts. There is not a standard process for meditative drawing, and unfortunately, research on the practice is exceedingly limited. However, a general process to the practice involves first scanning one's body for tension or stress and then adjusting one's body and the paper for comfort. Second, the student might engage in some deep breathing practices to induce a mild sense of calmness or focus prior to drawing (nowhere near as long or systematic as diaphragmatic breathing). The next step involves gripping the pen lightly and making contact with the paper. Lastly, the student is encouraged to draw in a way that involves focusing one's attention to making various patterns in nonjudgmental way (i.e., students should not try their hardest to draw perfectly). Therefore, it is a process-oriented practice as opposed to an approach for generating art.

Cultivation of Attitude of Openness, Curiosity, and Acceptance

Collectively, efforts to cultivate an attitude of openness, curiosity, and acceptance all encourage students to shift out of rigid thinking and closemindedness. There are numerous ways to attempt to achieve this aim, many of which come from the CBT literature, such as using perspective taking activities; exploring similarities and differences between seemingly disparate concepts; having students share information about their culture, family, or background; having students engage in self-directed inquiry; and so on. What is important is that efforts to cultivate attitudes of openness, curiosity, and acceptance are calibrated to the specific needs of students based on their own life experiences.

When to Use/Not Use Mindfulness Training

In a world in which people are distracted by a range of competing demands, especially one in which social media are becoming a dominant form of communication, it is easy to say that we should all be less distracted and more mindful. Even if this is true, mindfulness training must be delivered in a way in which it is accessible by students with a range of abilities and disabilities. Therefore, mindfulness must be calibrated to specific students. As a relaxation strategy, elements of mindfulness might be accessible for almost all students; however, many students with cognitive limitations, developmental disabilities, and other limitations will struggle to glean key messages from higher-level meditation practices. Such students might benefit more from some of the previously mentioned and less abstract relaxation training exercises that can be reinforced for performing (similar to contingency reinforcement, see Appendix Exhibits 4.3–4.8).

ADDITIONAL BEHAVIORAL REGULATION STRATEGIES

Several other therapeutic approaches fit under the CBT self-regulation umbrella, even if they do not pertain to treating a constellation of internalizing or externalizing disorders. Instead, their application may be more related to specific disorders and clinical presentations. In this vein, two such approaches are discussed in the following text. Among other approaches for high-risk patients that warrant treatment in clinical settings or with an integrated treatment team (e.g., didactical behavioral therapy [DBT], multisystemic family therapy [MSFT]), these approaches have been selected because of their applicability to school-based practice (Chu, Johns, & Hoffman, 2015; Sulkowski, McGuire, & Tesoro, 2015).

Behavioral Activation

Behavioral activation is an intervention strategy that is employed to help individuals cope with social withdrawal and depressed moods (see Appendix Exhibits

4.9–4.14). Behavioral activation is based on the premise that people are less likely to engage in enjoyable activities when they feel depressed, apathetic, or lethargic. Often, people are less active when they are in a depressed mood. Essentially, when their activity level declines, they may become even more withdrawn, unmotivated, and torpid (Beck, 2011; Leahy & Holland, 2000). Hence, in such a state, they may experience a downward spiral that leads to greater degrees of depression, as they are not actively involved in the world or enjoying pleasurable or rewarding experiences.

To offset this decline, behavioral activation aims to help individuals be more active and gradually engage in social and personally beneficial or valued activities, whether or not they are initially enjoyable when depressed. Engaging in this process alone can be challenging because the task of engaging in previously avoided activities can be daunting for individuals who are depressed, display low motivation, or may feel lost in their head or sorrow when doing so. Therefore, engaging in behavioral activation with a therapist can help increase students' motivation to be more active as well as encourage their efforts to stick with activities that may seem more distressing or exhausting at first until their mood lifts and these activities are pleasurable. Additionally, with the help of a therapist, behavioral activation can be complimented with cognitive restructuring (see Chapter 5, Exposure and Response Prevention and Cognitive Behavioral Therapy), relaxation, and mindfulness strategies to help with negative thoughts and feelings if activation strategies do not initially induce pleasure or the lifting of depressed mood.

To apply behavioral activation with students, a therapist should first help students to identify and list a variety of activities that they can pursue that might elicit pleasure or even tepid enjoyment. To optimize students' success, activities should be carefully chosen so they are not overly daunting and unachievable, which could contribute to greater feelings of depression and hopelessness. Thus, it would not be reasonable to encourage a student in the midst of an episode of depression to begin a highly challenging new hobby (e.g., playing guitar) that likely will contribute to feelings of frustration in the short term and will not result in feelings of mastery. Instead, it is more apt to encourage students to engage in simpler and more realistic tasks that do not require a lot of effort yet encourage them to step out of their current "discomfort zone" and experience a different experience, even if it is only distracting at the outset. Among countless others, some of these might include the following:

- Planning to spend time with a friend or family member
- Becoming physically active on a daily basis
- Trying a new hobby
- Joining a new group or club at school
- Being in public places and interacting with others
- Volunteering to help others
- Providing support for people with disadvantages or who are experiencing significant adversities and life challenges
- Going to bed and getting up at set times regardless of how one feels
- Committing to work with animals and sticking to a schedule

While working with students to assign behavioral activation tasks, therapists may want to encourage students to first engage in activities that are easy to complete and then assign increasingly challenging activities throughout the course of treatment after the students display consistent success with the easier activities. In this regard, if a student starts regularly attending intramural sports after school and enjoying participating in this club, he or she could be encouraged to sign up for a sporting team. Moreover, in addition to beginning with easier activities that encourage success and enjoyment, students also may experience more success if they start off by completing a fewer number of activities and then gradually increasing their number each subsequent week. Lastly, whenever possible, it is beneficial for activities selected as part of the behavioral activation process to be as personally meaningful as possible. Therefore, even if a student does not seem motivated to make any changes for his or her benefit, he or she can be encouraged to "experiment" with helping others or giving back to society. In this vein, students can be encouraged to volunteer at a humane society if they report that they love animals, a local community mental health center if they have empathy for the suffering of individuals with mental health issues, or any nonprofit organization that is consistent with their values and beliefs. Further, they can be reinforced for their prosocial efforts by the therapist and instructed to volunteer to see if they feel any better or experience a lift in their mood while helping others.

After a list of activities is identified for inclusion in behavioral activation therapy, students are then encouraged to plan their weekly schedule that includes these activities in session. To help students understand how engaging in several activities can impact their moods with behavioral activation, the final step of the process includes encouraging students to monitor their moods before and after activities are attempted and completed. Monitoring their progress can help students recognize their individual accomplishments as well as recognize when they are not feeling depressed, hopeless, or dysthymic. Overall, this process can elevate their mood, increase their motivation for other life activities, and encourage them to keep moving forward in their daily pursuits and with future goals. Furthermore, having a therapist periodically review a log of a student's moods may help him or her become more mindful of when he or she is feeling well or at least okay as opposed to feeling depressed or significantly distressed. Moreover, this process can help therapists identify patterns of behavior that may warrant further discussion or intervention. Behavioral activation may be repeated until the student's activity monitoring data illustrate that he or she is consistently experiencing more pleasurable feelings before and after activities are completed.

When to Use/Not Use Behavioral Activation

Behavioral activation can be used to help students cope with major depressive disorder (MDD) and persistent depressive disorder (PDD), as well as with related symptoms such as lethargy, indolence, and social withdrawal. However, it should not be used if an indication of suicidality and if any medical problems like hypothyroidism exist that could be contributing to depression. To protect their immediate well-being, students with suicidal risk need to be immediately and carefully evaluated by a requisite and credentialed professional expert to ensure their safety. Individuals with medical problems, such as hypothyroidism, need to be seen by a physician to help disentangle their medical and psychological problems. Behavioral activation also should not be implemented as a treatment option for students who have a history of nonresponse to active forms of therapy (e.g., CBT, behavior modification) or those who demonstrate poor treatment adherence for reasons that inhibit their ability to engage in a consistent pattern of behavioral improvement (e.g., psychosis, substance dependence, burgeoning personality disorders, nonresolved traumatic/abusive experiences, personal safety issues).

Habit Reversal Training

The history of habit reversal training (HRT) can be traced back to the early behavioral work of Azrin and Nunn (1973) for tics and anxiety-related habits. This work, which has been incorporated into a multicomponent approach to HRT, includes the following: awareness training, competing response training, and providing social support to individuals experiencing tics or body-focused repetitive disorders (e.g., trichotillomania, excoriation/pathological skin-picking disorder).

Awareness training focuses on increasing a student's ability to anticipate tic and/or a body-focused repetitive urge. Regarding children with tics, awareness training often includes helping students identify premonitory urges (i.e., disquieting feelings prior to performing a tic—like the feeling before sneezing) associated with tics that often go unnoticed. However, students with body-focused repetitive disorders do not experience the same sensation, so awareness training instead tends to focus on the antecedents of engaging in hair pulling or skin picking, which often include hyperarousal (e.g., anxiety, nervousness, excitement, feeling tense) or boredom/tedium.

Once students develop greater awareness of the antecedents to their tics or body-focused problematic behaviors, competing response training is initiated. This is the second part—and the most crucial part—of the HRT treatment model. Competing response training involves teaching students to perform behaviors that are incompatible with performing a tic or body-focused problematic behavior. For example, if a student has a head jerk tic, a competing response may be to have the student press his or her chin to his or her chest (Sulkowski et al., 2015). With competing response training, students are taught to initiate such a response as soon as a warning sign is present such as a premonitory urge or an antecedent to a problematic body-focused repetitive urge.

Typically, for tics, competing responses should be as close to the opposite of the tic behavior as possible, which would make them incompatible with the performance of the tic (Woods, Piacentini, & Walkup, 2007). Therefore, if a child had a vocal tic, he or she could be encouraged to place his or her tongue to the roof of his or her mouth to block the performance of the vocal tic. In practice and application, competing responses should be maintained for as long as the urge to perform the tic or body-focused action exists.

The last step of the HRT model involves providing social support. This process involves working with family members and individuals at school who can assist and encourage students to employ competing responses—and even reinforce them to do so. In this role, if the student is not utilizing his or her competing responses, the person providing social support should prompt him or her to do in an encouraging manner. Awareness training is not perfect, and many students with tics and body-focused behavioral problems may have some difficulty recognizing when they are engaging in undesired behaviors. Therefore, gentle prompts from a social support person can help them remember to apply competing responses.

REFERENCES

Azrin, N., & Nunn, R. (1973). Habit-reversal: A method of eliminating nervous habits and tics. *Behaviour Research and Therapy, 11*(4), 619–628. doi:10.1016/0005-7967(73)90119-8

Beck, J. S. (2011). *Cognitive behavior therapy: Basics and beyond* (2nd ed.). New York, NY: Guilford Press.

Chu, B. C., Johns, A. M., & Hoffman, L. J. (2015). Transdiagnostic behavioral therapy for anxiety and depression in schools. In R. Flanagan, K. Allen, & E. Levine (Eds.), *Cognitive and behavioral interventions in the schools* (pp. 101–118). New York, NY: Springer.

Felver, J. C., Celis-de Hoyos, C. E., Tezanos, K., & Singh, N. N. (2016). A systematic review of mindfulness-based intervention for youth in school settings. *Mindfulness, 7*(1), 34–45. doi:10.1007/s12671-015-0389-4

Hayes, S. C., & Shenk, C. (2004). Operationalizing mindfulness without unnecessary attachments. *Clinical Psychology: Science and Practice, 11*, 249–254. doi:10.1093/clipsy.bph079

Holmes, E. A., Arntz, A., & Smucker, M. R. (2007). Imagery rescripting in cognitive behaviour therapy: Images, treatment techniques and outcomes. *Journal of Behavior Therapy and Experimental Psychiatry, 38*(4), 297–305. doi:10.1016/j.jbtep.2007.10.007

Leahy, R. L., & Holland, S. J. (2000). *The clinician's toolbox. Treatment plans and interventions for depression and anxiety disorders.* New York, NY: Guilford Press.

Otto, M. W., Simon, N. M., Olatunji, B. O., Sung, S. C., & Pollack, M. H. (2011). *10-minute CBT: Integrating cognitive-behavioral strategies into your practice.* New York, NY: Oxford University Press.

Renshaw, T. L., & Cook, C. R. (2017). Introduction to the special issue: Mindfulness in the schools—historical roots, current status, and future directions. *Psychology in the Schools, 54*(1), 5–12. doi:10.1002/pits.21978

Sulkowski, M. L., McGuire, J. F., & Tesoro, A. (2015). Treating tics and Tourette's disorder in school settings. *Canadian Journal of School Psychology, 31*(1), 47–62. doi:10.1177/0829573515601820

Woods, D. W., Piacentini, J. C., & Walkup, J. T. (Eds.). (2007). *Treating Tourette syndrome and tic disorders: A guide for practitioners.* New York, NY: Guilford Press.

Exposure and Response Prevention and Cognitive Behavioral Therapy

INTRODUCTION

Cognitive behavioral theory (CBT) proposes that thoughts, feelings, and behaviors are interconnected, which allows for different points of intervention. One common evidence-based behavioral intervention approach is called behavioral exposure, exposure therapy, exposure with response prevention (ERP), or exposure with ritual prevention. Collectively, these terms often are used synonymously in the CBT literature. Over a century of clinical trials supports the efficacy of this behavioral approach with a range of psychiatric and behavioral conditions (American Psychological Association, 2016; Anxiety and Depression Association of America, 2015; International OCD Foundation, n.d.). However, ERP is the first-line treatment for obsessive-compulsive disorder (OCD) and other obsessive-compulsive–related disorders (OCRDs) that have compulsive features such as rituals and avoidance (Jordan, Reid, Mariaskin, Augusto, & Sulkowski, 2012). For convenience, *exposure therapy* is used as an encompassing term unless noted otherwise in this chapter.

EXPOSURE AND RESPONSE PREVENTION THERAPY

Exposure therapy involves repeatedly exposing a person to a feared stimulus, situation, thought, image, or emotional experience that he or she typically would avoid, tolerate with significant or impairing distress, or engage in ritualistic behaviors to neutralize the distress experienced. Next, the person is encouraged not to engage in any avoidant or distress-reducing rituals in order to get used to his or her feelings. This process is called habituation, and it is not unique to humans. Squirrels in the wild are afraid of humans (a perceived threat), yet squirrels in a city park may even approach humans to beg for food—they have habituated to the presence of humans and no longer fear them (see Appendix Exhibits 5.1 and 5.2 for counselor checklist and parent information handouts).

As an example of conducting a behavioral exposure with a student, a student with contamination-related OCD might be encouraged to touch a dirty doorknob and then refrain from washing his or her hands, applying hand sanitizer, or using an avoidance-related safety object (opening the door with a paper towel). After touching the doorknob, the student should be encouraged to simply wait for his or her distress to decrease naturally or for the person to habituate to the contamination feeling.

The process of habituation breaks two associations that result in individuals engaging in compulsive rituals or avoidant behavior. First, the individuals learn that they do not need to fear or avoid a distressing stimulus or situation. Second, they learn that they can tolerate the stimulus or situation without engaging in compulsive or avoidant behaviors to make themselves feel better. Thus, the ultimate goal for exposure therapy is to teach the student to habituate to a range of stimuli and situations in a gradual and systematic manner and then generalize therapy to real-world situations as they occur outside the context of therapy. The student should learn to face his or her fears in a safe therapeutic environment with gradual success as a goal. Moreover, these students should feel like they stepped out of their comfort zone a little bit, experienced distress from doing so, habituated to whatever was causing the distress, and walked away feeling like they pushed their comfort zone edge and experienced success.

Although the exact processes behind the efficacy exposure therapy continue to be researched, through repeated exposures, adaptive learning and cognitive restructuring are thought to occur as clients extinguish their avoidance behaviors and challenge their cognitive distortions about their fears. Furthermore, this process is thought to have neurodevelopmental effects on the brain, leading to new neural connections that inhibit the old fear pathways contributing to anxiety (Craske, Treanor, Conway, Zbozinek, & Vervliet, 2014). For instance, individuals with social anxiety disorder fear social situations (the feared stimulus), avoid social interactions (the avoidance behavior), and frequently worry about judgment or negative evaluation from others (a cognitive distortion). To address these functional limitations, clients would be exposed to situations in which they interact with others to reduce their avoidant behavior, thinking errors, and anxiety (Zaboski et al., 2019). Over time, they learn that their distorted thoughts about social interactions were not valid and that avoiding people and social situations was not necessary.

It is important to highlight how exposure therapy should be conducted in a gradual and systematic manner that elicits a moderate amount of distress. Pushing these students to do tasks that are too daunting or intense too soon could cause them to feel "flooded" with anxiety or distress, and they may fail to habituate. Instead, they may learn that the stimulus or situation should indeed be avoided or not tolerated. Conversely, however, not encouraging them to step out of their comfort zone also might not lead to habituation because the stimuli or situations they are being exposed to do not elicit enough distress. In other words, they can already tolerate these stimuli or situations, so therapy will have a null effect. With the previous points in mind as a guiding principle, the core components of exposure therapy are discussed next.

Starting Exposure Therapy

When starting exposure therapy, therapists should provide developmentally appropriate psychoeducation for clients about how this therapeutic approach can help. Because exposure therapy can be somewhat abstract and counterintuitive for children and adolescents, drawing a graph (Figure 5.1; see Appendix Exhibits 5.20 and 5.21) can help with elucidating this process. Figure 5.1 places anxiety severity on the

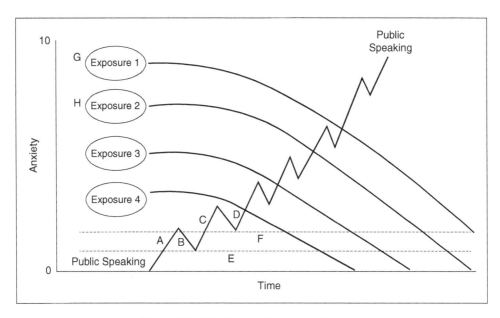

Figure 5.1   The basics of exposure therapy.

y-axis and time on the *x*-axis, and it visually displays the habituation process through repeated exposures. It also lists the interaction of how reducing anxiety results in an increase in desired behavior, which, in this case, is public speaking (see Appendix Exhibits 5.3 and 5.4 for exposure therapy graph teaching sample and worksheet).

With exposure therapy, it can be hard to know if change is happening if it is not being assessed. Therefore, some type of scale should be used to get an approximation of how much anxiety or distress the student is experiencing during exposures. Typically, during the psychoeducational process, a 10-point scale of "subjective units of distress" (SUDs; Wolpe, 1969) is introduced and discussed. On this scale, 1 could be described as feeling perfectly peaceful or relaxed, and 10 could be described as panicking or even fearing for one's life. The SUD scale will be used in therapy to help guide the therapeutic process and ensure habituation (see Appendix Exhibits 1.4 and 1.5 for examples for young children and Exhibits 5.5–5.7 for examples for adolescents).

Following the introduction of the SUD scale, students can be taught how their compulsive or avoidant behaviors are causing their problems to actually get worse over time and, essentially, how they have been a crutch that provides short-term help but if not cast away become a hindrance and result in long-term problems. This can be illustrated by describing how their avoidant behaviors only temporarily reduce distress by actually drawing this out on paper or a whiteboard. For example, a student could be asked how he or she would feel if he or she stuck his or her hand under the desk and touched a wad of gum. The student might say, "Ew, gross—that would be about 7 SUDs," and then the therapist could draw the student's anxiety raising to a 7 on a graph. The therapist could then say, "Well, what if you could go to the sink and wash your hands?" which might prompt the student to say, "I'd feel a lot better; my SUDs would drop to about a 3." The therapist could then ask, "How would you feel if a student next to you sneezed on your book?" which might prompt the student to say, "Oh, that would be even worse! That would cause 9 SUDs!" Following this, the therapist could ask, "What if you had sanitizer at your desk and cleaned the book," to which the student might say, "It would still be kind of gross, but my SUDs probably would drop to about a 5."

The main point of going through such a discussion with the student during psychoeducation is to illustrate the temporary relief that engaging in compulsive or avoidant behaviors provides and how such behaviors are incapable of providing lasting relief. Second, this process illustrates how performing such behaviors produces a roller-coaster type of function in that anxiety or distress spikes up when exposed to certain stimuli or situations but then drops precipitously through performing compulsive or avoidant behaviors, which prevents the student from habituating to the former. Therefore, instead of "riding the anxiety roller coaster," the student can be encouraged to "surf the habituation wave." Doing the latter involves smoothing out the peaks and valleys and instead experiencing habituation through being exposed to moderately distressful stimuli or situations and then "riding them out" by not engaging in compulsive or avoidant behaviors.

There are some other points to cover during psychoeducation that are particularly related to engaging in exposure therapy. The first is that exposure therapy is relatively simple to understand conceptually, but engaging in actual therapy will not always be easy. Therapy fundamentally involves facing one's fears; however, this can and should be challenging sometimes. For optimal treatment outcomes, it is important to go all the way through the anxiety/fear hierarchy and do the most intense exposures (this is discussed in the following text).

Second, the therapist should reinforce the completion of homework or "between-session practice." Just meeting with a therapist once a week is better than nothing—yet this is far from best practice. With the guidance of the therapist and the recruitment of others (e.g., parents, teachers, other adults at school, occasionally older siblings), the student should be encouraged to practice exposures at home, school, and in the community to help replicate what was done in therapy and help these gains generalize more broadly.

Third, the therapist should reinforce the point that the overall goal is for the student to experience success with facing fears and to feel like he or she stands a little taller from engaging in exposures. Additionally, the therapist should establish that the student would never be required to do anything that the therapist would be unwilling to do personally and that he or she is willing to go first to model the exposure. Of course, this can be anxiety provoking for the therapist, so it is important to model calmness when asked "to go first."

Fourth, the therapist should emphasize that treatment is not completely linear. There will be ups and downs and good days and hard ones—but the overall trend is what is most important. This is why it is important to keep in-session logs and homework-related SUD rankings to illustrate tangible progress on a rough day. Fifth, it is important for the therapist to probe the student's understanding of the information provided during psychoeducation. This can be done by having the student describe what treatment involves, how he or she could benefit from it, what SUDs are, or any of the other exposure therapy components in his or her own words. Lastly, students should have the opportunity to ask any questions that they have about exposure therapy or anything else related to treatment.

Functional Assessment

Following psychoeducation, therapists using exposure therapy should conduct a thorough evaluation to understand the nature of the student's distress. This functional assessment (Abramowitz, Deacon, & Whiteside, 2012) considers external antecedents/triggers (e.g., teachers, classrooms, academic subject, specific peers) and triggering thoughts (e.g., "This presentation in front of my class is going to be horrible!"; "If I touch this doorknob, I'll get sick and die."). Next, consider the consequences of the anxious thought coming true (If I mess up, I'll be humiliated forever) and other cognitive effects of the anxiety (such as intolerance of uncertainty, fear of panic attacks, thought distortions, and overestimates of feared events coming true). Lastly, functional assessment involves understanding the behaviors used to decrease the anxiety that these thoughts cause; for instance, avoidance (skipping class, refusing to complete assignments, school refusal), overt compulsive behavior (perfectionism, repeatedly asking for reassurance from others, excessive studying/practicing, nail biting), and mental rituals (e.g., repeatedly telling oneself that "it will be okay," avoiding thoughts about anxiety-provoking situations).

During this process, therapists should also assess for behavioral accommodation. Accommodation refers to efforts from other people (family, teachers, friends) to decrease a person's distress or anxiety (Storch et al., 2015). Note that accommodation in this sense does not refer to reasonable academic or behavioral accommodations given to students for disabilities. Rather, accommodation in the context of anxiety disorders relates to positive or negative reinforcement of anxiety-related symptoms. This may include a parent who allows a child to skip a day of school to avoid a public speaking assignment, a friend who supplies hand sanitizer to a person with contamination fears, or a teacher who allows a socially anxious student to sit outside the classroom during instruction. As in these examples, inappropriate accommodations may inadvertently serve to enable or maintain maladaptive behaviors. When teachers or parents engage in accommodation of maladaptive behaviors with children, it can be important to also provide consultation to the teachers and psychoeducation for the parents to simultaneously change these enabling influences. Keep in mind that accommodations are not typically malicious; in fact, they tend to reflect a genuine concern and motivation to improve a situation for someone with anxiety. Nevertheless, accommodations often need to be removed or modified throughout treatment, requiring ample consultation and psychoeducation for clients, parents, guardians, and school-based personnel about the mechanisms that maintain anxiety. Essentially, accommodations work like compulsive rituals or avoidant behaviors in that they prevent habituation from occurring.

Types of Exposures

There are many ways to structure exposure therapy sessions. As briefly mentioned above, flooding involves prolonged exposure to the most anxiety-provoking stimuli first (Abramowitz, 1996), while a systematic approach utilizes a gradual introduction to feared stimuli (Abramowitz et al., 2012). Although flooding techniques are effective in the hands of veteran exposure therapists, particularly for specific phobias (Wolitzky-Taylor, Horowitz, Powers, & Telch, 2008), a more gradual approach to exposure therapy is generally warranted. Because compulsions and avoidance behaviors strengthen anxiety, starting with easier exposures helps clients fully learn to resist compulsive/avoidance urges when faced with an anxiety-provoking situation. Relatedly, beginning with challenging exposures may interfere with habituation to anxiety or distress if clients have not yet developed the skill to resist their compulsive or avoidant behaviors (Blakey & Abramowitz, 2016).

In addition to systematic/flooding techniques, therapists can also choose from imaginal and in vivo (taking place in person) exposures. Clinicians conduct in vivo exposures in natural settings and imaginal exposures in a client's mind. One popular type of imaginal exposure is the Worry Script. Worry Scripts are short (usually two to three paragraphs), hypothetical stories that involve a worst-case scenario related to one's fear coming true (Robichaud, 2013). To identify a client's core fear, the downward arrow technique may help (see Appendix Exhibit 5.8 for the Downward Arrow Technique worksheet; additional exposure therapy worksheets may be accessed at cbt4panic.org/imaginal-exposure-example-script). With this technique, a therapist repeatedly asks what would happen next until a client cannot respond any further. For example, a conversation might progress like this:

Therapist:	What would happen if you entered the lunchroom?
Client:	I would get anxious.
Therapist:	So you walk into the lunchroom and get anxious. Then what?
Client:	No one would let me sit with them.
Therapist:	I can see why that would cause you anxiety. What would happen next?
Client:	Other kids would stare at me.
Therapist:	Then what?
Client:	Everyone would get super quiet.
Therapist:	Wow, how would you handle that awkwardness?
Client:	I'd just run out of there!
Therapist:	Yeah, I can't blame you for wanting to escape an uncomfortable situation. What would happen after that?
Client:	I guess I would never have any friends.
Therapist:	Then?
Client:	I'd be alone.
Therapist:	What would happen if you were alone?
Client:	I . . . don't really know. I'd be miserable I guess.

After using the downward arrow technique, the therapist might help the client write a script about entering the lunchroom, having nowhere to sit, receiving stares from her peers, experiencing an uncomfortable silence, running out of the lunchroom in tears, losing her friends, and being alone. Scripts should include as much detail as possible while conforming to the two to three paragraph rule. Worry scripts and other imaginal exposures are typically appropriate starting points for most hierarchies, serving as stepping stones for the in vivo or real-life challenges later in treatment (see Appendix Exhibit 5.9 for Worry Script Worksheet). Thus, under most circumstances, therapists are encouraged to progress from imaginal exposures to in vivo exposures as early as possible, as these tend to engender the biggest treatment changes (Craske et al., 2014).

The Fear Hierarchy

The fear hierarchy is a list of increasingly challenging exposures (imaginal and in vivo) that the client completes through treatment (see Appendix Exhibits 5.5–5.7 for fear hierarchy worksheets). The hierarchy is a living document to which items will be added or modified as needed and involves continuous consultation with the client. Indeed, when creating the hierarchy, it should be emphasized that the students will not be required to complete any particularly daunting exposure tasks in the immediate future and they will not be requested to do any tasks before they are ready and have had success with easier ones. This approach provides modeling opportunities and strengthens rapport. Table 5.1 is a sample hierarchy for a socially anxious client who is afraid to enter the lunchroom and eat in front of others.

Several features of the hierarchy are worth discussing. First, hierarchy items should *always* be ethical, legal, and aligned with school codes of conduct (see Olatunji, Deacon, & Abramowitz, 2009). In addition, fear hierarchies should generally contain items that are commonly encountered in our lives and that do not lead to adverse consequences. Walking into a lunchroom, eating in front of others, and eating with peers all satisfy these requirements. Second, unless a client is prohibitively anxious about doing exposures that elicit SUDs ratings from 3 to 5, it is preferable not to start with exposures that are 1s and 2s because doing so increases the number of treatment sessions required with little benefit (remember that 1 is rated as a "totally peaceful" experience). Like other applications of CBT, exposure therapy should be time-limited, goal-directed, and efficient. This premise is especially true in school settings where counseling time duration may be limited to 30 minutes a session as compared to a typical 1-hour session in outpatient or clinic settings.

Third, many hierarchy items are similar yet have minor variations (e.g., run in and out of the lunchroom versus casually walk into the lunchroom). When designing a hierarchy, think about the knobs that can be turned on each exposure: duration, setting, number of people present, the activity completed (e.g., video games versus eating), or the intensity of the experience (e.g., confusedly wandering around to find a seat vs. sitting down immediately). Including small modifications to exposures allows the therapist to develop challenges that represent a variety of SUDs ratings, increasing the ease of gradually transitioning from one exposure to the next.

Fourth, all of the included hierarchy items contain two parts: the exposure stimulus (e.g., walking into the lunchroom, reading the worry script) and the response prevention (no avoidance/reassurance). In this case example, the student frequently engaged in safety behaviors, such as reassurance seeking, in which she would ask, "Am I going to be okay?" as well as avoidance, in which she would avoid the lunchroom altogether. Although the response prevention components in the sample hierarchy may seem redundant, we include them for each case we treat. While monitoring safety behaviors, clinicians already in the habit of documenting them will be accustomed to updating the hierarchy when new ones appear. Moreover, this practice allows for more effective communication between staff members and family assisting with exposures (e.g., teachers, parents), as they will understand which safety behaviors to look for. Hierarchies should be provided to clients during and at the conclusion of treatment, and it can be helpful for them to have a reminder of which safety behaviors they need to resist. Having complete documentation on the hierarchy also provides for smoother referrals to new service or intervention providers, who will not need to complete a fear hierarchy from scratch or guess at the anxiety-avoidance relationships.

Fifth, the hierarchy includes items that were rated past the 10-point SUDs scale (10+). These items are overlearning items and serve as exceptions to the rule that

TABLE 5.1   Exposure Hierarchy Activities for a Fear of Entering the School Lunchroom and Eating

SUDs	Hierarchy Item
3	Write a worry script about going into the lunchroom; no avoidance/reassurance
4	Read the worry script out loud to the therapist; no avoidance/reassurance
4	Read the worry script out loud to a family member; no avoidance/reassurance
4	Draw pictures of the lunchroom in color; no avoidance/reassurance
3	Draw pictures of the lunchroom with pencil (black and white); no avoidance/reassurance
4	Play video games outside the lunchroom; no avoidance/reassurance
7	Play video games inside the lunchroom for 5 min; no reassurance/avoidance
8	Play video games inside the lunchroom for 10 min; no reassurance/avoidance
9	Play video games inside the lunchroom for 15 min; no reassurance/avoidance
9	Complete schoolwork inside the lunchroom for 15 min; no reassurance/avoidance
5	Run in and out of the lunchroom when no one else is in there; no avoidance/reassurance
5	Walk casually into the lunchroom when no one else is in there; no avoidance/reassurance
6	Walk slowly into the lunchroom when no one else is in there; no avoidance/reassurance
8	Complete a relay race against the therapist in the lunchroom when no one else is there; no avoidance/reassurance
8	Play video games in the lunchroom when a few peers are present for 10 min; no avoidance/reassurance
9	Play video games in the lunchroom when a few peers are present for 20 min; no avoidance/reassurance
4	Eat a small snack outside the lunchroom; no avoidance/reassurance
4	Eat a larger snack outside the lunchroom; no avoidance/reassurance
7	Eat a small snack inside the lunchroom; no avoidance/reassurance
9	Eat a small lunch with preferred peers in the lunchroom; no avoidance/reassurance
7	Eat all your lunch in the lunchroom during lunchtime for 5 min; no avoidance/reassurance
8	Eat all your lunch in the lunchroom during lunchtime for 10 min; no avoidance/reassurance
8	Eat all your lunch in the lunchroom during lunchtime for 15 min; no avoidance/reassurance
9	Eat all your lunch in the lunchroom during lunchtime for 20 min; no avoidance/reassurance
9	Eat all your lunch in the lunchroom during lunchtime for 25 min; no avoidance/reassurance
10	Eat all your lunch in the lunchroom for all of lunchtime; no avoidance/reassurance
10	Walk into the lunchroom confidently, sit down with peers, and eat lunch; no avoidance/reassurance
10+	Walk into the lunchroom and pause as you try to find a seat; no avoidance/reassurance
10+	Walk into the lunchroom and start eating a snack while you try to find a seat; no avoidance/reassurance
10+	Walk into the lunchroom and drop a pencil on the floor in front of others; no avoidance/reassurance
10+	Walk into the lunchroom and loudly say "hi" to a peer who is sitting farther away; no avoidance/reassurance
10+	Walk into the lunchroom and wave to peers who are sitting on the other side of the room; no avoidance/reassurance
10+	Sit in the lunchroom while eating your food and reading your worry script; no avoidance/reassurance

SUDs, subjective units of distress.

challenges should be experienced by most people in everyday life. The process of overlearning, or pushing the norm, is akin to studying a little more than needed. Just as on a test you may not know what a teacher might ask, you never know what might trigger anxiety. Keep in mind that although some of these 10+ items may seem extreme, they still represent real, albeit less common, experiences that people encounter. Without preparing clients for such experiences (e.g., going into a lunchroom and not being able to find a seat or tripping in front of others), the risk of relapse increases (Abramowitz et al., 2012).

Regarding the previous point, some guidelines on overlearning may be helpful. Because some items can seem so daunting to some children and adolescents, occasionally it may be beneficial to leave them out of the initial hierarchy building and propose them later after a stronger therapeutic alliance has been built and the client has succeeded with some easier exposures. As is the case with all hierarchy items, overlearning items should always be ethical and legal. For example, although having a student steal something from the school lunchroom would trigger his or her social anxiety, this is highly unethical, against school codes of conducts, and is therefore not an appropriate exposure. At the same time, some items can seem extreme, while being highly ethical and highly beneficial (e.g., rubbing a public entrance doorknob repeatedly and then touching one's face for a child with contamination obsessions or an irrational fear of germs). When in doubt about an exposure, it is best to consult with a colleague, particularly other professionals trained in delivering exposure therapy. Moreover, as a general principle, it does not hurt to "start low and go slow" when working with new clients or students until it becomes clearer how they habituate. Lastly, the primary goal of exposure therapy is to challenge core fears and elicit anxiety and have the client habituate—not to embarrass or belittle him or her. In the aforementioned hierarchy example, the client was willing to challenge her anxiety by fake tripping in front of others, and her willingness to complete this exposure was a testament to her treatment progress. However, if she were unwilling to complete this challenge out of a reasonable fear of embarrassing herself in front of classmates, working with the client to modify this exposure would be possible so that the same therapeutic effect could be achieved without the immediate social consequences such as maybe fake tripping while walking down a street or in a grocery store. This would mitigate risks associated with having the client's anxiety increase without habituation occurring or other unintended problems occurring such as being teased or harassed by peers.

Implementing Exposures

With consent and assent obtained from the child and parent(s), initial psychoeducation complete, and a draft of the hierarchy finished, behavioral exposures can commence. Throughout this process, recognize that facing one's fears is challenging, and like other therapies, exposure therapy requires a strong therapeutic alliance, particularly in the beginning of treatment (Kendall et al., 2009). Using the fear hierarchy, the therapist and the student should collaborate on where to start, favoring a gradual and systematic approach. When a starting place is agreed on, three general elements constitute an effective approach to conducting exposure: It should be (a) gradual, (b) prolonged, and (c) repeated.

To illustrate these elements, it is helpful to return to the fear hierarchy that was previously discussed. One exposure task was playing video games outside the lunchroom without avoidance/reassurance. Assuming that the fear hierarchy is followed, this exposure would satisfy (a), as it would follow the completion of several easier challenges. To complete a prolonged exposure (b), we might encourage our client to do this exposure for 10, 15, or 20 minutes without any reassurance/ avoidance behaviors. To satisfy element (c), a therapist might assign 10 trials of 2-minute exposures in which the child plays video games outside the lunchroom. Additionally, repeatability also refers to repeated exposures between therapy sessions, in other words, electing to complete the exposure again during the next session or for homework.

Importantly, when clients are engaged in exposures, practitioners should look carefully for subtle safety behaviors and mental rituals. Safety behaviors could include subtle forms of avoidance such as being around a "safe person," carrying a safety object (e.g., cell phone, toy, picture), or wearing special clothes. Mental rituals could be a special mantra that a client performs, a nonreligious/excessive prayer, or some other mental event that is compulsively performed to reduce distress or anxiety. During exposure-based therapy, the therapist should be attentive to the former and actively ask clients if they are doing anything to reduce their distress or anxiety when exposures are being attempted. Safety behaviors and mental rituals, like compulsive and avoidant behavior, effectively interfere with habituation and are counterproductive to therapy.

Additionally, while conducting behavioral exposures, therapists should never reassure anxious behaviors. Thus, when working with an anxious student, it would be contraindicated to tell a client that "Everything will be okay," "Nothing bad will happen," or "There is nothing to worry about." This is not to say that therapists shouldn't be warm, empathetic, and genuine. However, the reality is that nobody knows what the future holds and providing false reassurance tends to just magnify doubts that the client may be having (e.g., "My therapist is just being nice like my teacher—how can he know that my parents will never get in a bad car accident?").

However, in contrast to providing reassurance, therapists *should* praise a client's effort: "You are doing a great job with this challenge," "Your progress is excellent," "I have a lot of respect for your courage right now." Lastly, therapists should not accommodate anxious behaviors. If a child is part-way through an exposure and wants to quit, the therapist should encourage finishing the exposure trial or engaging in at least one more trial before taking a break or moving to something else temporarily. At the very least, to avoid reinforcing avoidant behavior, the exposure should be reintroduced during the course of treatment (preferably as soon as possible).

The pace of exposure therapy should be matched with the client's progress, measured by how quickly anxiety is decreasing, how quickly the client is moving through the fear hierarchy, and how effectively the client is learning that her or his distorted thoughts are illogical. Exposures may take time. One arbitrary determination of how long an exposure should last is when the SUD decreases by half. Another benchmark we discuss with children/adolescents is to do an exposure until it is extremely boring. Once the exposure has "become boring," it is an indicator that the activity is no longer evoking fear or distress and the client has acclimated to the task. In any case, the fear hierarchy is not a checklist. Therapists should incorporate old exposures throughout treatment and blend items on the hierarchy.

Maximizing Exposure Effectiveness

In the early implementation of exposure-based treatments, habituation was emphasized. Again, habituation refers to a reduction of anxiety over time (either within a session or between sessions). The astute reader may have noticed that this chapter introduces a habituation-type explanation of how exposure works during psychoeducation (see Figure 5.1). Although this explanation is appealing to clients, and exposure therapists often use habituation as a guideline for treatment (e.g., SUDs decreasing), neither within- nor between-session habituation strongly predicts treatment outcomes (Baker et al., 2010). And though anxiety often decreases during exposures, the magnitude of that decrease is not predictive of overall improvement (Craske et al., 2008). At present, exposure is thought to operate through inhibitory learning (see Craske et al., 2014), in which exposures create new connections that inhibit the old fear connections. These connections are created through doing prolonged exposures that violate one's expectations. Thus, in this paradigm, expectancy violation is emphasized over decreases in anxiety.

Although habituation is a more concrete way of providing psychoeducation to clients, inhibitory learning theory should be applied in clinical practice to maximize therapy outcomes. This can be done in several ways. First, therapists can create expectancy violations by asking clients *before* they complete an exposure questions such as "What will happen if we do this exposure?" and "How likely from 0% to 100% is [the feared outcome] to occur?" Next, do the exposure until either (a) those expectations are violated or (b) a specific goal is achieved (e.g., I've introduced myself to 10 people). Following the exposure, assess whether the feared outcome happened and what was learned (e.g., "You introduced yourself to 10 people. What happened? Did anyone actually yell at you?").

Another way to utilize inhibitory learning is through deep extinction trials, in which exposures are combined. For instance, in our sample hierarchy above, a deep extinction trial would involve reading a worry script while eating a full meal in the crowded lunchroom. Even though these exposures are more anxiety provoking, they are highly effective, combining multiple challenges to ensure that clients generalize their skills across stimuli and settings. One of the significant benefits of school-based counseling is the opportunity for generalization by applying these techniques across classrooms with multiple teachers and peer groups, in varied environments such as physical education or lunchtime, and across differing times of day. Therapists can also vary the stimulus intensity. For example, it can be empowering to clients to repeat easy exposures they did 10 sessions ago, and it can reinforce prior learning to remember that their fear still has not come true. Consider that a client with an intense contamination fear may benefit from the reminder that, despite his prediction on session 2, the doorknob he touched did not give him an incurable disease. Lastly, exposures should be done in multiple settings to ensure that learning is not just taking place in the therapist's office.

When to Use or Not Use Exposure Therapy

Exposure therapy can be used to treat a range of anxiety (e.g., social anxiety disorder, specific phobia, and separation anxiety disorder) and obsessive-compulsive and related disorders (e.g., OCD, body dysmorphic disorder), but it should not be used for all students or for all situations. The first consideration in using exposure therapy is time. In less than 30 minutes, it can be difficult to violate anxiety-driven expectations. Following an initial assessment, therapists should consider the severity of a case and whether enough time is allotted to provide adequate treatment. Therapists should also consider whether they themselves can engage in the exposures required to treat specific cases. For a case of OCD with contamination fears, therapists should feel comfortable engaging in exposures with clients, such as eating food that has been placed on a tabletop or touching doorknobs without handwashing.

Exposure therapy does not work with all of the OCD spectrum disorders, specifically skin picking, hair pulling, and hoarding, although emerging research and scholarship suggest that it can be used as an adjunctive treatment approach (Sulkowski, Jacob, & Storch, 2013). Exposure therapy should not be used for psychosis associated with schizophrenia spectrum or other psychotic disorders. In school settings, exposure should be used cautiously for children who exhibit marked emotional reactions to anxiety (e.g., aggression, panic, emotional agitation). Although exposure therapy can be effective for this population, school personnel may lack the resources needed to manage these behaviors safely. Exposure therapy is effective for children and adolescents with depression; however, therapists should assess the nature and severity of these symptoms carefully. Exposure therapy is often helpful for co-occurring mild depression, particularly if those symptoms are secondary to the anxiety. In school settings, more severe depression, particularly with suicidality or self-injurious behaviors, should first be addressed through safety planning, evidence-based treatments for depression (e.g., dialectical behavior therapy, behavioral activation), or outside mental health referrals if needed prior to considering exposure therapy.

COGNITIVE RESTRUCTURING

Cognitive restructuring is a therapeutic technique that is commonly used to challenge cognitive distortions and correct negative thinking patterns that contribute to depression, anxiety, anger, or other problems (see Appendix Exhibits 5.10 and 5.11 for a counselor's checklist and parent/guardian information forms). It is based on the premise that one's irrational thoughts and beliefs about a specific event can lead to unhealthy emotions and behaviors that maintain depression, anxiety, and related problems (Beck, 1991; Beck, 1995, 2011). Thus, cognitive distortions can include any number of ways that individuals think in maladaptive, nonobjective, and irrational ways, and the primary objective of cognitive restructuring is to help individuals challenge and reframe their cognitive distortions or replace them with thoughts that are more adaptive, objective, rational, or based in reality (Friedberg, McClure, & Garcia, 2009). Through this process, individuals often experience improvements in their affective state or mood because of the integral link between thoughts and emotions. Additionally, they often experience improvements in their functional behavior because they may not be held back by self-defeating, personally invalidating, fear-based, or irrational thoughts.

To illustrate the previous link, consider some of the thoughts that often are experienced by a person with depression: "I'm worthless," "I can't do anything well," "Nobody likes me," and "I'll never feel any better." Now imagine being bombarded by these thoughts dozens of times throughout the day and not being able to do anything about them. From this example, one can imagine how a person's mood might begin to suffer from feeling overwhelmed by negative thoughts that they might feel powerless to manage. Moreover, a person may start to internalize and believe these thoughts, which can then negatively impact his or her behavior and throw him or her into a spiral in which he or she is no longer doing activities and tasks that bring him or her pleasure and enjoyment in life such as socializing with others and engaging in hobbies. Additionally, this may lead to further life problems as students may stop completing school work; withdraw from friends, family members, and teachers; and generally shut down. This process can be described as a "depression downward withdrawal spiral." Without therapy, it can be hard for individuals to liberate themselves from this cascading process when they are being affected by multiple negative cognitive, mood, and physical factors, possibly leading to life-threatening critical factors (see Figure 5.2 and Appendix Exhibit 5.12 for a visual description).

Whereas behavioral activation targets physical factors (see Chapter 4, Emotional and Behavioral Regulation Strategies) and involves increasing the amount of pleasurable experiences a person has on a regular basis, cognitive restructuring aims to target a different point of intervention: the cognitive factors domain. By disputing, reframing, and replacing these distortions, maladaptive thoughts, and self-defeating beliefs, individuals can experience relief from thoughts that torment them as well as concomitant improvements in their mood or affective state. Thus, as a therapeutic method, therapists can use cognitive restructuring to help students become more aware of their thinking, evaluate the validity of their thoughts, challenge problematic cognitions, and change their beliefs to better suit them and help them succeed in school and life (Sulkowski, Joyce, & Storch, 2012).

Consistent with this model, a triggering or anxiety-provoking event occurs, which then leads to experiencing anxiety-related thoughts (Beck, 1995). For example, a child might stutter while giving a speech in front of his or her peers and experience cognitive distortions such as "I'm so dumb," "Everyone noticed—this is so embarrassing," or "Now I'm going to get a bad grade." This might then cause the child to experience physical symptoms such as becoming flushed, having sweaty palms, feeling his or her heart race, feeling a little shaky, or even experiencing somatic symptoms such as having "butterflies in one's stomach," having a stomachache, or feeling like he or she could pass out. In such a state, the student might want to avoid similar situations (being absent for the next time he or she has to speak in front of peers) or tolerate them with significant distress or through performing compulsive behaviors (e.g., having safety objects present).

Although less commonly discussed in the CBT literature, the relationship between anger-inducing or -sustaining thoughts (e.g., personalizing something negative, blaming others) also influences the presentation of angry feelings and anger-related problematic behaviors (e.g., being physically aggressive, acting hostile toward others, destroying property; Beck & Fernandez, 1998). Similar to the depression downward withdrawal spiral's four domains, Figure 5.3 depicts an anger upward escalation spiral (also see Appendix Exhibit 5.13). When negative factors across the domains coalesce, becoming more intense and sustained, individuals can experience highly maladaptive behaviors. Without therapy, it can be difficult for them to free themselves from this cascading process, as compounding negative cognitive, mood, and physical factors possibly lead to more negative outcomes for both themselves and others.

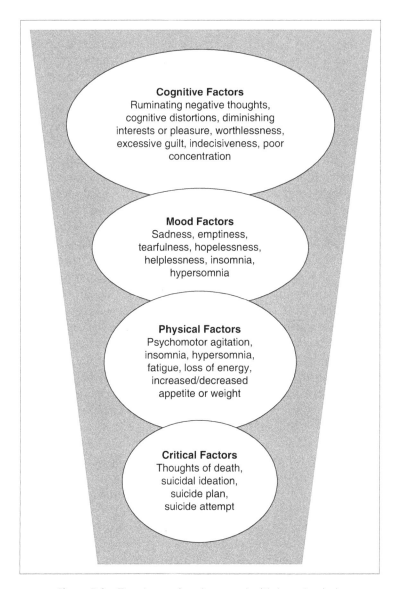

Figure 5.2 The depression downward withdrawal spiral.

Source: From Joyce-Beaulieu, D. (2019). *Easy application of CBT for internalizing and externalizing disorders.* Presented at the Marion County District School Psychologist Training, Ocala, FL.

As the anger upward escalation spiral builds, an anger escalation sequence begins (see Figure 5.4 and Appendix Exhibit 5.14). This sequence follows a pattern of reciprocal negative cognitive interpretations and physiological arousal in response to life events that results in negative behavior responses. For example, some type of situation or event triggers a negative cognitive appraisal ("He did it on purpose," "She's looking at me funny," "They're all out to get me"), which is then related to an increase in arousal/anger. Following this, there could be a negative behavioral response that could further escalate the situation (e.g., getting into a fight, saying something provocative or hurtful), which could then lead to additional negative cognitive appraisals, feelings of anger, and problematic behavioral responses.

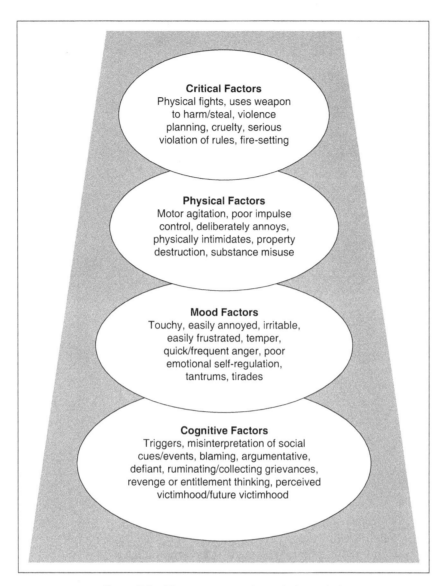

Figure 5.3   The anger upward escalation spiral.

Source: From Joyce-Beaulieu, D. (2019). *Easy application of CBT for internalizing and externalizing disorders.* Presented at the Marion County District School Psychologist Training, Ocala, FL.

The CBT Triad

The first step of cognitive restructuring involves teaching students about the relationship between their thoughts, emotions, and behaviors. This relationship is often represented by a triad (see Figure 5.5 and Appendix Exhibit 2.1) in that thoughts impact feelings that then impact emotions, which then impact behaviors and finally subsequent thoughts (Beck, 1995, 2011). It should come as little surprise that this triadic model resembles the depression trap, the anxiety escalation, and the anger escalation models that were previously discussed. This is because, similar to how cognitive distortions can negatively impact one's feelings and behaviors, more adaptive thoughts can improve the former. This is the core of cognitive restructuring: to teach clients more adaptive ways to think by challenging their cognitive distortions.

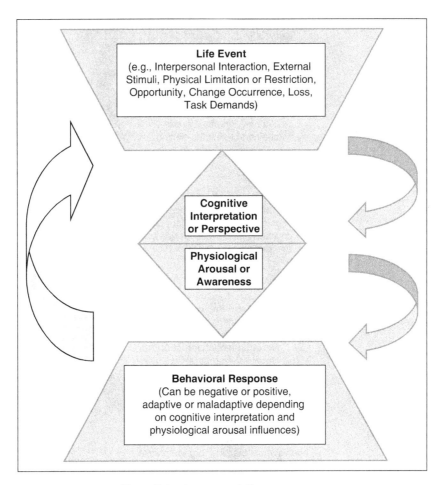

Figure 5.4 Anger escalation sequence.

To help establish the link between thoughts, feelings, and behaviors, it is helpful for a therapist to offer the student examples such as "consider the impact of a positive thought (e.g., the thought of finding a $100 bill lying on the sidewalk), and then think about how you would feel (e.g., excited, joyful) and what you might then do (e.g., buy something desirable, save for a rainy day). Just hearing this might make you feel a little excited as you think of what you could do with $100!" Now, on the other hand, try a different thought experiment that illustrates the same relationship between thoughts, emotions, and behaviors. "Right now, think about a friend having lost her pet. Try to think of how she would feel. What emotions would you feel? How do you feel just reading this right now? How might these uncomfortable feelings impact your behavior? Perhaps you might hug the person you were just thinking of or tell her how you understand when you see her."

After students comprehend that their thoughts can elicit negative emotions and behaviors, they can be prompted by the therapist to identify some of their problematic thoughts. These thoughts are generally difficult for individuals to identify without help because they tend to seem to occur spontaneously and automatically as opposed to because of conscious reflection. Additionally, they often are rooted in what individuals perceive to be an emotional truth (e.g., "I think that I am a loser"

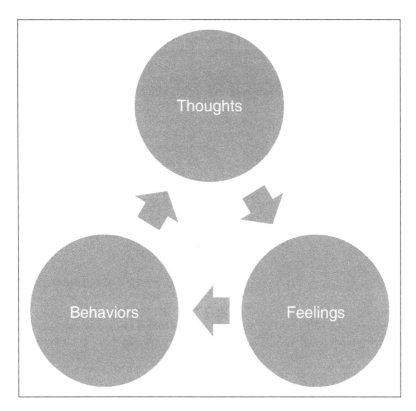

Figure 5.5   General cognitive model: Cognitive behavioral therapy triad.

→ "I feel like a loser" → "I must be a loser"), which then tends to inflate the salience and significance of these thoughts, as well as people's willingness to accept them as true.

Because individuals often believe that their automatic thoughts are true in the same way that a goldfish might think that the entire world is covered in water, as a thought experiment, it can be helpful to encourage students to "get outside their head" or envision "thinking with someone else's brain" for a few minutes to critically evaluate their own thoughts. Additionally, they also can be encouraged to view their own thoughts from another person's perspective to help distance themselves from their thoughts, which can be an effective thought experiment for students with depression who often are much harsher with their self-appraisals than they are when appraising others. Collectively, these strategies are discussed at greater length next with content related to Socratic questioning.

Specific Cognitive Distortions

In the CBT literature, there are dozens of identified cognitive distortions. However, Table 5.2 provides definitions and examples of the more common thinking errors found among children and adolescents experiencing a range of internalizing and externalizing forms of psychopathology (Friedberg et al., 2009; Leahy & Holland, 2000; Mennuti, Christner, & Freeman, 2012). Although individual students can display quite different clusters of cognitive distortions, there are some that are

TABLE 5.2 Common Cognitive Distortions and Thinking Errors

Cognitive Distortions (Automatic Thoughts, Thinking Errors, Thinking Traps, Stinkin' Thinkin')	Descriptor and Examples
Blaming (Finger Pointing, Who-Dun-It, Shame Game, Lame Blame)	Shifting responsibility for negative events to others. The opposite of personalization: holding other people solely responsible for events for which the person doing the blaming is at least partially responsible. "I shouldn't get detention. It is all their fault."
Catastrophizing (Disaster Forecaster, Doctor Gloom/Doom) *Note:* Catastrophizing is a subtype of magnification/minimization (Burns, 1980, 1989)	Views the future with disastrous outcomes (e.g., grossly exaggerated and tragic) based on perceptions of minor negative events, portraying a negative event or situation as a major disaster or tragedy (more so than most others would view the event). "I didn't get a date for the prom; my life is over now."
Control fallacy (Poor Me)	Child perceives self as a helpless victim of an external force or circumstance. "I can't help it if I'm no good at schoolwork, I have ADHD." "The teacher is so hard. I can't win."
Dichotomous thinking or polarized thinking (All or Nothing, No Middle Riddle; One-Eyed Ogre)	Putting experiences in one of two extreme categories does not recognize a continuum of experiences or outcomes; may be expressed in superlatives, perceiving things in black or white terms and absolutes as opposed to gradations or shades of gray. "People are all bad." "I am an absolute failure."
Discounting the positive (Disqualifying the Positive, Countless Thinking, Ignoring the Good)	Youth has a negative affirmation bias, clinging to a negative self-view despite positive outcomes, discounting positive events or negating their existence. "Getting into that college was pure luck."
Emotional reasoning (Prisoner of Feelings, The Roller Coaster)	Child feels that his or her current feelings are the truth and lacks awareness that feelings are not facts, viewing and describing events through an emotional filter. Essentially, a person's emotional tone inordinately colors his or her experience. "I feel energized around her; therefore, I must be totally in love."
Entitlement beliefs (The Princess, The Prince, The Revenger)	An individual believes he or she is exempt from the requirements others may be held to or have special privilege. "I know this stuff; I don't need to turn in the homework."
Fairness fallacy (Right Knight, The Regulator)	Student believes he or she knows what is truly fair and has rigid expectations that others should share that view and act accordingly. "It's not fair that I got 2 days detention and they only got 1 day."
Fortune telling (The Crystal Ball). *Note:* Fortune telling is a subtype of jumping to conclusions (Burns, 1980, 1989)	This distortion involves predicting a negative future event (not necessarily projected out globally or long term) without evidence or supporting predictive information. "Even though I try, I won't make the team."
Jumping to conclusions (The Jumper, Too Fast Forward). *Note:* Jumping to conclusions has two subtypes: fortune telling and mind reading	Child responds to situation without all the information needed to make a sound assessment, settling on conclusions that are based on little evidence, if any. "The teacher looks tired; she won't check the homework so I don't need to do it."
Labeling (Mislabeling, The Name Game)	The child uses derogatory names to describe himself or herself holistically in response to isolated circumstances. "I am a loser."

(*continued*)

TABLE 5.2   Common Cognitive Distortions and Thinking Errors (*continued*)

Cognitive Distortions (Automatic Thoughts, Thinking Errors, Thinking Traps, Stinkin' Thinkin')	Descriptor and Examples
Magnification and minimization (The Amplifier, The Shrinker). Note: Catastrophizing is a subtype of magnification/minimization	The child attributes disproportional weight (greater or lesser) to perceived failures or negative events. Magnification is sometimes described as "making a mountain out of a molehill" or making a big deal out of something that is not as significant as it is portrayed. Minimization is portraying a significant event, situation, or personal accomplishment as being marginal or inconsequential. "Winning that trophy was just luck, not really important."
Mind reading (Tragic Magic Thinking). *Note:* Mind reading is a subtype of jumping to conclusions (Burns, 1980, 1989)	Individual thinks she or he knows what others are thinking about her or him without any facts (i.e., no conversation with the person or supporting evidence), making overly presumptuous judgments about other people based on one's own bias or based on their nonverbal communication. "I know from the way she looks at me that she just hates me."
Negative filtering (Wearing Dark Glasses, The Blues News)	Magnifying a negative aspect of an incident while ignoring the rest, focusing exclusively on negative aspects of a situation to the exclusion of positive or neutral aspects. "I stuttered on the very last word of my presentation. It went horribly!"
Overgeneralizing (The Repeat-Repeat)	Perceives a current event to be representative of all events or life overall, predicts same negative outcome repeatedly over time, thinks something will always occur because it happened once. Making broad assessments, judgments, or generalizations based on a single or small set of particulars or from insufficient experiences and evidence. "I am never going to be able to give a presentation since I had a panic attack last time."
Personalization (Me-Me, Mini-Me, It's All About Me)	Assumption that he or she is the cause of a negative event, despite a lack of evidence. Attributing personal responsibility for events over which a person has little or no control. "They must have canceled the show because my audition was miserable."
Should/must thinking (Bossy Thoughts)	Student thinks of own actions and those of others as needing to conform to rigid "should" and "must" rules. Thoughts can be guilt-ridden if directed at themselves or result in anger when directed at others. "They should give it up." "I really *should* get better grades, and I must start dieting."
Unfair comparisons or comparing (Foul Referee)	Student holds him- or herself to an unrealistic and unfair comparison. "My dancing is awful compared to the prima ballerina."
What If (The Guessing Game)	Student approaches situations second-guessing possible but highly improbable negative contingencies. "What if I don't wake up on time for the test?" "What if my brain goes blank?" "What if the teacher quits and I can't get help?"

Note: In the cognitive behavioral therapy (CBT) literature, some cognitive distortions are referred to by more than one term (depending on the author). Additionally, theoretical terms may be difficult for children and adolescents to understand; therefore, this table has alternate names for distortions from CBT literature as well as child-friendly versions of terms provided in parentheses.

ADHD, attention deficit hyperactivity disorder.

Sources: Boyes, A. (2013). 50 common cognitive distortions. *Psychology Today.* Retrieved from http://www.psychologytoday .com/blog/in-practice/201301/50-common-cognitive-distortions; Burns, D. D. (1980). *Feeling good: The new mood therapy.* New York, NY: William Morrow; Burns, D. D. (1989). *The feeling good handbook: Using the new mood therapy in everyday life.* New York, NY: William Morrow; Leahy, R. L., & Holland, S. J. (2000). *Treatment plans and interventions for depression and anxiety disorders.* New York, NY: Guilford Press; Mennuti, R. B., Christner, R. W., & Freeman, A. (Eds.). (2012). *Cognitive behavioral interventions in educational settings: A handbook for practice* (2nd ed.). New York, NY: Routledge.

typical of particular mental health symptoms. For example, blaming, dichotomous thinking, entitlement beliefs, fairness fallacy, jumping to conclusions, labeling, and should/must thinking are often consistent with acting-out, bullying, disruptive acts, or aggressive behaviors. Diagnoses such as conduct disorder and intermittent explosive disorder have a propensity toward quick blaming of others, mind reading, feeling justified in harsh judgment of others, and polarized thinking about their perception of right and wrong.

On the other hand, diagnoses with internalizing behavioral problems that may include pessimism, social withdrawal, anxiousness, and helplessness, or hopelessness features also are prone to manifest as a cluster of distortions. These include catastrophizing, control fallacies, discounting the positive, ignoring the good, fortune telling, negative filtering, and unfair comparisons. Those with diagnoses such as anxiety, depression, reactive attachment, and phobias typically struggle with feeling victimized, overwhelmed, and lacking control of their own destiny. Both externalizers and internalizers can be prone to personalization, overgeneralizing, and emotional reasoning.

In a counseling session, a student can be encouraged to come up with an example of each cognitive distortion that applies to his or her own life or someone else. The student can then describe ways that the distortion is irrational, inaccurate, maladaptive, or problematic in another way and list more adaptive ways to think about the event or situation that is related to experiencing the cognitive distortion. However, cognitive restructuring is abstract, and it is challenging for many students to understand how to effectively evaluate their thoughts or understand how their mind works, especially for young students or students who have limited metacognitive skills. Therefore, a therapist may have to provide specific examples for the student to follow or use props such as cartoons or puppets that the student can identify with and observe. In this vein, a therapist could cut pictures out of magazines or print them off the Internet that depict people engaged in dramatic situations (e.g., falling off a bike, getting back a test with a failing grade on it) and have the child describe a thought that the person in the picture might be thinking. Then, if the student describes a thought that suggests the presence of a cognitive distortion, the therapist can encourage replacing it with better or different thoughts that are likely to make the person feel better. Lastly, it is important to note that because terms such as *cognitive distortions* and *maladaptive thoughts* are jargon terms and not likely to be well received by students, therapists should avoid using these terms when working with them. Instead, in collaboration with the student, the therapist could come up with clever substitute words for these terms such as *stinkin' thinkin'*.

Once a student can begin identifying cognitive distortions, the therapist can enhance this process and help the client start challenging such distortions or coming up with different ways to think and behave in hypothetical situations that are grounded in real-world experience. In this regard, the ABC model (i.e., antecedent–beliefs–consequences; see Appendix Exhibits 2.2, 2.3, 2.5–2.9) can be used to help understand the functional relationship between triggers or activating events and related feelings and behaviors. The three-step ABC model originates from the work of Ellis (1991), and it utilizes the term *antecedent* to describe the initial behavior or situation and the automatic thoughts related to it. Then, *beliefs* are noted and reviewed to determine if they are rational or irrational, and finally, *consequences* are identified to help students understand the complete functional relationship between the antecedents (As), behaviors (Bs), and consequences (Cs). In the ABC model, negative events and rational beliefs do not necessarily erase the negative feelings, but there are healthy and unhealthy responses to negative events. For example, a child who loses a favorite pet can have irrational beliefs of self-blame and guilt, even if he or she did nothing but love the pet and could do nothing to prevent its natural death. Moreover, through identifying specific cognitive distortions, he or she could realize that more adaptive and maladaptive ways exist to think about the death of the pet. For example, instead of personalizing the death and feeling guilt or shame, the child could reflect on loving the pet, growing together, and appreciating the role the pet had in the family. Essentially, the cognitive model provides a structure for illustrating that thoughts, feelings, and behaviors influence each other and can directly influence outcomes. Deconstructing and teaching the relationship between the As, Bs, and Cs can be challenging, however. Therefore, therapists should use strategies such as thought records to elucidate the often abstract functional relationships between thoughts, feelings, and behaviors.

Thought Journaling and Records

Thought records are commonly used to identify and challenge cognitive distortions, and they extend cognitive interventions downward to have greater utility for student populations. They are also directed toward the three-step ABC model and even can be crafted to extend the model to also include "D," disputing cognitive distortions by coming up with alternative thoughts/ways of thinking, and/or "E," evaluating the perceived efficacy of the alternative thoughts as they compare to the initial distortion.

Simply stated, this intervention involves keeping a record of cognitive distortions or maladaptive thoughts and related experiences that can be used to challenge them therapeutically. When encouraging students to keep a thought record, the therapist should tell them to pay attention to changes in their mood or affective state and then jot down what was happening right before this change was noticed (the antecedent, or "A") and what they were thinking about immediately after (the consequence, or "C"). Thought records can easily be created by folding a regular blank sheet of paper into three or four columns that can be used for a student to record the aforementioned information. Through using them, thought records help students directly see the functional relationship between their own thoughts and feelings as well as events that trigger changes in both domains. Examples of thought records can be found in the Appendix Exhibits 2.6 and 2.7). Additionally, when these thoughts include misperceptions about what others are thinking (e.g., mind reading), perspective-taking scenarios and exercises may help expand thinking options. Asking students to generate alternative and positive interpretations of events also may be helpful (see Appendix Exhibits 5.15–5.21).

As briefly illustrated previously, the logical extension of thought records involves using them therapeutically. In this regard, the therapist can work with the student to identify specific cognitive distortions, label them, and dispute (D) or challenge them (see Appendix Exhibit 2.7). For example, a child with generalized anxiety disorder might notice that he becomes anxious whenever he hears news stories about terrorist attacks. When exposed to such information, he may compulsively call his parents to make sure they are safe, refuse to leave the house, or ask for reassurance that nothing bad will happen to him or them. Because the student has never been exposed to any serious threats or acts of violence, such concerns are disproportionally related his reality, especially because his risk for personal harm from a terrorist attack is exceedingly small.

Using a thought record, the student could monitor all of the antecedent events that cause him to experience anxiety (e.g., watching scary and developmentally inappropriate videos online, watching the nightly news with his parents, asking peers about scary things) and his related thoughts. With this example, the student might identify watching a scary video about a terrorist attack (the antecedent "A") with the thought: "What if a terrorist attack occurs where my mom works?" or "What if the terrorists target my school?" The student should also list the consequences associated with ruminating about such remote possibilities ("I felt sick to my stomach," "I called my mom immediately to see if she's okay," "I avoided the school bus and made my parents pick me up").

Through working with the therapist, the student might identify that he is *catastrophizing* (viewing the future with unrealistic disastrous outcomes), *overgeneralizing* (looking at a small number of isolated events and thinking that they represent a much broader and immediate threat), *personalizing* (taking negative events that happened on the other side of the world or decades ago and applying them to a perceived personal risk), and engaging in *emotional reasoning* (letting one's own emotional state disproportionately color one's perceptions of reality). This then opens up an opportunity to dispute (D) the identified cognitive distortions. For example, the student might say, "Well, my thought that terrorists were going to attack my school is unlikely. I watched a scary video, which made me afraid and not think clearly and overreact." After disputing cognitive distortions, the student and the therapist can evaluate (E) the related process: "This is a better way to think about the situation. I feel less worried and more calm now after thinking about things differently."

Through reviewing information collected on thought journals or records (or through directly focusing on problematic thoughts that the student seems to harbor in session), therapists can help students better identify, understand, and eventually challenge these thoughts through using a list that included common cognitive distortions and thinking errors. Many of these have already been alluded to in other portions of this book; however, common cognitive distortions include all-or-nothing thinking, overgeneralization, disqualifying the positive, personalization, emotional reasoning, catastrophizing, negative filtering, and labeling. Table 5.2 presents a more comprehensive list of cognitive distortions, their description, and various examples.

Each year, an increasing number of apps emerge that can be used to monitor one's cognitive processes, identify cognitive distortions, consider different ways of thinking, and monitor one's progress. This is ideal, because students can download such apps on personal devices and literally have them at their fingertips. Every CBT therapist deals with frustrations associated with thought records or journals getting lost or between-session homework not getting completed. Using high-quality CBT apps can help minimize the former, as well as engage students in a familiar setting (i.e., in cyberspace). For information on apps as they emerge, the Anxiety and Depression Association of America (ADAA) rates apps based on their expected age level, ease of use, effectiveness, degree to which they can be personalized, the amount of feedback they provide, and level of research support (adaa.org/finding-help/mobile-apps).

Socratic Questioning

In addition to using thought records to identify and dispute cognitive distortions, therapists can also utilize the Socratic questioning. This intervention approach aims to help individuals discover maladaptive thoughts, determine ways in which they are maladaptive, and identify errors in their reasoning. Furthermore, it can be used independently or with thought records, which likely will have the greatest benefit. Through using this technique, therapists can descend deeper and past surface responses to uncover meaningful answers to the therapist's questions.

By no means is Socratic questioning a way to control a client's thoughts or challenge her or his autonomy. It also is not used to challenge deep-seated personal beliefs and values. Instead, it is a tool that the therapist shares with the client so that he or she can reduce the negative impact of cognitive distortions on his or her life. Additionally, while engaged in cognitive restructuring, asking the question *why?* often is not as effective as *what?* or an alternative question because it can cause individuals to become defensive or say "I don't know" if they feel judged. As applied, Socratic questions should be mixed in with the typical therapeutic dialogue or discussion. Being peppered with questions causes people to become defensive or shut down, and it can feel invalidating. Therefore, the traditional counseling skills should be utilized while doing cognitive restructuring. It always is still important to develop and maintain rapport, provide positive regard, show genuine interest in what the client is saying, and use nonverbal attends to prevent therapy from feeling stale, inauthentic, stilted, or even ingenuous.

Often, new CBT practitioners (or individuals who want to begin practicing CBT in school settings) report feeling that they are at a loss on how to do cognitive restructuring. By no means is this their fault. Cognitive restructuring scripts can seem artificial in real-world settings. In contrast to a short script or vignette, does a therapist have the seemingly perfect response to a client or does a real student have the advanced awareness of a scripted client? While reading the examples in this chapter, you might have thought: "I wouldn't have known to say that" or "The students I'm working with wouldn't say that or talk that way." This is probably true, but it is not a problem, and totally okay. The use of cognitive restructuring—and CBT for that matter—should evolve organically. Although it is a short-term form of therapy, clients and therapists move at different rates, and there are no rigid rules on the duration of treatment.

Furthermore, as a school psychologist, school counselor, or social worker, you likely already do things with students that fall under the CBT umbrella (you might just not think of them this way or apply them as systematically). Attentive and thoughtful counselors, educators, and therapists ask questions that encourage students to reflect on their thoughts, change their behaviors, and regulate their emotions more effectively. In fact, cognitive restructuring, in particular, can be reduced to a handful of questions that can be used to dispute cognitive distortions that have many different variations. These questions are as follows:

- What is the evidence for _____ ?
- What is a better way to think about _____ ?
- What are the advantages and disadvantages of_____ ?
- What might other people think about _____ ?

The following dialogue illustrates the application of these questions to encourage a student to think about his or her thinking as well as some related cognitive distortions. However, it should be noted that prior to engaging in such a dialogue, it is important to have adequate rapport and to validate the way a client is feeling:

Therapist:	How are you today?
Student:	Terrible. My life is completely over.
	[Catastrophizing, fortune telling, magnification]
Therapist:	Oh no. Would you tell me more about what happened?
Student:	"Yeah, my boyfriend just broke up with me. He's perfect. I'll never find someone like him, and I'll probably be alone forever!
	[Dichotomous thinking, fortune telling, jumping to conclusions]
Therapist:	I'm so sorry that you feel that way. I can tell that you care a lot about him and that you're very upset today.
Student:	Thank you. I do care a lot about him.
Therapist:	Can I ask you something?
Student:	Sure.
Therapist:	What evidence is there that he's perfect?
Student:	Well, I just think he's special even though he can be mean, and my friends don't like him.
Therapist:	I get it, and you have some friends who really have your back. What does your best friend think?
Student:	She thinks he's rude and that I can do way better.
Therapist:	Instead of thinking that your life is over and that you'll be alone, can you think of a different way to view your current situation?
Student:	Yeah, well, I guess I can. We've only been dating for a couple of months, and he's already getting kind of demanding. I just don't want to go to the upcoming dance alone. I'll get over it though. A lot of people just go to hang out in groups anyway.
Therapist:	I like how you can see the pluses and minuses of your relationship situation. Can you think of others?
Student:	Yeah. This will give me more time for soccer, and I won't feel guilty about dancing with other people at the dance.

Notice that the dialogue includes a range of different variations of the previously listed questions. As much as possible, it is important not to sound robotic or mechanical when challenging cognitive distortions.

Downward Arrow

The "downward arrow" technique (see Appendix Exhibit 5.8) is similar to using Socratic questioning; however, it is typically used to identify core beliefs as opposed to being used as an independent therapeutic technique (Burns, 1980). Additionally, it should be used with caution because it can expose clients to core beliefs about themselves that they are not yet ready to process. As an analogy, it is used to simultaneously peel back many layers of the onion and expose what is toward the core. The following dialogue illustrates the use of the downward arrow technique with a student with test anxiety to get to a deeper fear that the student harbors:

Therapist:	What are you so anxious about?
Student:	My math test on Friday!
Therapist:	What is so scary about the math test?
Student:	I'm afraid that I will fail the test.
Therapist:	What is so scary about failing the test?
Student:	If I fail the test, I might fail the class!
Therapist:	What is so disastrous about failing the class?
Student:	My parents will get really mad, and they might not let me go to college.

Notice how what stated as a surface-level concern (i.e., the upcoming math test) quickly gave way to a deeper concern through questioning (parental rejection worries). Beck (1995) has identified two deep core fears that are the root of most other fears, worries, and concerns:

1. A fear of being inadequate or helpless
2. A fear of being unlovable

Considering how deeply ingrained such fears may be and how overlaid they may be with other fears, avoidant behaviors, and even self-rejecting or hurtful behaviors, extreme caution is needed when exploring core fears. If attempted, such a process should be client led and include other cognitive, behavioral, and emotion-regulation strategies; and the therapist should pace the process to ensure the well-being of the client.

When to Use and Not to Use Cognitive Restructuring

Cognitive restructuring can be used with students who display a range of internalizing forms of psychopathology. In addition, it can be used with students who have low self-esteem, biases, limiting beliefs, negative attributions (e.g., global and stable), or maladaptive thoughts, in general. However, therapists should refrain from using cognitive restructuring as a therapeutic approach for children who display obsessive or ruminating symptomatology, especially if these obsessions are highly ritualized, as is the case with those who have OCD. Cognitive skills required for cognitive restructuring include the ability to engage in self-reflection and reasoning, consider the perspective of others, and understand cause–effect relationships. Therefore, as noted in Chapter 2, Cognitive Theoretical Foundations, this method of treatment should not be used with students who have a low cognitive functioning, very young children (i.e., preschool and first- to second-grade students), and any other students who display poor insight and a very limited metacognitive ability. Therapists may have to determine the student's level of insight and metacognitive skills through interviewing the child, teachers, parents, or others who know the student well.

As a final caveat, it is not clear exactly why individuals benefit from cognitive restructuring or various cognitive interventions. Surely changing thoughts can influence emotions and behaviors consistent with the standard CBT model. However, the mere understanding that thoughts are malleable and not rigid also can have a therapeutic benefit. When stuck in rigid thinking, individuals tend to believe that their current thoughts are real, accurate, and irrefutable. However, through the process of engaging in cognitive restructuring, or other therapeutic approaches (e.g., mindfulness), it becomes clear that one's own thoughts often are inaccurate and disproportionally influenced by one's feelings, having incomplete information, previous experiences, or myriad of other factors. Therefore, part of the efficacy of cognitive interventions may lie less in the specific therapeutic activities and more in the client's enhanced understanding that thoughts often are distorted and amenable to change. With this in mind, accuracy in identifying the exact cognitive distortion is less important than understanding that a distortion is present and that there are different ways to think about reality.

REFERENCES

Abramowitz, J. S. (1996). Variants of exposure and response prevention in the treatment of obsessive-compulsive disorder: A meta-analysis. *Behavior Therapy, 27,* 583–600. doi:10.1016/S0005-7894(96)80045-1

Abramowitz, J. S., Deacon, B. J., & Whiteside, S. P. (2012). *Exposure therapy for anxiety: Principles and practice.* New York, NY: Guilford Press.

American Psychological Association. (2016). *Beyond worry: How psychologists help with anxiety disorders.* Retrieved from http://www.apa.org/helpcenter/anxiety.aspx

Anxiety and Depression Association of America. (2015). *Clinical practice review for social anxiety disorder.* Retrieved from https://www.adaa.org/resources-professionals/clinical-practice-review-social-anxiety

Baker, A., Mystkowski, J., Culver, N., Yi, R., Mortazavi, A., & Craske, M. G. (2010). Does habituation matter? Emotional processing theory and exposure therapy for acrophobia. *Behaviour Research and Therapy, 48,* 1139–1143. doi:10.1016/j.brat.2010.07.009

Beck, A. T. (1991). *Cognitive therapy and the emotional disorders.* New York, NY: Penguin Books.

Beck, J. S. (1995). *Cognitive therapy: Basics and beyond.* New York, NY: Guilford Press.

Beck, J. S. (2011). *Cognitive behavior therapy: Basics and beyond* (2nd ed.). New York, NY: Guilford Press.

Beck, R., & Fernandez, E. (1998). Cognitive-behavioral self-regulation of the frequency, duration, and intensity of anger. *Journal of Psychopathology and Behavioral Assessment, 20*(3), 217–229. doi:10.1023/A:1023063201318

Blakey, S. M., & Abramowitz, J. S. (2016). The effects of safety behaviors during exposure therapy for anxiety: Critical analysis from an inhibitory learning perspective. *Clinical Psychology Review, 49,* 1–15. doi:10.1016/j.cpr.2016.07.002

Burns, D. D. (1980). *Feeling good: The new mood therapy.* New York, NY: William Morrow.

Craske, M. G., Kircanski, K., Zelikowsky, M., Mystkowski, J., Chowdhury, N., & Baker, A. (2008). Optimizing inhibitory learning during exposure therapy. *Behaviour Research and Therapy, 46,* 5–27. doi:10.1016/j.brat.2007.10.003

Craske, M. G., Treanor, M., Conway, C. C., Zbozinek, T., & Vervliet, B. (2014). Maximizing exposure therapy: An inhibitory learning approach. *Behaviour Research and Therapy, 58,* 10–23. doi:10.1016/j.brat.2014.04.006

Ellis, A. (1991). The revised ABC's of rational-emotive therapy. *Journal of Rational-Emotive and Cognitive-Behavior Therapy, 9,* 139–172. doi:10.1007/BF01061227

Friedberg, R. D., McClure, J. M., & Garcia, J. H. (2009). *Cognitive therapy techniques for children and adolescents: Tools for enhancing practice.* New York, NY: Guilford Press.

International OCD Foundation. (n.d.). *How is OCD treated?* Retrieved from https://iocdf.org/about-ocd/ocd-treatment

Jordan, C., Reid, A. M., Mariaskin, A., Augusto, B., & Sulkowski, M. L. (2012). First-line treatment for pediatric obsessive–compulsive disorder. *Journal of Contemporary Psychotherapy, 42*(4), 243–248. doi:10.1007/s10879-012-9210-z

Joyce-Beaulieu, D. (2019). *Easy application of CBT for internalizing and externalizing disorders*. Presented at the Marion County District School Psychologist Training, Ocala, FL.

Kendall, P. C., Comer, J. S., Marker, C. D., Creed, T. A., Puliafico, A. C., Hughes, A. A., . . . Hudson, J. (2009). In-session exposure tasks and therapeutic alliance across the treatment of childhood anxiety disorders. *Journal of Consulting and Clinical Psychology, 77*, 517–525. doi:10.1037/a0013686

Leahy, R. L., & Holland, S. J. (2000). *Treatment plans and interventions for depression and anxiety disorders*. New York, NY: Guilford Press.

Mennuti, R. B., Christner, R. W., & Freeman, A. (Eds.). (2012). *Cognitive behavioral interventions in educational settings: A handbook for practice* (2nd ed.). New York, NY: Routledge.

Olatunji, B. O., Deacon, B. J., & Abramowitz, J. S. (2009). The cruelest cure? Ethical issues in the implementation of exposure-based treatments. *Cognitive and Behavioral Practice, 16*, 172–180. doi:10.1016/j.cbpra.2008.07.003

Robichaud, M. (2013). Cognitive behavior therapy targeting intolerance of uncertainty: Application to a clinical case of generalized anxiety disorder. *Cognitive and Behavioral Practice, 20*, 251–263. doi:10.1016/j.cbpra.2012.09.001

Storch, E. A., Salloum, A., Johnco, C., Dane, B. F., Crawford, E. A., King, M. A., . . . Lewin, A. B. (2015). Phenomenology and clinical correlates of family accommodation in pediatric anxiety disorders. *Journal of Anxiety Disorders, 35*, 75–81. doi:10.1016/j.janxdis.2015.09.001

Sulkowski, M. L., Jacob, M. L., & Storch, E. A. (2013). Exposure and response prevention and habit reversal training: Commonalities, differential use, and combined applications. *Journal of Contemporary Psychotherapy, 43*(3), 179–185. doi:10.1007/s10879-013-9234-z

Sulkowski, M. L., Joyce, D. K., & Storch, E. A. (2012). Treating childhood anxiety in schools: Service delivery in a response to intervention paradigm. *Journal of Child and Family Studies, 21*(6), 938–947. doi:10.1007/s10826-011-9553-1

Wolitzky-Taylor, K. B., Horowitz, J. D., Powers, M. B., & Telch, M. J. (2008). Psychological approaches in the treatment of specific phobias: A meta-analysis. *Clinical Psychology Review, 28*, 1021–1037. doi:10.1016/j.cpr.2008.02.007

Wolpe, J. (1969). *The practice of behavior therapy* (2nd ed.). New York, NY: Pergamon Press.

Zaboski, B. A., Joyce-Beaulieu, D., Kranzler, J. H., McNamara, J. P., Gayle, C., & MacInnes, J. (2019). Group exposure and response prevention for college students with social anxiety: A randomized clinical trial. *Journal of Clinical Psychology, 75*(9), 1489–1507. doi:10.1002/jclp.22792

SIX

Applied Cognitive Behavioral Therapy Session Activities

INTRODUCTION

Counseling children and adolescents requires the ability to adapt theoretical terms and concepts that are more abstract in nature to the individual's developmental level. Such adaptation is essential to cognitive behavioral therapy (CBT), as cognitive ability and maturity are key considerations in ensuring that students understand the relationship between their thoughts, feelings, and behaviors in order to make change. In this sense, the students' capacity to experience insightful self-awareness, conceptualize in-depth ideas, and understand causal interactions is paramount to their ability to participate in CBT in a meaningful way. A student's chronological age is another key developmental consideration. Early Piagetian developmental theory postulates that children in the preoperational stage (i.e., 2–7 years old) are likely to function from an egocentric perspective. Consequently, these children may have limited insight into their own thinking patterns and those of others during social interactions. Therefore, relying on behavioral modification approaches to change behavior may be more efficient. Although children under 7 who are especially bright also may benefit from more advanced strategies, children in the concrete operational stage (i.e., 7–11 years old) tend to have better reasoning skills than younger children, especially if concepts are demonstrated and illustrated through concrete examples. For these children, CBT may be more effective when counselors embed concrete examples and activities in their treatment plan. This chapter provides a number of suggestions for ways to incorporate concrete examples and activities that assist this age group in understanding CBT processes. Finally, children in the formal operational stage (i.e., ages 12 and older) possess a greater capacity to reason deeply and conceptualize abstract concepts. Consequently, CBT is deemed to be a good match for their metacognitive skills. In fact, research by Durlak, Fuhrman, and Lampman (1991) found CBT outcomes consistent with early Piagetian developmental theory in that children in the formal operations stage (ages 11 and older) have twice the positive effects utilizing CBT as children ages 2 to 10. For adolescents and young adults, discussion can dominate the sessions; however, even individuals of this age can benefit from visual aids, such as using a whiteboard to illustrate concepts, providing handouts to review strategies, offering journaling formats, or incorporating technology apps.

Bearing such developmental considerations in mind, CBT interventionists (e.g., school mental health providers) should be thoughtful in their approach when introducing and reviewing key concepts to school-age youth. A number of activities can be successfully implemented within school systems, especially for students who present with mild- to moderate-level mental health needs (Joyce-Beaulieu & Sulkowski, 2015). The remaining sections in this chapter review sample-applied strategies and related activities that school mental health providers can use when working with the students they serve. The options are of course unlimited, and there are numerous free-access published worksheets or activities for inspiration in customizing sessions for students. As motivation to engage in the counseling process is essential, activities that students find fun or related to their personal interests are likely to increase participation. The sample activities in this chapter reflect two age ranges of techniques: middle-age (ages 7–11) and adolescent students (ages 12+). Additionally, low-intensity counseling strategies such as use of technology apps are reviewed. The Appendix in this book also offers a variety of worksheets illustrating CBT concepts.

COUNSELING ACTIVITIES FOR CHILDREN AGES 7 TO 11

Teaching the Relationship Between Thoughts, Feelings, and Behaviors

- **Comparing the Negative Fall and the Positive Launch**: To introduce students to the core philosophy behind CBT, pictorial illustrations of the interaction between one's thoughts, feelings, and behaviors can be introduced at the beginning of the intervention period (see Appendix Exhibits 2.1–2.7). To help students further understand how the central idea behind CBT is relevant to their personal experiences, the *Comparing the Negative Fall and the Positive Launch* activity can be implemented (see Appendix Exhibit 2.4). During this activity, students are prompted to provide an example of a negative thought (e.g., "I know I will fail in school") and a positive thought ("I can work hard to improve my grades"). From there, the students are encouraged to generate examples of subsequent feelings and behaviors that they may experience as a result of their respective thoughts. For younger children, the counselor can emphasize that positive thoughts will likely lead to positive feelings and helpful behaviors, hence leading one to move in a positive direction, as in the case of a rocket ship successfully launching upward. Additional activities such as launching paper rockets may further illustrate the concept.
- **Hula-Hula-Hula Loop**: Having students draw circles (also called *Thought Circles* or *Thought Bubbles*), followed by writing thoughts that they have experienced in the circles/bubbles, can be a starting point for promoting students' awareness of their own thinking patterns. To further demonstrate the distinction between thoughts, feelings, and behaviors, the game of *Hula-Hula-Hula Loop* might be particularly useful for younger children. In this game, the counselor arranges three hula hoops on the floor labeled thoughts, feelings, and actions. The student is then encouraged to jump in each hoop as they describe a recent sequence of their own thought patterns. If the student

describes a negative sequence (e.g., "Other kids will pick on me. I feel scared. I am going to withdraw), he or she is coached to reframe the sequence as he or she moves through the hoops again (e.g., "My classmates have said kind words to me. I feel good. I am going to play with them during recess").

■ **What I Feel Inside:** When teaching students to become aware of their own physiological precursors to negative feelings and behaviors (e.g., the expression of anxiety and anger), counselors can prompt students to identify the stress reactions that they typically experience when faced with a triggering situation. Activities such as *What I Feel Inside* (see Appendix Exhibit 1.5) and *My Feelings Map* (see Appendix Exhibit 4.2) might be especially appealing to younger students. When completing these activities, students are prompted to identify their physiological reactions to anger and anxiety-provoking situations using a pictorial (and age-appropriate) figure/map of the human body. While older students may only include written descriptions of their physiological reactions next to respective body parts (e.g., writing the words *jaw clenching* near the face of the figure), younger children may wish to color the picture to further illustrate how they feel inside. Because students may struggle with generating examples on their own, the counselor may need to read a list of possible symptoms aloud before the student begins these activities.

Building Feeling Vocabulary

■ **Name Game and Order That Feeling:** Building students' feeling vocabulary can be profitable for helping them gain effective communication skills to articulate their feelings in a more nuanced and appropriate way rather than jumping to superlatives or catastrophizing language. For example, children with a propensity for catastrophizing will often use expressions such as "I am red hot mad" or "I am scared to death." They typically do not recognize a myriad of other feeling word options, for example, "I am disappointed, upset, hurt" or "I am confused, worried, unsure." The *Name Game* is one approach to executing this objective. In this activity, students are prompted to quickly name pictures of expressed emotions without using the same word twice. Adding a timer and encouraging students to beat the clock may also make the activity fun and engaging. From a developmental perspective, counselors may also wish to use pictures of a student's favorite television character or those that represent a student's personal interests (e.g., pictures of famous singers if the student enjoys listening to music). Another related activity is the *Order That Feeling* game. In this activity, the counselor provides the student with a list of words that can be used to express a positive or negative feeling. From there, the counselor asks the child to move the words along a ruler from least to most. As an example, when given the words *calm, unsettled, upset, agitated, frustrated, mad, angry,* and *furious,* the student would be expected to order them from the least (i.e., calm) to the most significant expression (i.e., furious). Considering that younger children may benefit from concrete illustrations of abstract terms, the counselor may also wish to pair the words with pictorial representations of the presented terms. For example, a student may mention that a favorite movie character is the Incredible Hulk. As such, the counselor can couple the aforementioned words with several variations of the Hulk's appearance.

Cognitive Restructuring

■ Hot Thought, Cool Thought: Having students distinguish adaptive versus maladaptive thoughts can be useful for facilitating their ability and tendency to replace negative thoughts with positive thoughts. One way to do so is by playing a *Hot Thought, Cool Thought* game with the student. For this activity, students are presented with a series of pictures representing hostile or confrontational exchanges between the people in the pictures. When each picture is presented, the student should be asked to articulate a "hot thought" (e.g., "My mom wants to make me miserable") that one of the characters may be thinking, followed by generating a replacing "cool thought" (e.g., "I may be disappointed, but my mom probably cares about my safety"). Counselors may need to model this activity before prompting the students to complete the game on their own.

■ Face Reader: Some children may experience difficulties as a result of misinterpreting others' behaviors. Negative misinterpretations of others' expressions/actions are a hallmark of externalizing behaviors and also a propensity of children with social phobia and a fear of negative appraisal by others. As such, utilizing photos of expressions and actions (e.g., sad face, child swimming in the pool, child shocked) to first discuss what the student thinks the person in the photo is thinking and feeling and then reexamining other alternative thoughts/feelings that could go with the expression may be helpful for this group of children. In the aforementioned examples, alternative interpretations of a sad face could be boredom, a child swimming in the pool could be interpreted as fun or scary, and a child shocked could be interpreted as excited or confused. All in all, the objective is to help students understand that their perspective of what others are doing and feeling does not have to be negative, others have a range of feelings, and we often do not know what they are thinking without asking them. Thus, jumping to conclusions may not be in our best interest.

■ Detective Effective: One common method of encouraging clients to restructure their thinking is to prompt them to identify evidence that supports or challenges their thinking. Thus, playing the *Detective Effective* game with young children can be a fun way of encouraging them to look for such facts or evidence. To play this game, children can use a magnifying glass to collect samples in plastic bags while "gathering" physical evidence reflecting whether a statement is true (e.g., "School ends at 2:45 p.m.," "My science teacher has an ant farm in her classroom"). Following the evidence-gathering stage, all the facts they collected are discussed and the students decide if the original statements are true. From there, the game moves from a concrete exercise to a social exercise, wherein students are prompted to consider how they might refute their own automatic negative thoughts by looking for evidence to refute their thinking (e.g., "Do all your peers dislike you? How will you find out the facts? What did you learn when talking to your classmates?").

■ Puppet Master, Cutting the Fuse: For this activity, students are prompted to personify anger as a puppet master controlling them. Next, children are prompted to list anger-inducing thoughts around the puppet master (e.g., "My teachers are mean," "I can't do anything right"). From there, students should be prompted to draw/imagine themselves cutting their anger fuse/the string attached to their body with their mind before they "blow up." Showing young children a picture of an actual puppet master controlling a puppet with several strings may be particularly useful for illustrating this activity in a more concrete manner.

COUNSELING ACTIVITIES FOR AGES 12 AND OLDER

Sentence Completion and If/Then Questionnaires

In cases in which youth struggle with articulating thoughts, a sentence completion technique may be helpful in eliciting responses. Sentence completions can be created by the counselor to include both innocuous questions mixed with select topic areas the counselor would like to explore. It is often advisable to start the exercise with a few items that are easy to answer and nonthreatening before asking questions related to core issues (e.g., anger, withdrawal) that may be uncomfortable for the student. Additionally, the language utilized will need to be developmentally appropriate and sensitive to the student's reading level. Although sentence completion is generally filled out by the student, for those with less willingness to write or less ability to write, the items could also be read and the counselor can complete the responses. Utilizing this process can at times identify themes in common word choices or phrases that identify thinking patterns. Examples of child and adolescent sentence stems for anger management are provided in Appendix Exhibits 1.1 and Exhibit 1.2. Another format for discovering thinking errors is using if/then questionnaires (see sample in Appendix Exhibit 1.3). If/then questionnaires can be created by the counselor to target a variety of counseling needs (e.g., depression, withdrawal, anger, anxiety). Both sentence completion technique and if/then questionnaires can be adapted to the reading and developmental levels of the student.

Thought Journaling

Thought journaling (sometimes also called thought records or daily mood logs) is another option for helping individuals discover and better understand their own thinking patterns. Generally, students are provided an explanation of the cognitive behavioral model or ABC model, and a thought record form is provided for documentation in between counseling sessions. Students are instructed to use the thought record to note their thoughts, feelings, and actions following any stressful or negative event. One benefit of the thought record is that it can be reviewed by the adolescent later after he or she is past the emotional state of having a negative circumstance and over time can foster insight into his or her own thinking patterns. For children, the counselor may wish to review thought records with the child during intervention to assist him or her in understanding negative patterns. The thought record also can help demonstrate progress over time as thoughts become more positive and thus change behaviors and outcomes.

Multiple examples of thought records are provided in Appendix Exhibits 2.5 to 2.10, and there are several versions of the ABC framework. The first exhibit

(2.5) displays a simple three-column ABC model. This can be presented in a four-column format (see Appendix Exhibit 2.6), which breaks consequences down into both short and long term to help children understand the sustaining effect of behaviors and thoughts. An alternating four-column form also can provide prompts to assist the student in practicing how to self-challenge irrational beliefs (see Appendix, ABCD sample, Exhibit 2.7). This last form may be more helpful after a student has mastered the three-step form or has begun successfully challenging distortions in the counseling intervention sessions. Another approach to thought records is to create forms specifically targeting symptoms (e.g., depression, perfectionism, posttraumatic stress disorder). The Cognitive Behavioral Self-Help Resources website offers freely available download forms for dozens of customized thought records, activity diaries, and thought-challenging forms (www.get.gg/gallery.htm).

Identifying Distortions Through Media

Socratic questioning technique is an effective method for helping individuals identify their own cognitive thinking distortions. However, there are times in therapy when students have low insight or resistance to the technique. Another form of learning this skill is to access the process through media. For example, we might ask a teenager to share lyrics from favorite songs or videos. YouTube can be an easy accessible way to review song lyrics with the ability to stop them and discuss what the songwriter is expressing. Are the thoughts healthy, unhealthy, catastrophizing, and so on? Some teens find the process of identifying words from others as less threatening than confronting their own statements and thoughts. Through the discussion, replacement lyrics and thoughts can also be generated to illustrate how the feelings evoked by the words or thoughts might change with a more positive message. The lyrics individuals gravitate toward can often be insightful. As an example, lyrics such as "I can't live if living is without you" can easily be identified as catastrophizing, and given the developmental stage of adolescents, a truly painful first heartbreak over a relationship is common. Thus, an adolescent may share this level of hopelessness and helplessness. Rephrasing the lyric to "It hurts because I miss . . ." or "In time, I'll be fine" presents a more positive option. The counselor might also ask the teen to identify contrasting positive lyrics or phrases from movies as a homework assignment.

INCORPORATING TECHNOLOGY: LOW-INTENSITY CBT INTERVENTIONS

From the original landline phone to the home computer, and now wireless smart phones and portable laptops, the current generation of students are more tech savvy than any group before them. In light of the technological advances in the 21st century, it is unsurprising that children and adolescents may be especially attracted to using a range of CBT-related activities that are readily available on their personal devices. Fortunately, innovative electronic applications have surfaced over the last two decades, granting individuals 24-hour/day access to important information and wide communication options. The use of technology to provide brief CBT is one of several applications known as low-intensity CBT intervention. Low-intensity therapy methods are not labor intensive for the counselor, and they may include programmed phone reminders or mood checks, emailed or texted positive messages, electronic bulletin boards, chat rooms, self-help books or websites, instant text messaging, phone apps, or computer-guided CBT programs.

Many professionals argue that this technology also can be utilized as a potent method of bringing CBT applications on a moment's notice at any time, to any location, to serve those with mental health and behavioral needs (Bennett-Levy et al., 2010). Some authors describe low-intensity CBT methods as an opportunity to provide graduated or "stepped care," which is self-paced and can improve cost-effectiveness and thus increase access to therapy (Bennett-Levy et al., 2010; Bower & Gilbody, 2005). Additional benefits include the self-correcting nature of low-intensity methods, the ability to generalize to a variety of contexts throughout the child's day, and intervention delivery of service in the spirit of least restrictive settings noted in the Individuals with Disabilities Education Improvement Act (IDEIA, 2004) guidelines. In fact, whether the goal is to extend practice opportunities and reinforce concepts learned within CBT sessions or to reach those individuals who are less willing to participate in counselor-led sessions, there is research to support positive effects for low-intensity CBT approaches.

As discussed by Joyce-Beaulieu and Sulkowski (2015), low-intensity interventions are also beneficial in that they typically are self-administered, flexible enough to fit into the student's schedule outside the school day, and free or of minimal cost. In contrast, computer software CBT programs may be expensive and thus require school systems to purchase these tools for the counselor and students. School personnel also may need to provide dedicated computer space and monitoring of students' utilization of these devices to ensure students have adequate access to the available resources and computers are used appropriately. Online bulletin boards and chat rooms require special safety considerations as well, considering that these two methods may not be monitored by a mental health professional. Bulletin boards involve the asynchronous posting of information, whereas chat rooms have real-time responses by participants (Griffiths & Reynolds, 2010). In this regard, sites that are open to the public with little oversight may allow access to the general public for commenting and responding, which increases the propensity of students being exposed to inappropriate, harmful, or ill-informed content. Case in point, peers utilizing such sites will have varying levels of insight and symptomatology; thus, the wherewithal of a student to exercise prudent judgment in accepting suggestions from others is very important. Additionally, the research support for these forums is mixed (Griffiths, Calear, & Banfield, 2009; Griffiths, Calear, Banfield, & Tam, 2009). When mental health professionals are involved, these individuals may monitor comments, edit or block inappropriate content, and require membership from users to prevent nonmembers from accessing the content. If school mental health providers advocate for student use of online bulletin boards and chat rooms, counselors should be well informed of the creditability and professional monitoring available, communicate this information to students and parents, and strongly encourage students to be cautious with self-disclosure. Examples of more credible chat rooms/bulletin boards include those sponsored by government and/or mental health agencies (e.g., Mental Health America, www.mentalhealthamerica.net/find-support-groups).

Overall, low-intensity methods are valuable ways to empower students to access affirmations, cope skill reminders, and self-monitor their own feelings and mood states. For example, studies have indicated decreased negative effects of depression, stress, anxiety, panic attacks, and phobias, and increased predictability for suicide risk assessment utilizing technology applications such as mobile apps, computer interview, self-exposure, and self-help guided therapy texts (Arean et al., 2016; Greist et al., 1973; Kenwright, Marks, Graham, Fanses, & Mataix-Cols, 2005; Marks, 2001; Rathbone & Prescott, 2017; Swinson, Soulios, Cox, & Kuch, 1992). Additionally, there is empirical support for the utilization of self-directed computer-aided programs (Barak, Hen, Boniel-Nissim, & Shapira, 2008; Spek et al., 2007). Regardless of the type of low-intensity CBT technique selected for a student, several strategies can make the supplemental supports more effective:

- Low-intensity interventions should not be used as a standalone method for support.
- Explain the limits of confidentiality in utilizing Internet-accessed media and/or communicating by phone.
- Introduce and model the technique in session with corrective feedback to assure the student knows how to apply the strategies. For example, demonstrate downloading a phone app for diaphragmatic breathing and practice with the adolescent to assure he or she can easily use the prompts and pull-down menus or tabs.
- Monitoring and adjusting frequency of strategies may include initially setting a higher frequency of positive affirmation messages on an app and then changing both the message and frequency over time as the child responds to the technique or needs to focus on additional areas. Some apps offer built-in data graphs that the therapist and child can review, which may inform frequency needs and indicate patterns for the time of day or situations that are most stressful for the student.
- Reviewing the utilization and progress of low-intensity CBT methods at the beginning of each new session and answering any questions regarding the materials may be helpful. For example, if a student is using thought records to challenge worry thoughts, it would be important to review those record sheets for patterns and session discussion points and/or to monitor correct understanding of the process.
- Additionally, offering students a variety of low-intensity methods and personal choices may increase utilization, especially if the methods change over time to enhance novelty and maintain interest.

Although not a conclusive list, Table 6.1 highlights some low-intensity applications and their corresponding targeted therapy objectives. Many of the apps are available free of charge and can be easily accessed by youth. These resources include coached breathing, guided imagery, progressive muscle relaxation, and journaling thought records. Each strategy can be taught during counseling sessions with modeling and corrective feedback and then self-reinforced throughout the week utilizing supplemental low-intensity CBT methods.

TABLE 6.1   Low-Intensity Cognitive Behavioral Therapy (CBT) Applications

CBT Applications	Description	Skills
Beating the Blues	This computer-aided software program offers empirically supported strategies for reducing depression symptoms (www.beatingtheblues.co.nz/what-is-it-practitioners.html).	Computerized CBT program
Breathe to Relax	This app is designed to help users utilize diaphragmatic breathing. A variety of learning tools is available, including readings, video demos, and progress monitoring tools.	Diaphragmatic breathing
CBT-I Coach	This app offers verbally coached breathing exercises, guided muscle relaxation with a graphic visual of the adult human body, and guided imagery with a choice of visual backgrounds for three locations (i.e., forest, country road, and beach).	Diaphragmatic breathing, muscle relaxation, guided imagery
CBT Thought Record Diary	This app allows users to understand, evaluate, and change their thoughts and feelings. Users can document negative emotions, analyze maladaptive thinking patterns, examine their thoughts, and change their thinking patterns.	Thinking tools
CBT Tools for Kids	This app is designed to help children and adolescents increase their emotional self-awareness and manage their feelings. Key features include an emotion tracker, emotional graph/history log, and relaxation skills tools (e.g., audio clips that youth can listen to to help them become calmer).	Self-monitoring, relaxation techniques, thinking tools
Get Self-Help	This website offers a variety of free worksheets specifically tailored to CBT, anger, depression, emotion regulation, relaxation, stress, and more (www.getselfhelp.co.uk//index.html).	Anger management worksheets, worksheets for managing anxiety, thought monitoring and recording worksheets, worksheets for relaxation training, and more
Negative to Positive: Erase Negative Thought Patterns	This app offers several scenic background options and verbal coaching for relaxation and challenging negative thought patterns.	Relaxation techniques, thinking tools

(*continued*)

TABLE 6.1 Low-Intensity Cognitive Behavioral Therapy (CBT) Applications (*continued*)

CBT Applications	Description	Skills
Mindshift	This app is designed to help users learn to relax and develop more effective ways of thinking. Some key features include anxiety and mood check-ins with graphs and journal entries, electronic coping cards, and guided imagery audio.	Positive affirmations
Therapist Aid	This website offers a variety of free worksheets specifically tailored to CBT, anger, depression, emotion regulation, relaxation, stress, and more (www.therapistaid.com/therapy-worksheets/cbt/none).	Anger management worksheets, worksheets for managing anxiety, thought monitoring and recording worksheets, worksheets for relaxation training, and more
ThinkUp	This app allows users to select positive affirmations from a professionally edited list or create their own affirmations. Users can also record themselves saying the affirmations aloud, add music to help with relaxation, and track their daily practice of positive affirmation use.	Positive affirmations
Unique Daily Affirmations	This app also allows users to select available positive affirmations or create their own affirmations. Users can also record themselves saying the affirmations aloud, and set phone alerts and email reminders to view the affirmations throughout the day.	Positive affirmations
Additional Applications	This website provides a list of apps that can be used to help individuals manage anxiety and depression (adaa.org/finding-help/mobile-apps).	Variety of CBT skills (contingent upon the purpose of the app)

REFERENCES

Arean, P. A., Hallgren, K. A., Jordan, J. T., Gazzaley, A., Atkins, D. C., Heagerty, P. J., & Anguera, J. A. (2016). The use and effectiveness of mobile apps for depression: Results from a fully remote clinical trial. *Journal of Medical Internet Research, 18*(12), e330. doi:10.2196/jmir.6482

Barak, A., Hen, L., Boniel-Nissim, M., & Shapira, N. (2008). A comprehensive review and meta-analysis of the effectiveness of internet-based psychotherapeutic interventions. *Journal of Technology in Human Services, 26*, 109–160. doi:10.1080/15228830802094429

Bennett-Levy, J., Richards, D. A., Farrand, P., Christensen, H., Griffiths, K. M., Kavanagh, D. J., . . . Williams, C. (Eds.). (2010). *Oxford guide to low intensity CBT interventions.* New York, NY: Oxford University Press.

Bower, P., & Gilbody, S. (2005). Stepped care in psychological therapies: Access, effectiveness and efficiency. *British Journal of Psychiatry, 186*, 11–17. doi:10.1192/bjp.186.1.11

Durlak, J., Fuhrman, T., & Lampman, C. (1991). Effectiveness of cognitive-behaviour therapy for maladaptive children: A meta-analysis. *Psychological Bulletin, 110*, 204–214. doi:10.1037/0033-2909.110.2.204

Greist, J. H., Gustafson, D. H., Stauss, F. F., Rowse, F. L., Laughren, T. P., & Chiles, J. A. (1973). Computer interview for suicide-risk prediction. *American Journal of Psychiatry, 130,* 1327–1332. doi:10.1176/ajp.130.12.1327

Griffiths, K. M., Calear, A., & Banfield, M. (2009). Internet support groups (ISGs) and depression: Do ISGs reduce depressive symptoms? *Journal of Medical Internet Research, 11,* e40. doi:10.2196/jmir.1270

Griffiths, K. M., Calear, A., Banfield, M., & Tam, A. (2009). Internet support groups (ISGs) and depression (2): What is known about depression ISGs? *Journal of Medical Internet Research, 11,* e41. doi:10.2196/jmir.1303

Griffiths, K. M., & Reynolds, J. (2010). Online mutual support bulletin boards. In J. Bennett-Levy, D. A. Richards, P. Farrand, H. Christensen, K. M. Griffiths, D. J. Kavanagh, . . . C. Williams (Eds.), *Oxford guide to low intensity CBT interventions* (pp. 295–301). New York, NY: Oxford University Press.

Individuals with Disabilities Education Improvement Act. Public Law 108-446, U.S. Code § 1400 (2004).

Joyce-Beaulieu, D., & Sulkowski, M. (2015). *Cognitive behavioral therapy in K-12 schools: A practitioners' workbook.* New York, NY: Springer Publishing Company.

Kenwright, M., Marks, L. M., Graham, C., Fanses, A., & Mataix-Cols, D. (2005). Brief scheduled phone support from a clinician to enhance computer-aided self-help for obsessive-compulsive disorder: Randomized controlled trial. *Journal of Clinical Psychology, 61,* 1499–1508. doi:10.1002/jclp.20204

Marks, I. M. (2001). *Living with fear* (2nd ed.). New York, NY: McGraw-Hill.

Rathbone, A. L., & Prescott, J. (2017). The use of mobile apps and SMS messaging as physical and mental health interventions: Systematic review. *Journal of Medical Internet Research, 19*(8), e295. doi:10.2196/jmir.7740

Spek, V., Cuipers, P., Nyklicek, I., Riper, H., Keyzer, J., & Pop, V. (2007). Internet-based cognitive behavior therapy for symptoms of depression and anxiety: A meta-analysis. *Psychological Medicine, 37,* 319–328. doi:10.1017/S0033291706008944

Swinson, R. P., Soulios, C., Cox, B. J., & Kuch, K. (1992). Brief treatment of emergency room patients with panic attacks. *American Journal of Psychiatry, 149,* 944–946. doi:10.1176/ajp.149.7.944

SEVEN

Case Studies

INTRODUCTION

The first case in this chapter reviews a third-grade student's difficulty with self-regulation, frustration tolerance, and a cognitive distortion related to perfectionism perpetuated by *all or nothing* thinking. Counseling strategies included teaching relaxation techniques, the cognitive behavioral therapy (CBT) triad, and replacement thoughts for perfectionism. Counseling was coupled with a positive reinforcement behavioral plan for the classroom and home–school collaboration with parents. The second case study addresses separation anxiety characteristics by applying graduated separation exposures, relaxation training, and CBT to address *what if* and *catastrophizing* thinking errors. The third case reviews counseling for a 14-year-old eighth grader with social anxiety. Counseling involved exposure therapy and CBT for *catastrophizing* and *mind reading* thinking errors. The final case study reviews school intervention coupled with outpatient therapy for a 10th-grade student with obsessive-compulsive disorder (OCD). Exposure therapy was provided, and subjective units of distress (SUDs) data were utilized for progress monitoring. Although all cases presented reflect real interventions with students, personal identifiers have been eliminated and some details altered to further protect identity.

CHILD COUNSELING CASE STUDY: SELF-REGULATION

Reason for Referral

Asher is a 9-year-old third-grade student who was referred to school psychological services because of a low rate of work completion in writing and math that was negatively impacting his current grades in those subjects. Additionally, the teacher had concerns for his difficulty in self-calming after upsetting events, noting difficulty with behavioral self-regulation, especially if he perceived a task to be hard.

Background Information

According to an interview with Asher's father, he is the older of two children and lives with both of his parents. He does not take any medications, and there is no history of significant illness or injury. Additionally, his father reports no significant stressors and notes English is the only language spoken by the family. Asher was described as an energetic, fun, and playful child. His father noted that Asher gets along well with siblings and children in the neighborhood with the exception of occasional outbursts if he thinks a game is too hard. He also noted that more recently Asher has had some crying episodes at the grocery store and synagogue, when upset over being asked to stand, sit, or stay quiet for an extended period of time. According to school records, he has consistently met or exceeded all of his school benchmarks during kindergarten through second grades. His attendance is good, and vision, hearing, and speech screenings are all within normal limits. This year, his academic performance started out strong; however, more recently, he has stopped completing class assignments and seems to become easily frustrated. When frustrated, he will put his head down, stop speaking to others, and often cry, sometimes inconsolably. During a parent–teacher conference, his parents noted they see this behavior at home as well and observed some perfectionistic characteristics, including tearing up papers he does not think are exactly right to redo and refusing to take homework back to school if it is not perfect. Classroom observations, by the school psychologist, indicated Asher's task frustration occurred only in subjects he found undesirable or more difficult (e.g., writing assignments, math that required showing steps he used to achieve an answer, homework review sessions). Once Asher became upset, he appeared to lack recovery strategies.

Intervention Plan

For the first area of intervention, his work completion, a positive reward plan was implemented. A week of baseline data indicated he was completing on average 50% of the class assignments. Asher was to receive points for completing each class assignment and also for turning in his homework daily. The teacher agreed to praise effort as well as correct answers and to encourage him to try his best on difficult items, noting she was proud of him for working. If he completed 85% of his work each day, he earned a prize from the treasure box, and a praise note went home to his parents. In collaboration with his parents, they agreed to also encourage Asher to follow the work completion plan at school and offered a weekly special activity on Saturdays (e.g., movie, trip to park) for meeting his goals 4 out of 5 days.

The second area of intervention, counseling, was designed to teach Asher self-calming skills for his frustration and to encourage perseverance. Baseline social–emotional data utilizing the Behavior Assessment System for Children, Third Edition (BASC-3) rating scale completed by his teacher indicated clinically significant anxiety characteristics and at-risk concerns for depression, attention problems, atypicality, and withdrawal. Given that anxiety was the only domain of clinical concern, reducing this was the primary counseling goal. Teaching relaxation techniques for self-calming and replacing a perfectionistic *all or nothing* thinking pattern with more positive affirmations were targeted (see Figure 7.1).

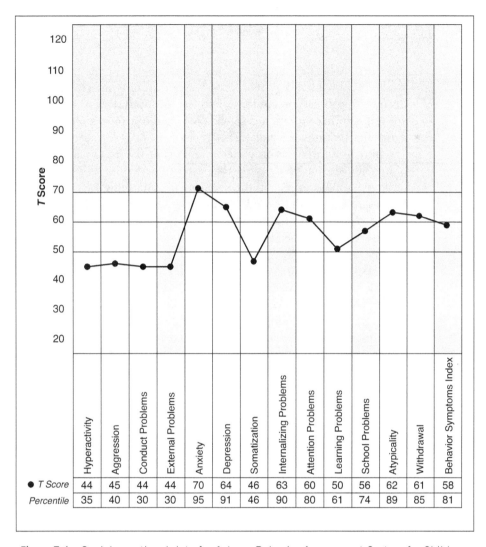

Figure 7.1   Social–emotional data for Asher—Behavior Assessment System for Children.

Counseling Sessions

The first session included introductions and rapport building, including a discussion of his interests in space travel, dinosaurs, and his favorite games in physical education class, as well as a discussion of confidentiality. Asher also was provided information on the purpose of the counseling sessions and an opportunity to describe his impressions of work frustration. He mentioned he knows he gets upset but indicated his brain freezes when things are hard and he is worried he will not get answers right, so he hides his head. If he is really upset, he mentioned tears come popping out and that is really embarrassing so he hides his face and does not talk. He also noted it makes him upset that papers have mistakes, so he throws them away or hides them sometimes. Lastly, the school psychologist reviewed the classroom behavior plan that was in place to reward him for completing work. The second through seventh sessions focused on the following:

1. Teaching Asher to recognize his physiological precursors to anxiety, which included feeling muscle tension, an upset stomach, and tearfulness. Recognizing these precursors provides the opportunity for him to initiate self-calming techniques quickly when those precursors first start (see Appendix Exhibits 4.1 and 4.2).

2. Teaching him three relaxation techniques (i.e., diaphragmatic breathing, use of a small meditative drawing that he could do discreetly at his desk, and progressive muscle relaxation; see Appendix Exhibit 4.8). Each relaxation technique was modeled and practiced in session. Additionally, the teacher agreed to praise use of these strategies when they were demonstrated in class, and his parents utilized the *Breathe to Relax* app at home to help him practice his techniques.

3. And lastly, counseling addressed his *all or nothing* cognitive distortion related to perfectionism. Asher was taught the CBT triad relationship between thoughts, feelings, and behaviors (see Appendix Exhibit 2.1). Additionally, the school psychologist used the Comparing the Negative Fall and the Positive Launch paradigm and the Coping Statements/Positive Affirmation Worksheet (see Appendix Exhibits 2.4 and 5.18) to help Asher generate alternative thinking options when he feels frustrated. His parents and teacher also provided negative self-talk statements from Asher to the school psychologist, and these were used as practice examples for generating alternative interpretations. Some of the replacement thoughts/affirmations he created for himself included "I will try my best," and "If I make a mistake, so what, everyone does."

The final two sessions included reviewing techniques with Asher and sharing outcome data from his teacher on his behavior plan success. A booster session in 3 months also was recommended.

Intervention Results

Asher's baseline preintervention work completion rate was 50%, and by the end of counseling, this had risen to 94%. Figure 7.2 shows social–emotional rating data at 6 months post intervention from his teacher with lowered anxiety. She also reported he was maintaining good work completion rates.

CHILD COUNSELING CASE STUDY: UNSPECIFIED ANXIETY

Reason for Referral

Nita is a 10-year-old fourth grader who is new to the school and was referred by her mother to the school social worker because of a variety of anxiety-related and somatic complaints (i.e., vague references to headaches, stomachaches, fatigue, especially prior to leaving for school). A recent pediatrician visit indicates no illness, and the physician recommended counseling. Teachers note higher than typical

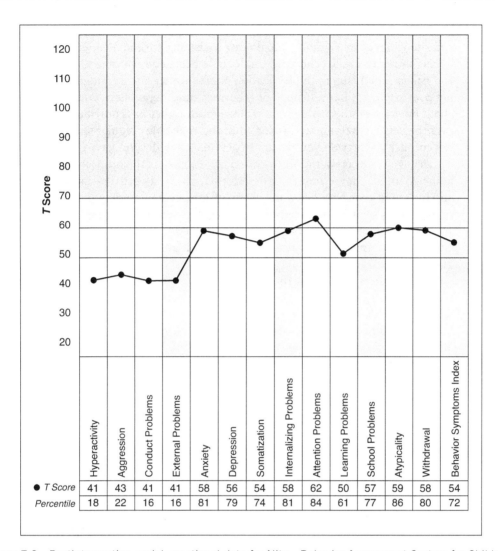

	Hyperactivity	Aggression	Conduct Problems	External Problems	Anxiety	Depression	Somatization	Internalizing Problems	Attention Problems	Learning Problems	School Problems	Atypicality	Withdrawal	Behavior Symptoms Index
● *T Score*	41	43	41	41	58	56	54	58	62	50	57	59	58	54
Percentile	18	22	16	16	81	79	74	81	84	61	77	86	80	72

Figure 7.2 Postintervention social–emotional data for Nita—Behavior Assessment System for Children.

absences for the first 4 weeks of school (i.e., 6), clinging for 3 to 5 minutes when separating from her mother at drop-off, vague body pain complaints at times, and two to three outbursts per week when work is difficult or she is missing her parents and wants to go home.

Background Information

An interview was conducted with Nita's mother, noting Nita is an only child who lives with her mother, stepfather, and maternal grandmother. Her biological father passed away when Nita was age 4, and she is noted to speak of missing him one to two times a year. If the family is talking about her biological father, Nita also occasionally comments that she hopes nothing bad happens to her parents and extended family. For the past year, Nita's mother has home-schooled her as attendance became increasingly difficult at the end of second grade. However, it was noted that Nita's grandmother has recently received a cancer diagnosis that is considered terminal and she will require significant daily care assistance for the next few months. Thus, Nita's mother feels she is no longer able to dedicate enough time to home-schooling and has enrolled Nita in public school. Nita's mother also confided that she is feeling overwhelmed, has a history of recurrent mild depression, and is very worried about her own mother's prognosis. Nita's grandmother has contributed significantly over the years to helping to care for Nita, and they enjoy regular storytime together. Her mother is worried about what impact this loss will soon have on Nita. The family heritage is Choctaw and Euro-American. English is the only language spoken at home. With parent consent to share information, Nita's pediatrician was contacted. She indicated that Nita has a diagnosis of unspecified anxiety disorder. Although symptoms of separation anxiety were present, given the complexity of her current situation, including adjustments to entering school, family stressors for elder care, and history of maternal depression, unspecified anxiety was considered the better diagnosis at this time.

Nita is currently in a fourth-grade classroom, pending assessment of her current academic levels, although teachers report that Nita does appear to know foundational knowledge consistent with beginning fourth graders. Grades for kindergarten through second grade were satisfactory, although it was noted Nita had a Section 504 plan in second grade with accommodations due to panic attacks. Her current teachers mentioned Nita appears to be having some difficulty adjusting to the school routine and a structured work schedule. She also can become frustrated with difficult tasks and asks to go home at times if she is missing or worried about her parents. Her recent vision, hearing, and speech screenings are within normal limits.

Intervention Plan

The first priority for intervention was family support; thus, through a series of home visits and coordinating community services, the family was connected with hospice social workers to prepare for end-of-life care for the grandmother and community mental health supports for the mother. Additionally, in-home visits coached both parents on structuring school morning routines, holding firm on expectations that Nita will attend school each day, and drop-off procedures, and provided information on after-school activities that were available, if needed. Nita's mother agreed to a drop-off plan that would gradually move from escorting Nita to class and long goodbyes to drop-off at the parking circle and one to two positive statements about the school day. Teachers also closely monitored and assisted with the process over a 3-week period.

The second intervention component was exposure therapy addressing separation anxiety characteristics. This portion of the intervention included 3 weeks of daily graduated independence at drop-off separation from her mother. Two relaxation techniques, square breathing (inhale 4 seconds, hold 4 seconds, exhale 4 seconds, hold 4 seconds) and progressive muscle relaxation, also were initially taught to help Nita self-calm after she separated from her mother and was settling into the classroom morning routine (see Appendix Exhibits 4.4 and 4.8). However, these strategies had only modest effects. Thus, two additional strategies (i.e., mental breaks and guided imagery) were later added. Mental breaks were applied as a way to refresh Nita's cognitive energy when overwhelmed. The technique was initiated by her teacher when Nita showed the first signs of restlessness and frustration and included taking 2 to 3 minutes to change to a more pleasant task momentarily (e.g., close eyes to meditate, stand up and stretch, change work locations from desk to table). Guided imagery taught Nita to engage in momentarily imagining a relaxing scene or experience. With guidance from the social worker, Nita chose rain and forest sounds/scenery as her preferred imagery. Initially, a verbal script was tried; however, Nita had difficulty with the concept, so a phone app depicting scenery with soothing music was used in session and by the teacher (i.e., *Rain Sounds—Sleep & Relax*). For home use, Nita's parents chose the *Sleep Bug Pro* app.

Additionally, a third component, CBT, also was provided to address *what if* and *catastrophizing* thinking errors. The CBT cognitive model (see Appendix Exhibit 2.1) was explained, and a copy of the cognitive restructuring handout was provided to her parents (see Appendix Exhibit 5.11). To address *what if* thinking, an if/then questionnaire (see Appendix Exhibit 1.3) was customized to reflect Nita's statements (e.g., "If Mom doesn't pick me up, what am I going to do?" and "If something happens to Dad at work, what would happen?"). The school social worker then reviewed Nita's responses and used this to illustrate and practice reframing answers with positive thoughts (e.g., "Mom is here to pick me up every day and could send Dad or someone else if she can't" and "If Dad gets hurt at work, there is family like Uncle Walt to help him and us"). Baseline BASC parent ratings indicated clinically significant concern for somatization and attention problems, with at-risk range for hyperactivity, aggression, conduct problems, and anxiety (see Figure 7.3).

Counseling Sessions

The first session included introductions, a review of Nita's impression of her new school, and a discussion of her interests and favorite things. The purpose of counseling and advance notice regarding upcoming home visits as well as the limits of confidentiality also were reviewed. Nita indicated she liked some things about the new school but missed all the time at home with her mom and grandmother, and she especially likes the trips to McDonald's or the grocery store during the day. She noted she does not like getting up early for school or when she has to leave her mom as she is afraid something bad might happen and does not know what she can do if her mom is late or does not come back. In talking about her stepfather, Nita indicated that she loves him but gets afraid sometimes because he is a policeman and has to find bad guys. She worries that a bad person could hurt him and does not know what she would do if he gets hurt or sick like her grandmother. She also expressed worry about her grandmother and mentioned how things were changing at the house, including less storytime, nurses coming by sometimes, and having to be quiet.

Sessions were provided twice weekly and extended across 6 months as Nita needed time to adjust to so many changes in her life. At the third month, her grandmother passed away, which also created stress, relating especially to bereavement, and required additional counseling sessions. During this transition time, some of the relaxation techniques and drop-off routine exposures had to be reviewed as well. There also was a temporary setback in separation anxiety symptoms, although they ameliorated in a couple of weeks.

During the final 2 weeks of counseling, Nita's strategies were reviewed, and closure for the counseling was discussed. She also was informed that the social worker, school counselors, and teachers were always available if she needed help. Nita requested to bring three friends to lunch with her and the social worker in the

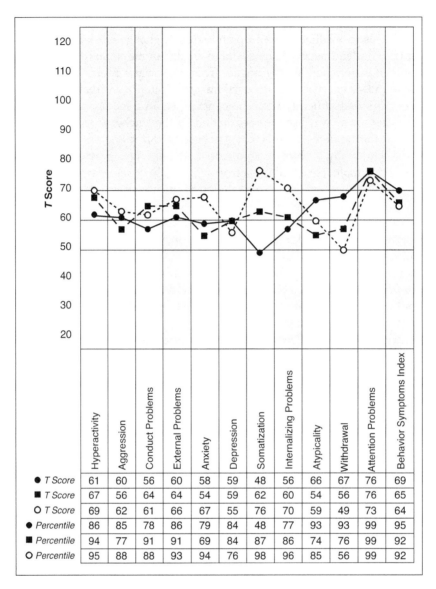

Figure 7.3 Behavior Assessment System for Children data (○ = preintervention, ■ = end intervention, ● = 3 months postintervention).

cafeteria for her last session. Additionally, parent BASC ratings were acquired at the end of the counseling intervention and again at 3 months after intervention

Intervention Results

Baseline data indicated Nita was averaging 1.5 days of absence per week (4 weeks = 6 absences) and experiencing two to three outbursts per week. She struggled daily with separation from her mother, often clinging and protesting for 3 to 5 minutes when her mother came to the classroom to drop her off. Baseline BASC parent ratings indicated clinically significant concern for somatization and attention problems, with at-risk range for hyperactivity, aggression, conduct problems, and anxiety. At the end of intervention, her attendance had improved to just five absences for the semester (2 days were for her grandmother's funeral), although tardies continued to be higher than typical for students. Academically, she was meeting benchmarks in reading, writing, and math. Her mother was consistently dropping her off at the parking circle, and clinging and *what if* and *catastrophizing* statements regarding harm to her parents had ceased. As noted in Figure 7.3, parent ratings at the end of counseling and 3 months after intervention were lower for hyperactivity, aggression, conduct problems, anxiety, and somatization. Ratings were somewhat higher for atypicality, withdrawal, and attention problems. Although parent ratings for withdrawal and attention remained high, these were not concerns experienced by teachers in the classroom. Continued monitoring of Nita's adjustment, attendance, and emotional well-being was recommended as well as booster sessions at 1 and 3 months after counseling. Additionally, frequent teacher communication with parents on Nita's progress was provided.

ADOLESCENT COUNSELING CASE STUDY: SOCIAL ANXIETY

Reason for Referral

Jamila is a 14-year-old eighth grader who was referred to the school counselor because of anxiety symptoms that were negatively impacting her school performance. Teachers noticed several absences and skipping of classes that coincided with group or individual presentation assignments, as well as social events (e.g., field trip, community Habitat for Humanity project). Additionally, her parents had requested school counseling based on recommendations from her outside therapist.

Background Information

Based on parental interview, Jamila is the youngest of three children and lives with both of her parents. Reportedly, all early developmental milestones were met within normal limits, and no significant physical illness or injury was noted. The primary language spoken in the home is English. Upon request, her parents signed for Consent to Share information between the school counselor and the outpatient therapist. The therapist indicated Jamila was first diagnosed with social anxiety last year and began receiving outpatient counseling following a parent-initiated psychiatric hospitalization 7 months ago for a panic attack. At that time, Jamila presented with chest pain, nausea, and an overwhelming sense of death. The precipitating event was noted as anticipation of a class presentation of her book report that also was being critiqued by the teacher for her final grade. The outpatient therapist was working with the parents on strategies to avoid enabling Jamila's social withdrawal (e.g., not allowing her to sleep in and arrive late or to stay home from school as well as making excuses for her when she wanted to avoid family social events or mosque) and noted this was improving. Additionally, Jamila was participating in exposure therapy within the clinic setting and had experienced some success. However, the therapist noted she requested collaboration with the school to provide opportunities for generalizing skills to a more naturalistic setting (as compared to the outpatient clinic) and for practice with social situations in school. Jamila's parents were highly supportive of adding a school-based counseling intervention.

According to school records, Jamila missed 16 days of school last year and had eight absences during the first quarter (i.e., 9 weeks) of school this year as well as 23 tardies. Additionally, she has discipline referrals for skipping five classes this quarter. She is behind academically because of missed assignments and in jeopardy of failing three classes. Her vision, hearing, and speech screenings are all within normal limits. Teachers describe Jamila as a kind, caring, and very polite student. They believe she is smart and capable, as demonstrated on her written work. However, they also note concern for her lack of participation in class; withdrawal from social interactions, including sitting with others at lunch; noticeable discomfort in group activities; and high number of nurse office visit requests. The school nurse indicates Jamila had 21 visits to his office for vague physical complaints (i.e., headache, nausea, stomachaches) this academic year with requests to go home. However, when the nurse contacted her parents, they noted Jamila has had a recent physical wellness exam and is not ill. The parents did not disclose her diagnosis of social anxiety at that time.

Intervention Plan

The intervention plan for Jamila targeted two components. First, exposure therapy was utilized to increase her participation in school academic activities, particularly those related to possible evaluation (e.g., group projects, presentations, community service project requirement). SUDs data were utilized to progress monitor exposures. Second, CBT with Socratic questioning was used to challenge two cognitive distortions: *catastrophizing* and *mind reading*. Pre- and postintervention progress monitoring data for social–emotional functioning utilized the Beck's Anxiety Inventory (BAI) self-report measure. Baseline indicated a raw score of 45 on the BAI (severe).

Counseling Sessions

It was decided in collaboration with teachers and Jamila's parents that 30-minute counseling sessions would be provided twice each week. The first week included introductions, rapport building, a review of the goals of the counseling, psychoeducation regarding social anxiety, and a discussion of the limits of confidentiality. Jamila shared her original hospitalization experience and mentioned that outpatient clinic therapy had helped, although she still found it hard to not be anxious in school. She expressed fear of evaluation in public and by teachers, noting it is "really embarrassing" when she "messes up" and she feels shame. She is afraid that if she makes an error, peers will not be friends, the teacher will fail her for the class, and she will never pass or graduate high school, which will ultimately mean she cannot have a good career. She also expressed a desire to perform well in school and finish the semester on grade level despite her apprehensions. Her preference is to avoid performance situations, and she would like the school to eliminate all those requirements. However, the school counselor explained that the goal would be to improve her ability to tolerate required performance events with a new perspective, rather than avoidance.

During the second week, the school counselor reviewed the concepts of exposure therapy (see Appendix Exhibits 5.1–5.7) and collaborated with Jamila in jointly developing a fear hierarchy that would include expanding her social interactions at school and participation in both a class presentation and a community service project with peers. Jamila noted that preparing her presentation for the social studies class and practicing alone at home were low-level tasks, sitting in the empty classroom and practicing her presentation in the room with only the counselor present were moderate anxiety-evoking tasks, whereas presenting to the teacher only and then with classmates present were high-anxiety situations. It was agreed that exposures would start the following week and move up the hierarchy as end-of-session SUDs rating reached 5 or less. Jamila was also informed that her attendance and nurse visits would be monitored and reviewed periodically with her parents with the goal of improving those. Her parents had agreed to an incentive program at home that included earning favorite activities and privileges Jamila requested (e.g., weekend visits to grandmother, gift certificate for the mall, upgraded smartphone) once significant improvement was accomplished.

During the third through ninth weeks, exposures were systematically applied and monitored with SUDs ratings, and data were reviewed with Jamila to help her understand how her autonomic anxiety responses were diminishing over time and how there were not horrific negative responses from others that she had predicted. Additionally, the school counselor infused discussions of two cognitive distortions, *catastrophizing* and *mind reading*. The Worry Script technique, the Four-Column Functional Assessment of ABCD worksheet, and the Perspective-Taking Worksheet strategies were applied as homework assignments and reviewed during sessions (see Appendix Exhibits 2.7, 5.9, 5.16, 5.17). In the 10th week session, closure of the counseling sequence was discussed, and Jamila completed the BAI. The last session reviewed her goals, strategies, and outcome data and ended in a cupcake celebration with the counselor.

Intervention Results

Jamila's baseline intervention data included 8 absences, 23 tardies, and 21 nurse office visits. Over the course of intervention, she had acquired only one absence and six tardies with no nurse office visits for the last 5 weeks. Her SUDs data for exposures had continued to start lower and reduce quicker (using 5-minute intervals), as she progressed through repeated exposures. She was able to give her class presentation, and although she described the process as stressful, she did persevere, acknowledging it was not as horrible as she thought it would be. She also managed to complete her community service project by volunteering in a nursing home with a group of four other students for a day. Her BAI moved from a diagnostic range of severe (45) to moderate (22) (see Figure 7.4). Continued monitoring of her attendance, participation, and a booster session at 3 months after intervention were recommended.

ADOLESCENT COUNSELING CASE STUDY: OCD

Reason for Referral

Susan is a 16-year-old 10th-grade student who was referred by her parents and outpatient therapist for supplemental school-based counseling related to OCD symptoms. Her teachers noted that she has a strong need for order at her desk and the surrounding area, which is intrusive to others at times, and perfectionistic

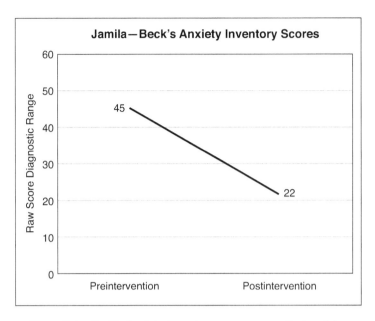

Figure 7.4   Beck's Anxiety Inventory progress monitoring data.

tendencies regarding work, and she can perseverate on details during timed tests, causing her not to finish all items. Both of her fathers expressed concern for her achievement and support for collaboration among her psychiatrist, outside therapist, and the school. Parental consent to share ongoing treatment and school intervention data with the outside therapist was granted.

Background Information

Susan is an only child adopted at the age of 9 by her fathers, and most of her prior home and medical history is unknown, although she did receive diagnoses of anxiety, OCD, and episodic depression from the age of 6. English is the only language spoken at home. Since her adoption, her general physical health has been good, and the prior diagnosis of depression has been removed. It was thought having a stable, caring home environment had ameliorated some symptoms. She is described as having two very good friends at school who also are in her after-school ballet class. Susan's parents also noted she can be delightfully funny with a keen sense of humor, is athletically inclined, and is very smart. They do share concern for how hard she drives herself at times for good grades, perfect appearance, and dance performance. She also reportedly exhibits a strong need for cleanliness as well as order in her room, clothing, and work. She is currently participating in a 1-hour intensive evening outpatient therapy program, three times weekly for 3 months, to address OCD symptoms, including unwanted and intrusive thoughts of perfectionism in handwriting, grooming, dance performance, and organization of her personal space. The program utilizes exposure therapy and CBT. Homework assignments for the program incorporate both the home and school environment; thus, the psychologist at the school was asked to provide services as well.

Teachers and classroom observation data confirm that Susan participates in some ritualistic behaviors (e.g., arranging her pens and pencils across the top of the desk from small to large, keeping her notebook centered, and picking up any items on the floor of surrounding students, placing those in the bin under their seats). She also has been noted to only use pencils on tests and worksheets so she can erase and rewrite answers, which happens frequently. Her habit of rewriting and carefully forming letters slows down her response time, which can interfere with completing timed tests. This is especially concerning for her performance on exams and high-stakes state testing. Her teachers are concerned it may also hinder her achievement on college entrance exams and her options for dual enrollment in college starting in 11th grade. Otherwise, Susan is described as a dedicated, hardworking, and enjoyable student to work with.

School records since fourth grade indicate good attendance and grades (i.e., mostly As) but somewhat average end-of-year exam and state testing scores. Hearing, vision, and speech screenings are within normal limits. She is administered medication for OCD at home, and there are no school nurse visits noted.

Intervention Plan

The school-based intervention plan was designed to supplement her outside OCD therapy program over the course of 3 months; thus, most of the psychoeducation, CBT training, and exposure therapy training components were delivered at the clinic. The school psychologist's role was to review concepts, as needed, and coordinate supplemental exposures in sessions and through the classroom. The goals from her OCD treatment program included identifying anxiety-provoking situations, participating in daily activities while tolerating intrusive thoughts, preventing avoidance and accommodating behaviors (e.g., rewriting answers, straightening items on desk/floor), and maintaining a SUDs rating of ≤5 for exposures. The clinic had administered the Children's Yale-Brown Obsessive-Compulsive Scale (CY-BOCS) as a baseline measure. She received a 21 for her global severity score, indicating moderate interference in daily functioning related to her obsessions/compulsions. For obsession-related items, Susan indicated current symptoms, which included fear of acting on unwanted impulses, fear of not being perfect, and worry about things being unclean or messy. She presented with compulsions related to need for symmetry, need for perfect grooming, and cleaning. She was not to engage in repeated rituals such as checking her appearance in mirrors frequently, rewriting work, and reorganizing personal items. Her therapist noted she had fair insight into these characteristics.

Counseling Sessions

During the first counseling session with the psychologist at the school, Susan was advised as to the nature of the counseling intervention referral, provided an overview of the exposures that would be conducted over the coming weeks based on the fear hierarchy she had completed with her OCD program, and advised as to the limits of confidentiality. Over the course of 3 months, the psychologist at the school structured and monitored exposures in collaboration with the outside provider. These included leaving items on the top of her desk messy without rearranging them, completing assignments in pen so she could not erase, wearing mismatched nail polish, and tolerating smudges of dirt on her chair, desk, and book bag. The ABC Method and ABC Record Form formats were used to guide debriefing discussions following each exposure (see Appendix Exhibits 2.2 and 2.5), as this was consistent with the OCD therapy program paradigm for explaining the relations among activating events, beliefs, and consequence. School counseling sessions were closed at the end of Susan's outpatient treatment program given her progress.

Intervention Results

Susan's baseline CY-BOCS score was 21, indicating moderate interference of OCD symptoms with her daily functioning. Postintervention, her CY-BOCS score was 8, which falls in the mild range. As noted in Figure 7.5, her SUDs score drop during exposures from peak discomfort at the beginning to the end of the exposure remained below 5, starting on January 31 till the end of treatment. It should be noted that January 24 was an easy low-level distress item on the fear hierarchy Susan created. Exposures moved up sequentially to more difficult items higher on her fear hierarchy each session.

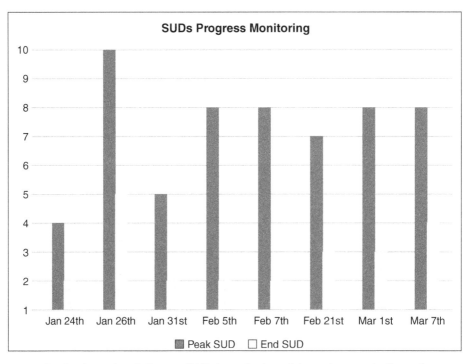

Figure 7.5   Subjective units of distress (SUDs) monitoring of decay from peak discomfort progress.

Appendix: Counseling Worksheets and Handouts

Exploring Thought Patterns

Exhibit 1.1   Student Sentence Completion Exercise
Exhibit 1.2   Adolescent Sentence Completion Exercise
Exhibit 1.3   If/Then Questionnaire

Subjective Units of Distress (SUDs)

Exhibit 1.4   Subjective Units of Distress Scale: Feeling Thermometer
Exhibit 1.5   Subjective Units of Distress Scale: What I Feel Inside

CBT Cognitive Model

Exhibit 2.1   Cognitive Behavior Therapy Model
Exhibit 2.2   Three-Step ABC Model
Exhibit 2.3   ABC Model: Alternate Consequences
Exhibit 2.4   Comparing the Negative Fall and the Positive Launch
Exhibit 2.5   ABC Record Form
Exhibit 2.6   Four-Column Functional Assessment of ABCs
Exhibit 2.7   Four-Column Functional Assessment of ABCD
Exhibit 2.8   Three-Step ABC Figure Worksheet Example
Exhibit 2.9   Three-Step ABC Worksheet
Exhibit 2.10   ABC Worksheet

Identifying Feelings

Exhibit 4.1   Physiological Stress Reaction List
Exhibit 4.2   My Feelings Map

Relaxation Training

Exhibit 4.3   Counselor's Checklist for Relaxation Training
Exhibit 4.4   Relaxation Training: Information for Parents/Caregivers
Exhibit 4.5   Relaxation Log
Exhibit 4.6   Relaxation Journal Worksheet Example
Exhibit 4.7   Relaxation Journal Worksheet
Exhibit 4.8   Relaxation Script Examples

Behavioral Activation

Exposure Therapy

Cognitive Restructuring

EXHIBIT 1.1

Student Sentence Completion Exercise

1. My best class is _____

2. I am good at _____

3. When I grow up, I want to be _____

4. Other kids _____

5. My family is _____

6. The worst thing is _____

7. At home _____

8. What upsets me is _____

9. People think _____

10. The best _____

11. My mind _____

12. Most girls _____

13. At school _____

14. I feel _____

15. Boys are _____

EXHIBIT 1.2

Adolescent Sentence Completion Exercise

1. My favorite class subject is _____

2. The best thing I do is _____

3. My career goal is _____

4. My friends are best at _____

5. The best thing my family could do is _____

6. If I could change something, I would _____

7. My parents' ideas are _____

8. The most perturbing thing is _____

9. People don't know I think _____

10. In my personal life _____

11. My thoughts often _____

12. Most females consider _____

13. My teachers think I am _____

14. My purpose in life is _____

15. Men are usually _____

EXHIBIT 1.3

If/Then Questionnaire

IF   I ace the test,   THEN   _____

IF   I make a mistake,   THEN   _____

IF   Others are nice to me,   THEN   _____

IF   I feel hurt,   THEN   _____

IF   I join the group,   THEN   _____

IF   I am mad,   THEN   _____

IF   My parents are happy,   THEN   _____

IF   I let people down,   THEN   _____

EXHIBIT 1.4

Subjective Units of Distress Scale: Feeling Thermometer

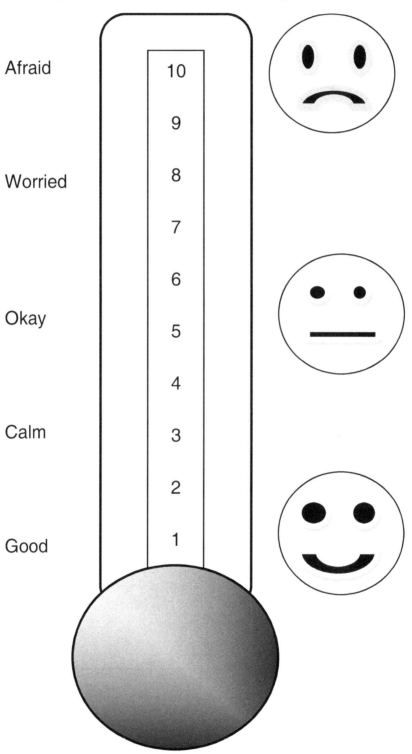

EXHIBIT 1.5

Subjective Units of Distress Scale: What I Feel Inside

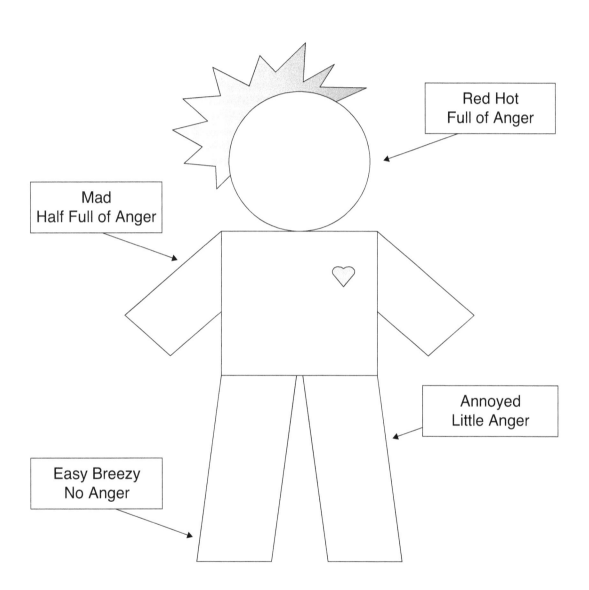

EXHIBIT 2.1

Cognitive Behavior Therapy Model

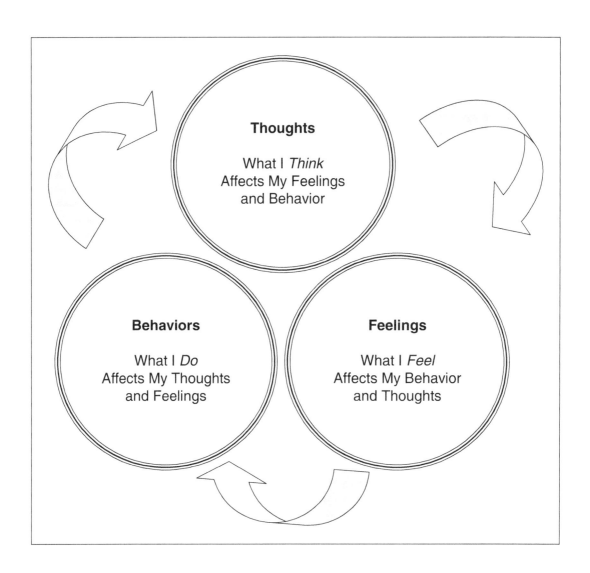

Thoughts

What I *Think*
Affects My Feelings
and Behavior

Behaviors

What I *Do*
Affects My Thoughts
and Feelings

Feelings

What I *Feel*
Affects My Behavior
and Thoughts

EXHIBIT 2.2

Three-Step ABC Model

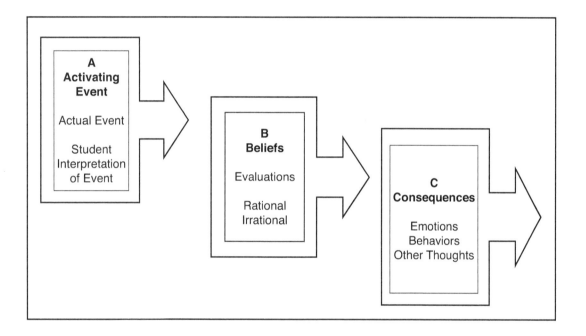

EXHIBIT 2.3

ABC Model: Alternate Consequences

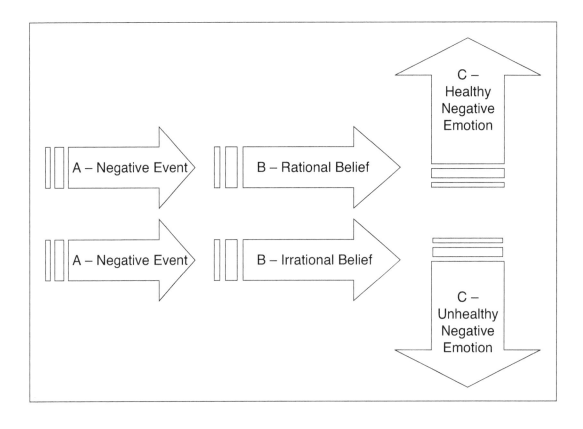

EXHIBIT 2.4

Comparing the Negative Fall and the Positive Launch

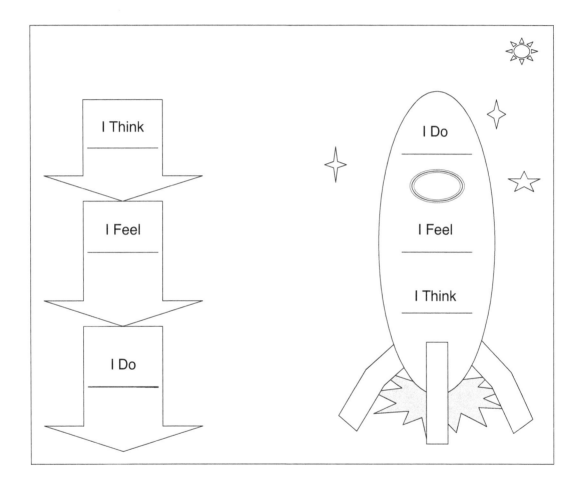

EXHIBIT 2.5

ABC Record Form

A—Activating Event	B—Beliefs	C—Consequences
(What happened? What action did you take? What was your first thought?)	(What automatic thought did you have?)	(What are the possible consequences?)
What type of thought was it?	Rational *or* irrational? What is something different that you could tell yourself?	What could you do differently next time?

Review notes:

EXHIBIT 2.6

Four-Column Functional Assessment of ABCs

A—Activating Event	B—Behavior	C—Consequences Short Term	C—Consequences Long Term
What happened immediately before?	What action did you take?	What was the immediate result? (What happened in 5 seconds, 1 hour, 2 hours?)	What are the long-term outcomes or results?

Review notes:

EXHIBIT 2.7

Four-Column Functional Assessment of ABCD

A—Activating Event	B—Behavior	C—Consequences	D—Disputing
What happened immediately before?	What action did you take?	What was the outcome?	Challenge your belief— Is it true or false? What is an alternative rational belief? What *facts* support this? What *facts* do not support this?

Review notes:

EXHIBIT 2.8

Three-Step ABC Figure Worksheet Example

Purpose: To help children/adolescents understand the relationship among experienced events, their beliefs about the events, and various consequences that they may endure.

Developmental considerations: Counselors may want to present visual illustrations to younger children (e.g., clip art or magazine cutouts) to help them understand the relationship among antecedent events, beliefs, and consequences.

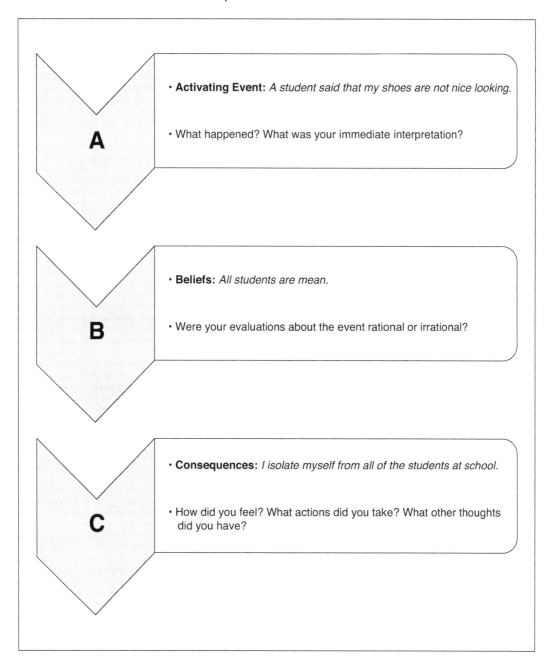

A
- **Activating Event:** *A student said that my shoes are not nice looking.*
- What happened? What was your immediate interpretation?

B
- **Beliefs:** *All students are mean.*
- Were your evaluations about the event rational or irrational?

C
- **Consequences:** *I isolate myself from all of the students at school.*
- How did you feel? What actions did you take? What other thoughts did you have?

EXHIBIT 2.9

Three-Step ABC Worksheet

Directions: In the following boxes, describe a situation/event, your belief(s) about the event, and the consequences/outcomes of your belief(s).

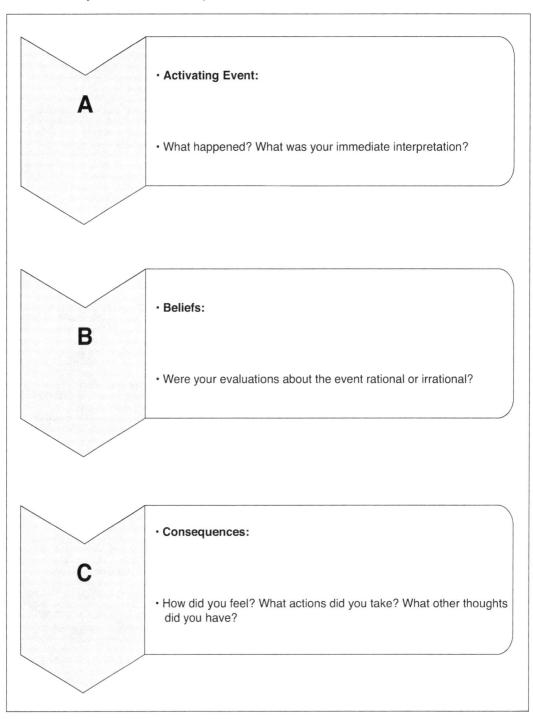

A

• **Activating Event:**

• What happened? What was your immediate interpretation?

B

• **Beliefs:**

• Were your evaluations about the event rational or irrational?

C

• **Consequences:**

• How did you feel? What actions did you take? What other thoughts did you have?

EXHIBIT 2.10

ABC Worksheet

Directions: In the following boxes, describe a situation/event, your belief(s) about the event, and the consequences/outcomes of your belief(s).

A (Activating Event)	Negative Event	Negative Event
B (Belief)	**Rational Belief**	**Irrational Belief**
C (Consequence)	**Healthy Emotion**	**Unhealthy Emotion**

EXHIBIT 4.1

Physiological Stress Reaction List

Directions: Mark each item that applies to you.

Head

☐ Forehead wrinkling

☐ Eyes squinting

☐ Eyes rolling

☐ Frowning

☐ Scowling

☐ Staring

☐ Lip pursing

☐ Lip smacking

☐ Dry mouth

☐ Swallowing

☐ Jaw clenching

☐ Teeth grinding

☐ Neck rolling

☐ Dizziness

☐ Feeling faint

☐ Feeling flushed/turning red

Shoulders/Back/Torso

☐ Shoulders pulling up

☐ Shoulders rolling forward

☐ Shoulder ache

☐ Backache

☐ Back tightening

☐ Indigestion

☐ Stomach growling

☐ Stomachache

☐ Rocking

☐ Heart racing

Arms/Hands

☐ Fist clenching

☐ Finger tapping

☐ Folded arms

☐ Sweaty palms

Legs/Feet

☐ Foot tapping

☐ Shaking

EXHIBIT 4.2

My Feelings Map

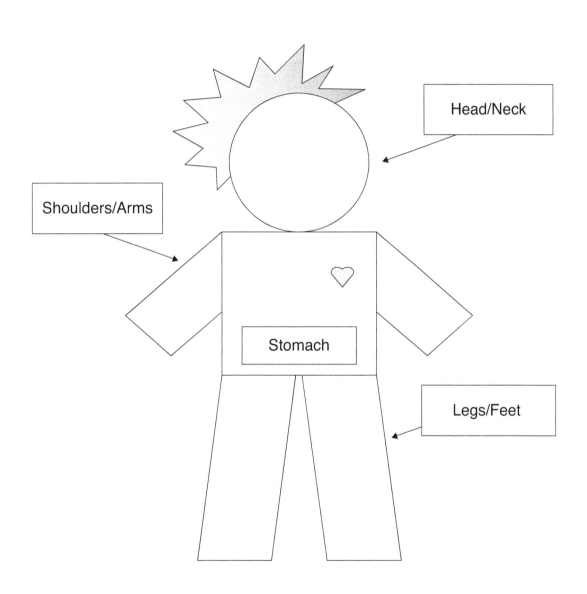

EXHIBIT 4.3

Counselor's Checklist for Relaxation Training

 Explain the relaxation training process to the parent/caregiver and student.

 Introduce the various relaxation techniques to the students
- Diaphragmatic breathing
- Progressive muscle relaxation
- Guided/visual imagery

 Rehearse the appropriate application of the various techniques during the counseling session (e.g., using relaxation scripts).

 Prompt the student to maintain a relaxation journal to help him or her monitor the effectiveness of relaxation techniques.

 In subsequent sessions, review the student's relaxation journal to identify critical patterns and engage in collaborative problem-solving regarding how to optimize the student's success.

 Continue to practice the application of the relaxation techniques and help the student identify when they can be used.

 Repeat the process until the student demonstrates a clear understanding of the correct application of the techniques.

EXHIBIT 4.4

Relaxation Training: Information for Parents/Caregivers

Relaxation Training

Relaxation training is a therapeutic technique that can be utilized to help individuals reduce high levels of anxiety and stress. Relaxation training is based on the idea that although most people encounter stressful and anxiety-producing events, people respond to stress and anxiety in different ways. Given that stressful and anxiety-producing events can cause individuals to feel overwhelmed and result in a heightened sense of anxiety, relaxation training is generally implemented to help individuals learn how to cope with stress and anxiety in a healthy manner by learning how to remain calm and slow their bodies down (e.g., manage a racing heartbeat). Counselors can teach children/adolescents a variety of relaxation techniques throughout their sessions.

The Relaxation Training Process

The first step in the process entails explaining to the student the idea behind and the value of relaxation training. After the counselor provides a general overview of relaxation training, the counselor then teaches the child/adolescent about various relaxation techniques. Finally, the counselor engages in various exercises and activities during the sessions to help the student learn how to correctly apply each technique (e.g., using relaxation scripts). Students are also encouraged to maintain a relaxation journal to learn how to monitor and evaluate the effectiveness of the techniques as a personal coping strategy. The relaxation journal can also be used to help the counselor identify critical patterns with the student and engage in collaborative problem-solving regarding how to optimize the student's success.

What Are Relaxation Techniques?

There are several relaxation techniques that children/adolescents can learn to help them remain calm and cope with stress and anxiety. These include the following:

1. *Diaphragmatic breathing*: Students learn how to engage in deep, slow, and relaxed abdominal breathing.
2. *Progressive muscle relaxation*: Students learn how to intentionally tense and relax various muscle groups in the body.
3. *Visual and guided imagery*: Students learn the method of actively imagining a pleasant and peaceful scene that they find calming (e.g., the beach, playing with the dog at the park, going to Disney World). This technique can also be applied to visualizing a positive outcome for an upcoming event that they find anxiety provoking (e.g., imagine performing well in the play, imagine scoring a point for the team).

Below Is an Example of a Guided Safe Place Imagery Exercise

We are going to close our eyes for a couple of minutes. Imagine yourself in a peaceful and soothing place. Imagine that you are on a beach. Picture details about this peaceful place. Is the sand warm? Are you at the beach with friends? See the waves washing onto the shoreline. Listen to the sound of the waves. What else do you hear? Listen to the calls of the seagulls. Imagine the wind blowing softly. Can you feel the cool breeze? How does it make you feel to be in this peaceful place?

EXHIBIT 4.5

Relaxation Log

Date/Time: _____

Relaxation Strategy Used: _____

Experience: _____ (What Happened)

Circle Rating *Before* Relaxation:

    Low   1   2   3   4   5   6   7   8   9   10   High

Circle Rating *After* Relaxation:

    Low   1   2   3   4   5   6   7   8   9   10   High

EXHIBIT 4.6

Relaxation Journal Worksheet Example

Purpose: Help children/adolescents understand the relationship among experienced events, their stress and anxiety level, and use of relaxation techniques (use SUDs to rate stress/anxiety).

Developmental Considerations: Present visual illustrations to younger children (e.g., smiley faces) to help them identify the level of stress/anxiety they experience with each situation.

Stressful Event	Anxiety or Stress Level	What Physical and Emotional Symptoms Did You Feel?	Relaxation Technique	Anxiety or Stress Level After Relaxation
My teacher notified the class about an upcoming test.	7	*My heart was racing; my muscles were tensed.* *My palms started sweating.* *I felt scared and nervous.*	*Deep breathing*	3
I found out my best friend is moving.	8	*My eyes got teary, my voice started shaking, and I couldn't talk.* *I felt overwhelmingly sad, like I would never have a friend or fun again.*	*Positive self-affirmations* *Took a walk to calm down, and imagine visiting my friend in the new neighborhood*	5
I have a physical education test for gymnastics in an hour.	9	*My leg muscles are tightening up, and I think I am getting a headache.* *I feel like I will fail.*	*Deep breathing* *Progressive muscle relaxation for legs* *Imagine self-performing well*	6
I lost my homework.	6	*My thoughts are spinning; I feel frozen and can't think what to do.* *I feel afraid to tell the teacher.*	*Take a few moments for deep breathing* *Imagine what I will tell teacher*	4
I have to sit by a new kid tomorrow.	5	*I don't know if he or she will like me. I don't know if I will like the new kid.* *I feel nervous and want to stay home from school.*	*Take a few moments to imagine a peaceful place* *Take a few moments to image that the meeting is fun*	

EXHIBIT 4.7

Relaxation Journal Worksheet

Directions: Reflect on an incident that happened within the last month. List your stress level and describe how you felt before you utilized a specific relaxation technique and list your stress level after you utilized the relaxation technique.

Stressful Event	Anxiety or Stress Level	What Physical and Emotional Symptoms Did You Feel?	Relaxation Technique	Anxiety or Stress Level After Relaxation

EXHIBIT 4.8

Relaxation Script Examples

Progressive Muscle Relaxation Technique

We are going to do some exercises that will help you learn how to stay calm and relaxed. First, sit back, close your eyes, and get comfortable—try to allow your worries and stressors to melt away as you become relaxed.

- Take some very deep breaths. Try to imagine your chest inflating like a large balloon—fill up your balloon as much as you possibly can. Now release your breath slowly—very slowly—and imagine exhaling your tension, all of your tension. Then, completely empty your tension so you're ready to breathe deeply again. [Repeat several times until the client starts feeling more relaxed.]
- Now turn your attention to your feet. Begin to tense your feet by curling your toes and the arch of your foot. Notice and witness the tension. [Have the client stay tense for about 5–10 seconds followed by about 20 seconds of relaxation.] Now release the tension in your feet. Notice the new feeling of relaxation. Notice how you feel different than you did when you were tense.
- Now begin to focus on your lower legs. Tense the muscles in the back of your legs. Get your muscles really hard, and pay attention to the tension. [Have the client stay tense for about 5–10 seconds followed by about 20 seconds of relaxation.] Now release the tension in your legs, and pay attention to the feeling of relaxation again. Remember to keep taking deep breaths. Now tense the muscles of your upper leg and in the middle of your body. You can do this by tightly squeezing your thighs together. Make sure you feel the tension. [Have the client stay tense for about 5–10 seconds followed by about 20 seconds of relaxation.] And now release. Feel the tension leaving your muscles.

MUSCLE GROUPS THAT MAY BE SELECTED

Right and left hand/forearm	Forehead	Upper back
Right and left upper arm	Eyes and cheeks	Lower back
Right and left upper leg	Mouth and jaw	Hips and legs
Right and left lower leg	Torso	Shoulders
Right and left foot	Stomach	Shoulder blades

Diaphragmatic Breathing

Touch your abdominal (or belly) muscles. Inhale slowly. Take a deep and powerful breath. Hold this breath for 3 to 5 seconds. Exhale slowly. Take another slow and deep breath. Hold this breath again. Now exhale slowly. Feel your hand moving slowly. Take another slow and deep breath. Exhale slowly. Release all of the tension. Now relax!

Guided Safe Place Imagery

Close your eyes. Imagine yourself in a peaceful and soothing place. Imagine that you are on a beach. Picture details about this peaceful place. Are you at the beach alone? See the waves washing onto the shoreline. Listen to the sound of the waves. What else do you hear? Listen to the calls of the seagulls. Imagine the wind blowing. Can you feel the cool breeze? How does it feel to be in this peaceful place?

EXHIBIT 4.9

Counselor's Checklist for Behavioral Activation

 Explain the behavioral activation process to the parent/caregiver and student.

 Help the student list a variety of activities that he or she can pursue.

 Help the student to generate a weekly schedule and include the activities on the schedule.

 Teach the student how to monitor his or her mood before and after various activities are completed.

 Encourage the student to monitor his or her moods throughout the week so that you all can discuss his or her progress in later sessions.

 In subsequent sessions, review the student's mood-level ratings, identify critical patterns with the student (e.g., activities that may not result in a significant mood change), and engage in collaborative problem-solving regarding how to optimize the student's success.

 Repeat the process until the student's activity-monitoring data show that he or she is consistently experiencing more pleasurable feelings before and after various activities are completed.

EXHIBIT 4.10

Behavioral Activation: Information for Parents/Caregivers

Behavioral Activation

Behavioral activation is an intervention strategy that is implemented to help individuals cope with social withdrawal and depressed moods. Behavioral activation is based on the premise that people are less likely to engage in enjoyable activities when they feel depressed. When their activity level declines, they may become even more withdrawn, unmotivated, and lethargic. Hence, there is a high probability that their depressed moods will continue to worsen. This may also cause these individuals to feel even more isolated and detached from others. Behavioral activation can help individuals gradually engage in pleasurable activities to decrease their avoidance and isolation, and improve their mood. Engaging in pleasurable activities can be challenging for individuals who are not motivated and are depressed. Thus, your child's counselor will support your child throughout the process to help your child succeed.

Behavioral Activation Process

First, the child is encouraged to identify and list a variety of activities that she or he can pursue. The counselor then encourages the child to engage first in activities that are easy to complete and then assigns increasingly challenging activities throughout the course of treatment. Students are also encouraged to start off by completing a few activities and gradually increase the number of activities that they are expected to pursue each week. After a list of activities is identified, the child is encouraged to plan his or her weekly schedule to include the chosen activities. To help students understand how engaging in several activities can impact their moods using behavioral activation, the final step of the process includes encouraging students to monitor their moods before and after the activity is completed, sometimes keeping a daily log. Monitoring their progress can help students recognize their individual accomplishments. This can elevate mood, increase motivation, and encourage them to keep moving forward. Behavioral activation may be repeated until the child's activity-monitoring data show that he or she is consistently experiencing more pleasurable feelings before and after various activities are completed.

What Kind of Activities Are Children Encouraged to Pursue?

Students are encouraged to engage in a variety of activities. Here are some guidelines that the counselor will follow when helping students identify activities to complete:

1. *Safe*: Activities should be safe.
2. *Achievable*: Activities should promote a sense of accomplishment.
3. *Reasonable*: Activities should be reasonable to complete.
4. *Meaningful*: Activities should be meaningful to the student.

An example of an activity monitoring table that might be assigned for homework is below.

0	1	2	3	4	5	6	7	8	9	10
None	Low				Okay				High	Extreme

Activity: Reading fiction, May 1.

	Depression Feelings	Pleasurable Feelings
Before	8	2
After	4	6

Activity: Going to the mall with friends, May 2.

	Depression Feelings	Pleasurable Feelings
Before	6	1
After	2	8

EXHIBIT 4.11

Activity Identification and Monitoring Worksheet Example

Purpose: To help students identify a range of activities that they can pursue and to monitor how each activity impacts their mood.

Developmental Considerations: Counselors may want to present visual illustrations to younger children (e.g., smiley faces) to help them identify their mood level in response to each activity.

List of Positively Rewarding Activities

1. Reading fictional material
2. Singing in my choir
3. Going to the mall with friends
4. Local sightseeing
5. Fishing
6. Bowling
7. Walking and jogging
8. Going to lunch dates with my sister
9. Attending family dinners
10. Camping

0	1	2	3	4	5	6	7	8	9	10
None	Low				Okay				High	Extreme

Activity: Reading fiction, May 1.

	Depression Feelings	Pleasurable Feelings
Before	8	2
After	4	6

Activity: Going to the mall with friends, May 2.

Before	6	1
After	2	8

EXHIBIT 4.12

Positively Rewarding Activities

Directions: List activities that might be fun and pleasurable for you. If you cannot think of any, work with a partner to help you identify a variety of activities. Let us see how many activities you can list. Ready, set, go!

_____   _____

_____   _____

_____   _____

_____   _____

_____   _____

_____   _____

_____   _____

_____   _____

EXHIBIT 4.13

Weekly Activity Schedule Worksheet Example

Purpose: To help students plan their weekly activities in advance.

	Sunday	Monday	Tuesday	Wednesday	Thursday	Friday	Saturday
8:00–9:00 a.m.	Walking	Walking	Walking	Walking	Walking	Walking	Walking
9:00–10:00 a.m.		Class	Class	Class	Class	Class	
10:00–11:00 a.m.		Class	Class	Class	Class	Class	Cleaning my house
11:00 a.m.– 12:00 p.m.	Singing in my choir						Cleaning my house
12:00–1:00 p.m.	Singing in my choir	Lunch date			Baking a cake		
1:00–2:00 p.m.							Fishing
2:00–3:00 p.m.	Family dinner	Mentoring	Sight-seeing	Mentoring		Mentoring	Fishing
3:00–4:00 p.m.	Family dinner	Mentoring	Sight-seeing	Mentoring		Mentoring	Fishing

EXHIBIT 4.14

Weekly Activity Schedule

Directions: List the activities that you will complete during each time block daily throughout the upcoming week.

	Sunday	Monday	Tuesday	Wednesday	Thursday	Friday	Saturday
8:00–9:00 a.m.							
9:00–10:00 a.m.							
10:00–11:00 a.m.							
11:00 a.m.–12:00 p.m.							
12:00–1:00 p.m.							
1:00–2:00 p.m.							
2:00–3:00 p.m.							
3:00–4:00 p.m.							
4:00–5:00 p.m.							
5:00–6:00 p.m.							
6:00–7:00 p.m.							
7:00–8:00 p.m.							

EXHIBIT 5.1

Counselor's Checklist for Exposure/Response Prevention (E/RP) Therapy

Explain the exposure/response prevention therapeutic process to the parent/caregiver and student.

Gather the parent/caregiver's consent and student's assent to participate in E/RP therapy.

Identify the student's fear-provoking triggers with the student.

Create a fear hierarchy with the student using the Subjective Units of Distress Scale (SUDS).

Expose the student to the fear-provoking stimuli.

Start with lower ranked fears and gradually move to higher ranked fears.

Encourage the student to endure the discomfort and utilize relaxation techniques to overcome his or her distress.

Assess the student's level of anxiety during the exposure exercises using the SUDS.

Repeat the process until the student's SUDS data indicate that the student consistently experiences low levels of anxiety (e.g., minor worry, calmness, and relaxation) when exposed to the stimuli.

EXHIBIT 5.2

Exposure/Response Prevention Therapy:
Information for Parents/Caregivers

Exposure/Response Prevention Therapy

Exposure/response prevention (E/RP) therapy is a therapeutic technique that is often utilized to help individuals face and overcome exaggerated fears. E/RP is grounded in the idea that a person must confront his or her fears to learn how to cope with them. When people avoid those situations that provoke anxiety and distress, their heightened fear is more likely to remain. Although the avoidance may serve as a protective response for the individual, constant avoidance can cause the anxiety to become worse as opposed to getting better. E/RP can help children and adolescents manage their fears and reduce their anxiety.

The E/RP Process

First, the counselor collaborates with the child to identify situations and circumstances that produce the child's fear. The child then creates a fear hierarchy with the counselor by ranking the level of anxiety that is experienced with each situation. Next, the child is voluntarily exposed to the fear-producing situations under the supervision of his or her counselor. During this exposure, response prevention will occur in which the counselor encourages the child to refrain from avoiding the fear-producing situation(s). Instead, the child is encouraged to endure any discomfort knowing it will soon subside. Students are first exposed to situations that provoke lower levels of anxiety and gradually are exposed to situations that provoke higher levels of anxiety. The child's anxiety level is assessed throughout the process to monitor his or her progress. The exposure discontinues when he or she is experiencing more relaxed and calm feelings in response to the fear-producing situation(s).

What Does the Exposure Entail?

Exposure exercises can be executed through several methods, ranging from less intense to highly intense. In the order of intensity levels, such methods include the following:

1. *Imaginal exposure:* The student imagines himself or herself in the fear-producing situation (e.g., presenting a book report in class).
2. *In-session exposure/role-playing:* The student acts out a scenario in which he or she is exposed to the fear-producing situation (e.g., practicing giving a book report with the counselor).
3. *Viewing visual images of the fear-eliciting situation:* The student views visual representations of the fear-producing situation (e.g., pictures and videos).
4. *In vivo exposure:* The student directly confronts the situation (e.g., gives the book report in front of differing audiences and then the class).

It is important to note that all exposures are agreed on in collaboration between the student and counselor, all are voluntary, the counselor is always present, and the counselor is also willing to model or participate in the exposure. An example of exposure self-ratings of anxiety and how those subside with each practice is given in the following graph. A–F on the graph indicate the "lightning bolt" pattern of ever-increasing fear that individuals may experience if they continue to avoid tasks/experiences they fear. For example, the initial fear of public speaking (A) will immediately decrease if a student avoids the task (B). However, the next time the task is required, the initial fear start point will be higher (C). This cycle of avoidance reinforces the likelihood of continued avoidance and exaggerated fear responses. In contrast, the first guided exposure with a counselor (G) may start out high, but fear subsides as an individual endures the activity. The next time the student participates in public speaking (H), the fear starts lower and goes down faster. This is called habituation (compare exposures 1, 2, 3, and 4). The gentle downward sloping graph response is often called the "rainbow effect."

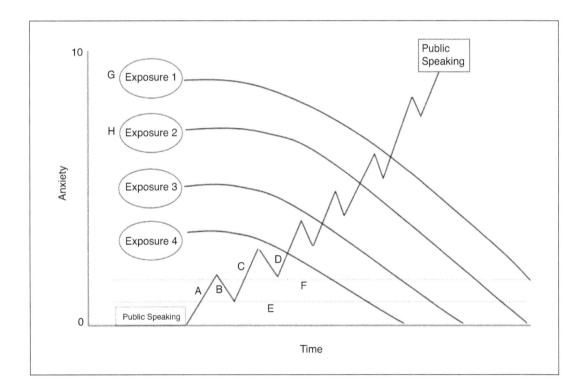

EXHIBIT 5.3

Exposure Therapy Graph Sample

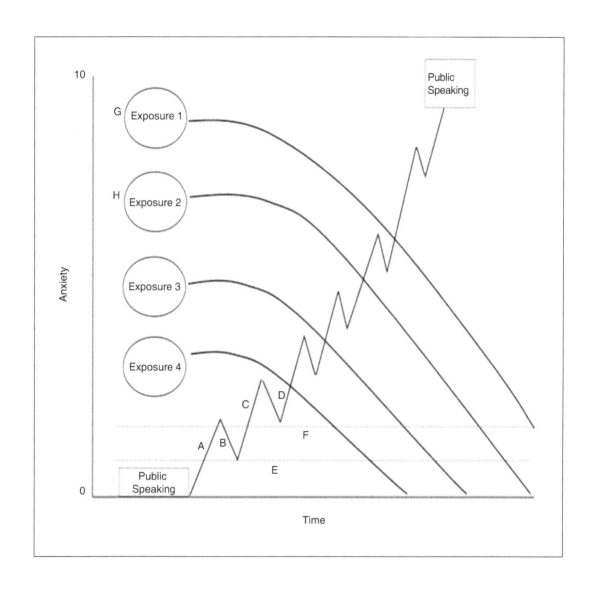

EXHIBIT 5.4

Exposure Therapy Graph

SUDS RATING								
10								
9								
8								
7								
6								
5								
4								
3								
2								
1								
0								
	TIME							

EXHIBIT 5.5

Exposure Hierarchy Teaching Example

Purpose: To help students rank their level of distress in response to situations of exaggerated fear.

Developmental considerations: May need to present visual illustrations to younger children (e.g., smiley faces) to help them identify the level of anxiety they experience with each situation (also see Appendix Exhibits 1.4 and 1.5 for scale examples for younger children). The hierarchy can be steps leading up to one highly feared situation (e.g., presenting in a classroom full of students for a grade) or multiple feared situations increasing in fearfulness (e.g., making a mistake on a paper, tripping in public, asking a stranger for directions, singing in public).

Situation	SUDs Ranking
Presenting in front of the entire class for a grade	10
Presenting in front of a classroom with the teacher for a grade	9
Presenting in front of the classroom with just two friends present	8
Presenting in a classroom alone	7
Rehearsing my presentation in front of a friend at home	6
Rehearsing my presentation in front of my parents/caregivers or sibling	5
Rehearsing my presentation in the mirror	4
Reading my presentation out loud	3
Preparing a PowerPoint presentation	2
Writing the class presentation date in planner	1

EXHIBIT 5.6

Subjective Units of Distress Scale

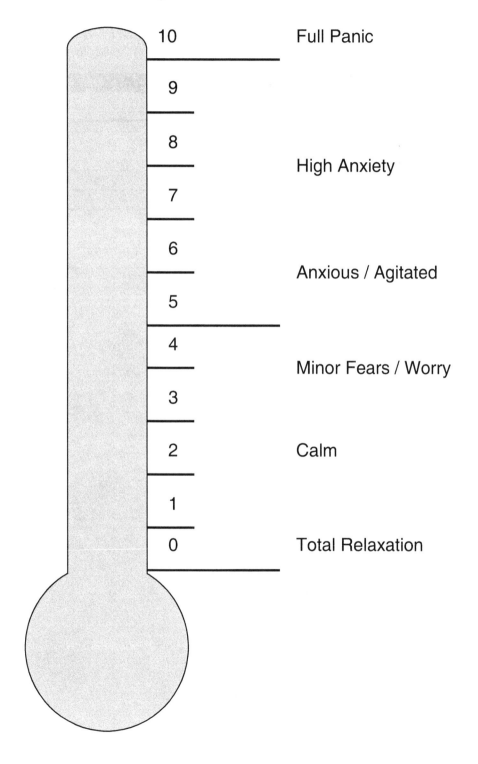

10 — Full Panic

9

8 — High Anxiety

7

6 — Anxious / Agitated

5

4 — Minor Fears / Worry

3

2 — Calm

1

0 — Total Relaxation

EXHIBIT 5.7

Exposure Hierarchy Worksheet

Directions: Write down the situations that cause you to feel anxious and afraid, and then add them to the first column, ranking them in order of how distressing they are. In the second column, write how anxious each one makes you, from 0 (totally relaxed) to 10 (full panic).

Situation	SUDS Ranking

EXHIBIT 5.8

Downward Arrow Technique

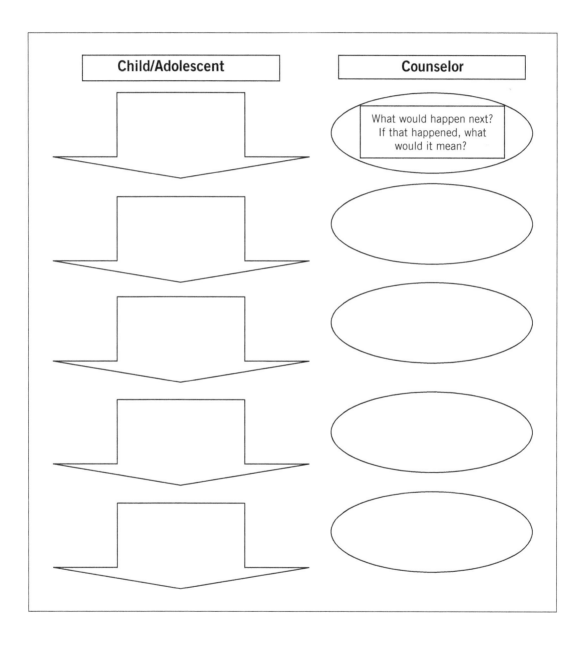

EXHIBIT 5.9

Worry Script Worksheet

Instructions: Using the space below, write down one thing you are worried about. Include as much detail as possible (how does it feel, sound, smell, what will happen next, what do you see). Also include why, when, and where you are worried.

Date: _____   Time: _____   Location: _____

What are you worried about?_____

_____

_____

_____

_____

_____

_____

_____

_____

_____

Summarize your worry in only one sentence: _____

_____

_____

_____

EXHIBIT 5.10

Counselor's Checklist for Cognitive Restructuring

 Explain the cognitive restructuring process to the parent/caregiver and student.

 Introduce the relationship between activating events and one's thoughts, emotions, and behaviors (e.g., utilize the ABC figure).

 Prompt the student to identify irrational and distorted thoughts.

 Challenge the student's distorted thinking through perspective-taking exercises, using the Socratic questioning method, and/or through reflective thought recording.

 Prompt the student to identify the specific cognitive distortions that exist.

 Help the student reframe his or her distorted and irrational thoughts and/or replace such thoughts with coping statements/positive affirmations.

 Repeat the process until the student's thoughts reflect a more balanced and rational manner of thinking.

EXHIBIT 5.11

Cognitive Restructuring: Information for Parents/Caregivers

Cognitive Restructuring

Cognitive restructuring is a therapeutic technique that is commonly used to challenge and correct negative thinking patterns that elicit depression and anxiety-related problems. It is based on the premise that one's irrational thoughts and beliefs about a specific event can lead to unhealthy emotions and behaviors that maintain depression and anxiety-related problems. Irrational thoughts are often referred to as cognitive distortions. Thus, the primary objective of cognitive restructuring is to help individuals challenge and reframe the cognitive distortions that are associated with their maladaptive emotions and behaviors. By disputing, reframing, and replacing unfavorable thoughts and beliefs, individuals are better prepared to manage and cope with their difficulties. Cognitive restructuring is a method that counselors can utilize to help students become more aware of their thinking and to change their distortions to more positive and rational patterns of thinking.

Cognitive Restructuring Process

The first step in the process entails teaching children or adolescents that their thoughts, feelings, and behaviors are interrelated and can influence each other (see diagram). After a child understands that his or her thoughts can produce negative emotions and behaviors, he or she can then be prompted to identify his or her problematic thoughts. These thoughts are generally brief, spontaneous, and not based on reflection. In order for the student to interpret such thoughts as problematic, several strategies can be employed. First, students can be encouraged to view their thoughts from another person's perspective. Counselors can also utilize a semi-structured questioning method to help the student discover his or her problematic thoughts, understand why such thoughts are problematic, and identify errors in his or her reasoning. Another approach includes encouraging the student to maintain a journal or record of events that occur and his or her succeeding thoughts, behaviors, and consequences. These activities can help the student challenge and become more aware of his or her thinking.

After the student identifies his or her thought(s) as irrational and problematic, the counselor then prompts the student to identify the specific type of cognitive distortion(s) that exist. This can further help the student understand the nature of his or her thinking. After the student identifies his or her irrational thought, why the thought is problematic, and errors in his or her reasoning, the counselor assists the student with generating a more rational thought to replace the distorted thought. This process can be repeated until the student's thoughts reflect a more balanced and rational manner of thinking.

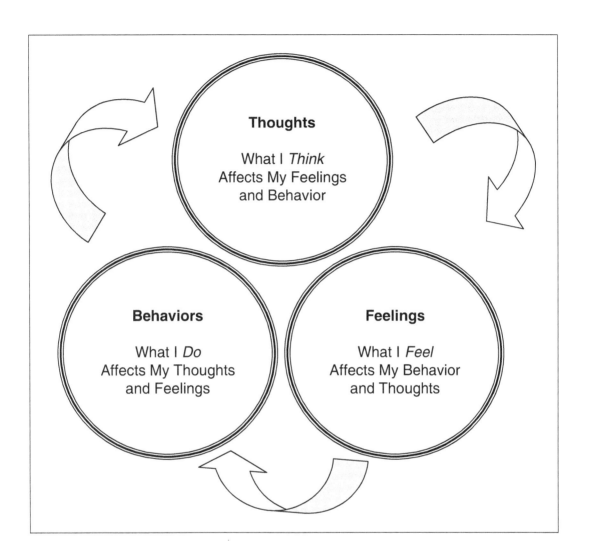

EXHIBIT 5.12

The Depression Downward Withdrawal Spiral

Cognitive Factors
Ruminating negative thoughts,
cognitive distortions, diminishing
interests or pleasure, worthlessness,
excessive guilt, indecisiveness, poor
concentration

Mood Factors
Sadness, emptiness,
tearfulness, hopelessness,
helplessness, insomnia,
hypersomnia

Physical Factors
Psychomotor agitation,
insomnia, hypersomnia,
fatigue, loss of energy,
increased/decreased
appetite or weight

Critical Factors
Thoughts of death,
suicidal ideation,
suicide plan,
suicide attempt

EXHIBIT 5.13

The Anger Upward Escalation Spiral

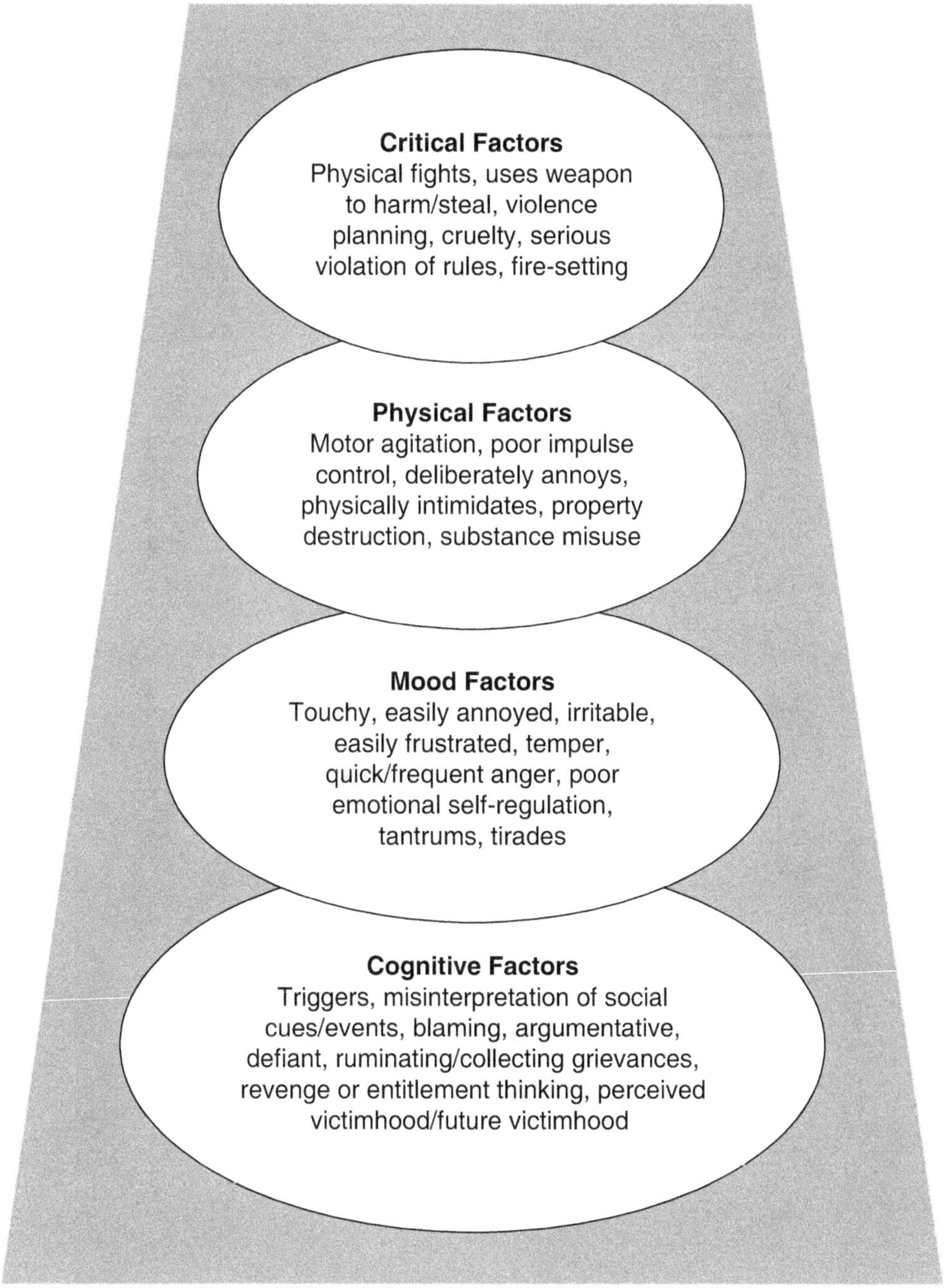

Critical Factors
Physical fights, uses weapon to harm/steal, violence planning, cruelty, serious violation of rules, fire-setting

Physical Factors
Motor agitation, poor impulse control, deliberately annoys, physically intimidates, property destruction, substance misuse

Mood Factors
Touchy, easily annoyed, irritable, easily frustrated, temper, quick/frequent anger, poor emotional self-regulation, tantrums, tirades

Cognitive Factors
Triggers, misinterpretation of social cues/events, blaming, argumentative, defiant, ruminating/collecting grievances, revenge or entitlement thinking, perceived victimhood/future victimhood

EXHIBIT 5.14

The Anger Escalating Sequence

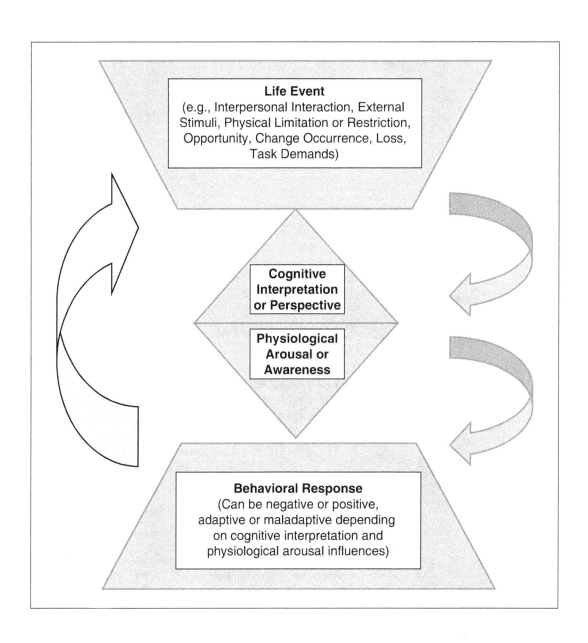

Life Event
(e.g., Interpersonal Interaction, External
Stimuli, Physical Limitation or Restriction,
Opportunity, Change Occurrence, Loss,
Task Demands)

**Cognitive
Interpretation
or Perspective**

**Physiological
Arousal or
Awareness**

Behavioral Response
(Can be negative or positive,
adaptive or maladaptive depending
on cognitive interpretation and
physiological arousal influences)

EXHIBIT 5.15

Perspective-Taking Scenarios

Directions: Review and discuss each scenario with the student. Emphasize to students that people may have different perspectives/points of view in response to various situations.

Scenario 1: The Case of the Missing Cards
Last week, John's favorite collection of baseball cards went missing. No one could solve the case, so John called a detective to investigate the incident.

■ What does a detective look for in an incident?

■ Why might the detective ask multiple people about what they saw?

Scenario 2: A Ride in the Sky
You were recently in a hot-air balloon that flew over a playground. You saw many things below during your ride.

■ Tell me what you saw happen. Be sure to talk about all of the children who were there.

■ What do you think each one was thinking?

■ How would each child see it differently?

Scenario 3: A Lunchtime Brawl
During lunch, 10 students were joking and throwing food at each other and at other students.

■ What if you were **in the group/another student/a teacher/a parent?** What do you think you will see, hear, and feel?

EXHIBIT 5.16

Perspective-Taking Worksheet Example

Purpose: To help children/adolescents understand that others may have different backgrounds, beliefs, and experiences, and interpret things differently.

Developmental considerations: Young children may need concrete activities to further illustrate the concept of perspective taking. Adolescents may benefit from examples using art or optical illusions (e.g., pictures with hidden images to illustrate how we can miss important details when we assess a situation too quickly).

THE PERSPECTIVE DETECTIVE

Activating Event	What Are Your Thoughts and Feelings About the Event?	What Are Some Possible Thoughts and Feelings That _____ Has About the Event?
My friends went to a party without me.	*Thoughts: They probably do not like me anymore.* *Feelings: I feel somber.*	*Person: Friend* *Thought 1: I want to be alone, so I'm not going to invite anyone else to go with me to the party.* *Feelings 1: I feel like I need a break from so many social events.* *Thought 2: Oh no, I forgot to invite Jane!* *Feelings 2: I feel gloomy.*
The teacher did not smile at me this morning.	*Thoughts: Something must be wrong with me. She is mad at me now.* *Feelings: Sad, nervous*	*Person: Teacher* *Thought I: I am running so late this morning, I need to hurry and get all the students seated.* *Feeling: I feel really rushed and frazzled.* *Thought 2: If I really hurry the students to be seated, we can start the lesson quickly and have more time for the video later.* *Feeling: I need to move the pace here and get focused.*
My mother is dating again and went to the movies without me.	*Thoughts: I feel left out and forgotten.* *Feelings: Sadness, loneliness*	*Person: Mother* *Thought 1: It feels good to have adult company and see a movie with a friend.* *Feeling: Relaxed and fun* *Thought 2: I love my children but also need some adult time.* *Feeling: I feel torn between wanting some free time from responsibilities and loving time with my children.*

EXHIBIT 5.17

Perspective-Taking Worksheet

THE PERSPECTIVE DETECTIVE

Activating Event	What Are Your Thoughts and Feelings About the Event?	What Are Some Possible Thoughts and Feelings That _____ Has About the Event?

EXHIBIT 5.18

Coping Statements/Positive Affirmation Worksheet Example

Purpose: To help students generate positive affirmations/statements to replace negative thoughts.

Developmental considerations: For students who have trouble generating positive affirmations/statements, the counselor may need to provide a list of positive affirmations for the student.

Negative Thought	Positive Affirmation
"I won't succeed at this task."	"I've done this before, so I am confident that I can do this."
"I hate myself."	"I am a good and likeable person."
"There's no way I can pass my test."	"I studied hard and I can give this my best effort."
"I'm a total failure."	"I have many gifts and talents."

EXHIBIT 5.19

My Coping Statements: Positive Affirmations

Directions: List positive affirmations/statements that you might use to replace negative thoughts that you have. If you cannot think of any, work with a partner to help you identify multiple affirmations. Let us see how many affirmations you can list. Ready, set, go!

Negative Thought	Positive Affirmation

EXHIBIT 5.20

Assertiveness Training Example

Purpose: To help students learn how to assert their feelings and rights.

Developmental considerations: Counselors may want to present visual illustrations to younger children (e.g., pictures) to help them understand the behavioral expectations.

A. Identify the problem:
   a. What happened?
   b. Why is it a problem?
   Another student told me that I'm not smart. It made me feel sad and depressed.

B. Describe your feelings using "I" statements:
   a. I feel_____ because_____.
   b. "I feel" should be followed by an emotion word/try to refrain from using "that you" or "like you."
   "I feel hurt because you told me that I'm not smart."

C. Describe the changes you want to see happen:
   a. Changes should be reasonable.
   b. Changes should consider the needs and feelings of the other person.
   "I would like for you and me to use kind words to each other."

D. Describe the potential consequences of being assertive:
   a. How would did you feel?
   b. What might happen?
   I may feel calm and happy.
   My classmate may agree to say more kind words to me.

EXHIBIT 5.21

Assertiveness Training Worksheet

Direction: Reflect upon an incident that happened within the last month. Describe the problem. Practice being assertive using the following prompts. Consider what might happen if you were more assertive.

A. Identify the problem:

    a. What happened?

    b. Why is it a problem?

B. Describe your feelings using "I" statements:

    a. I feel_____ because_____.

    b. "I feel" should be followed by an emotion word/try to refrain from using "that you" or "like you."

C. Describe the changes you want to see happen:

    a. Changes should be reasonable.

    b. Changes should consider the needs and feelings of the other person.

D. Describe the potential consequences of being assertive:

    a. How would you feel?

    b. What might happen?

Index

CPSIA information can be obtained
at www.ICGtesting.com
Printed in the USA
BVHW021647270223
659327BV00024B/453